WOMEN VS HOLLYWOOD

THE FALL AND RISE OF WOMEN IN FILM

WOMEN VS

HELEN O'HARA

HOLLY WOOD

THE FALL AND RISE OF WOMEN IN FILM

ROBINSON

ROBINSON

First published in Great Britain in 2021 by Robinson

3 5 7 9 10 8 6 4 2

Copyright © Helen O'Hara, 2021

The moral right of the author has been asserted.

A CIP catalogue record for this book
is available from the British Library.

ISBN: 978-1-47214-443-0 (hardcover)
ISBN: 978-1-47214-442-3 (trade paperback)

Typeset in Nexus Serif by Hewer Text UK Ltd, Edinburgh
Printed and bound in Great Britain by Clays Ltd, Elcograf S.p.A.

Papers used by Robinson are from well-managed
forests and other responsible sources.

Robinson
An imprint of
Little, Brown Book Group
Carmelite House
50 Victoria Embankment
London EC4Y 0DZ

An Hachette UK Company
www.hachette.co.uk

www.littlebrown.co.uk

To Mum and Dad,
thanks for taking me to the cinema

Contents

Introduction

HOLLYWOOD IS the American dream writ large. It's the promise that any plucky young person with grit and determination can become an icon. In its own mythos, it's open to all and welcoming to anyone with sufficient talent and a little luck. It's Lana Turner discovered drinking a soda at the Top Hat Cafe, John Wayne promoted from odd jobs around the studio, Harrison Ford working as a carpenter, and all of them being transformed into stars.

The truth, however, is often less shiny. If you're young, white, cis, straight, slim, able-bodied and rich enough to fund your way through photo sessions, gym classes and auditions, you're going to find opportunity knocking louder and sooner than it does for anyone else. The Hollywood dream has not been open to everyone and, with a large majority of roles and senior jobs going to white men, its scales have often been tilted against women.

Still, the legend is so pervasive that it's hard for people to accept that it's a rigged game. The sort of person who sets their sights on a movie career is generally the sort who believes that a little hustle will make it happen *if* you're good enough. So if you fail? If you face one disappointment after another? Maybe it's you. Maybe you're just not as good as Kathryn Bigelow, as Julia Roberts, as Amy Pascal. That's the pernicious effect of discrimination. It not only allows those with the power to sit in ivory towers preaching a meritocracy; it forces everyone else to question themselves and their talent, because no one wants to be a bad loser and suggest that maybe the playing field was tilted.

History shows that women have wanted to make movies since the very earliest days. One of the first people ever to make a narrative film was Alice Guy-Blaché; one of the highest-paid directors of the early silent era was Lois Weber. There were female action stars jumping off trains and facing down wild animals; there were women editors who shaped the history of film. It's never been a question of women not wanting it enough, or even not being good enough. Hollywood shut them out, sometimes quite consciously.

You may not accept that, but the stories from women in the industry in this book and the data amassed over the last few years show that it is absolutely the case. And that matters because the stories we tell on the big screen don't just reflect society, they can shape it. 1915's *The Birth of a Nation* rebirthed the moribund Ku Klux Klan. Less appallingly, the sight of Clark Gable without a vest in *It Happened One Night* devastated the undershirt market. Documentary *The Thin Blue Line* saw an unjust conviction overturned. Films have changed fashions, started crazes and shifted the stock market.

The stories we tell reflect what we value, who we empathise with and how we see the world. So maybe if our films were more egalitarian, our world would be too. If films showed women's stories mattering as much as men's, maybe that would be true in real life too. That may be optimistic, but it's not entirely far-fetched. We absorb our values from a hundred different directions, but the sheer, all-encompassing power of the cinema experience means that it could do a lot.

The good news is that Hollywood is changing and becoming more inclusive, and women are pushing, individually and collectively, for that change. These women may be genetically blessed, financially fortunate and endowed with the skincare regimes of the gods, but they're fighting the same pernicious attitudes as the rest of us, combating sex discrimination and trying to open doors that were previously closed.

'It's about not just getting rid of the problem people in the industry,' says Jasmin Morrison of Time's Up UK, 'but also giving people opportunity. These problems are not going to be solved overnight, or in a year, but it feels different now.'[1]

We're at a moment when real change seems possible, and I've tried in this book to explain why that is.

Much as I would love to have written the single, definitive take on women in film, this book isn't that; it would need to be about ten times longer for a start. So I set some ground rules for the sake of my sanity. I've focused on Hollywood only, because a look through 125 years of film history and into the future is wide enough without including the many other great cinema traditions around the world.

By default, most of the people discussed are therefore white and at least ostensibly straight and cis. Those are the people who were able to make a career and who made it into the Hollywood histories. I have tried to draw attention to those who struggled not just against sexism but racism, ableism and homophobia or transphobia as well – but few of those who faced such intersectional discrimination ever got their chance in the first place. So please bear in mind the stories that are *not* here, the people who never got their start because their skin was the wrong colour or because their sexuality or gender identity didn't match society's expectations.

This book uses terms like men and women almost as a binary, without much time on the wider spectrum of gender identity. That's to keep my language as simple as possible, but my intention is not to exclude non-binary or agender people. Some classic Hollywood figures might now be considered gender-queer, might have called themselves non-binary or even trans if they were alive today, but they didn't then and I didn't like to speak for them now. To be clear, however, people who experienced discrimination on the basis of their sexual identity (or sexual preferences, or race, or any combination of prejudices) belong here too, and I have done my best to highlight their stories.

As director Alma Har'el told me, 'Our global consciousness is skewed. You can see that women have been consistently written out of history. We can't expect people to fully grasp how biased they are because they have been educated from a young age to believe that men are visionaries and built the world, and they don't even know the contributions of women. We have to literally rewrite history. But the times are changing. The whole idea of gender is shifting.'[2]

It's worth noting that survivors of sexual assault or worse may find some of the discussion here triggering. The #MeToo movement is specifically discussed in Chapter 10, but there is non-graphic discussion of rape or assault in earlier chapters on the silent and studio eras, in discussion of censorship and briefly in Chapter 7.

This is not really a sober, balanced book; I've approached it more like a polemic and aimed to rebalance the stories endlessly written about Hollywood men: good, bad and ugly. Many men also suffered under the system described here, but those tales have already been told.

I want this book to be a celebration of the work women did in cinema, sometimes against extraordinary odds. There were female directors like Dorothy Arzner and Ida Lupino who, entirely alone in an otherwise all-male environment, still made impressive and personal films. There were stars who blazed across the studio system and whose names still echo in our culture. Unfortunately there'll also be stories of women who were held back by men, locked out of positions of power and generally stymied. Some readers may therefore conclude that I am anti-male. But I assure you, some of my best friends are men! At no point do I mean 'all men' (I don't use that phrase) so if you feel unjustly attacked by anything here, please mentally insert a 'not all men' where appropriate and go on about your day. For what it's worth, I believe that current gender roles hurt men as well as women, because they're unjustly attacked for liking things considered too feminine and their very identity is made contingent on adhering to strict gender norms in a way that is sometimes emotionally abusive. The little boy who's told not to play with his sister's dolls grows up to be the guy who will absolutely not watch a rom-com with his girlfriend because he doesn't like that soppy stuff. This is policed by women and men, and that's not fair.

In contrast, women are told – less explicitly, but no less emphatically – that male-focused stories are more important, more universal. The world wants us to watch men's films because the world assumes that stories about (cis, straight, white) men are normal. Everyone is harmed by this dynamic. With that in mind, you might detect some anger here, and at times you might despair, but overall I hope you leave this book feeling optimistic. I genuinely do believe that film can change the world, which is one of the many reasons I love it, and that it is an important and valuable thing to be taken out of our own heads for a couple of hours and put in someone else's life. There are fierce, powerful women (and men) out there pushing to widen the big screen so that there's room on it for all of humanity in all its glorious variation. This book is for all those who have paved the way and all those now trying to change the picture, whatever it takes.

1

The Wild West
When film could be female

THERE'S A story that Hollywood tells itself about the earliest days of film, a story about men. It tells us that cinema was invented by serious, bushily moustachioed Victorian men thanks to ingenuity, pluck and a can-do attitude. Early experiments by Eadweard Muybridge were followed by the commercial aptitude of Thomas Edison (a rare clean-shaven pioneer) and the great leap forward of the Lumière Brothers, who first projected film for audiences. These men had tall hats, high collars and even loftier ambitions, in keeping with the spirit of their age.

Within a year of that first Lumière show, moving pictures were screened all over the US. Within twenty years it was a major industry; within forty it would be the US's biggest export. Hollywood tells us all about the daring men who shaped this time: Cecil B. DeMille and D. W. Griffith; Charlie Chaplin and Buster Keaton. The problem is that its story is not the whole truth.

As soon as the technology existed, women used it to make films. They directed and produced and headed their own studios before they even won the vote. These women were locked into corsets and long skirts, their hair in elaborate Victorian up-dos. If married, they were unable to own property in their own right. But for all such limitations, they made movies. They thrilled audiences, launched careers and helped to establish the way films were shot. Some became so highly valued that they were paid more than any man in town. Some were so intrepid that they threw themselves on to moving trains or out of balloons just for entertainment. In 1917 alone, Universal Studios would credit eight female directors. In 2017, the same studio made just one film with a female director, *Pitch Perfect 3**. Admittedly, Universal in the 1910s was remarkably woman-friendly, but that's still a stunning statistic – and it shows that the current male dominance in filmmaking was *not* inevitable. Women have always wanted to make films.

So why is the popular vision of women in the silent era, if such a thing even exists, limited to a girl tied to the railway tracks ahead of an oncoming train? You know the picture. She's struggling ineffectually against her chains, little boots waggling and improbable ringlets swinging as her eyes plead with the camera for help. Obviously, she was put there by a bad dude who twirls his moustache and silently cackles. But never fear! Just in the nick of time a bright young thing in too much eye make-up is going to turn up to save her. That's what women looked like in the silent era: victims, right?

Wrong – and on several counts. For one, the imperilled ingénue was a figure of parody even then, a comic riff on old stage melodramas. Women in the silent era were far more likely to be leaping from trains to rescue hapless menfolk, as in the popular female-led action serials of the time, than they were to lie screaming on the tracks. Second, that terrified damsel was played by comedienne Mabel Normand in a 1913 film called *Race for a Life*, and she played it for laughs. The role was a departure from her usual slapstick persona, which saw her perform her own pratfalls and frequently rescue her male love interests. But still, it was all in a day's work: Normand had already made one hundred or so films. She would soon take a newcomer called Charlie Chaplin

---

* To be fair, they did also release several female-made films through their Focus Features subsidiary.

under her wing, helping him develop his 'Tramp' persona and teaching him how film acting worked.

All that context was deliberately stripped away. In the early days of the sound era, clips from silent films like this were held up to ridicule in order to promote the new technology and encourage audiences to fork out for the costs of converting theatres to sound. Soon the entire silent era was treated as Hollywood's awkward, acne-covered teen years: best forgotten, or mocked. So the stories of the women who worked on those films were also buried. There were more women directing, editing, and especially writing screenplays – 50 per cent by some estimates – than there ever were screaming for a man to save them.

Cinema was a great opportunity for women, a brand-new field where they could make an impact. Industry magazine *The Story World* wrote in 1923 that, 'Motion picture history has recorded women serving in practically every important position, from that of producer, owner and promoter of film companies down as far as "important" carries.' The great female directors of the era encouraged other women to follow in their footsteps, and mentored them along.

Few of those women are remembered today, at least partly because there were efforts – conscious and unconscious – to leave them out of the official histories or downplay their roles.

The first ever North American movie star was a woman. Florence Lawrence was the 'Biograph Girl', closely followed by Florence Turner, the 'Vitagraph Girl'. Both were known by the name of their studios, and those studios were in no hurry to tell audiences their real names. Even back then, they knew that a star's popularity would give them leverage in pay negotiations and enable them to move wherever they could find the best roles and biggest audience. But word got around anyway, and soon Lawrence was earning twice the usual Biograph rate while Turner sailed off to England at the height of her fame in search of more creative freedom.

The two Flos were soon eclipsed by another woman, Mary Pickford, who became the biggest draw of the 1910s and who would write the rule book on being a movie star. Pickford played near-children for much of her career, tomboy figures who were *just* old enough to have a love affair with some dashing fella (often her husband-to-be, Douglas Fairbanks). She worked collaboratively with many of her directors and wrote some of her own scripts, though her biggest triumphs came in conjunction with the screen-writer Frances Marion, of whom more later. Off-screen, Pickford showed an entirely adult sense of business savvy. She was the first star to earn $500 per week, and by 1916 she had approval over every aspect of her productions and was paid an astonishing $10,000 weekly – for comparison, an average government employee at the time earned just under $1,000 per year.[1] Pickford co-founded United Artists in 1919, alongside Charlie Chaplin, D. W. Griffith and Fairbanks, with the grand aim of taking their star power away from the studios' control and exploiting it themselves – a recurring theme in Hollywood history. Pickford and her team, for a moment, succeeded better than most: if UA was never a major producer, it consistently attracted creative talent. Meanwhile, Pickford's palatial home with Fairbanks, Pickfair, was the epitome of glamour in the 1920s and played host to the most spectacular parties on Earth, as she ruled Hollywood society and welcomed the king of Siam for dinner.

Inspired by Pickford, copycat tomboys tweaked the noses of the rich and powerful and challenged Victorian ideas of how girls should behave. Behind the scenes, a wealth of female talent worked to estab-lish the movie business as not just a new art form but *the* pre-eminent entertainment of the century.

Film could never have become a mainstream attraction without women. That's not just because they're half the audience; it's also because they were key to drawing in the other half. The prospect of ogling beautiful women on screen sold films to many male audience members, and the star power of women like Pickford and Lawrence lured in more. But it went beyond that. The industry that was not-yet Hollywood – no features would be made there until 1913 – was desperate to win over women because doing so would establish it as mainstream, family entertainment. So there was a brief, shining time when female filmmakers were courted and put front-and-centre of their films' publicity campaigns.

In 1907 the fledgling movie industry was struggling to convince people that it was a respectable enterprise for respectable people. For the first ten or fifteen years of their existence, moving pictures had been a carnival sideshow, a peekaboo novelty focused more on images than on story. Investors feared that it would stay that way, just a cheap thrill in disreputable establishments (inevitably, porn was an early adopter). Filmmakers with grander ambitions worked to convince middle-class patrons that cinema could be a substantive, morally uplifting pastime. Thomas Edison's very first demonstration of his Kinetoscope, on 20 May 1891 (four years before the Lumières' first true cinema show), was for 147 members of the National Federation of Women's Clubs. They each peered into a small wooden box, to see a man smiling, bowing and doffing his hat. Edison – a far better marketeer than inventor – knew that if you win over such women, you win over the masses.

It would be female viewers, and those who catered to them, that turned cinema from a flash-in-the-pan fad into the dominant art form of the twentieth century. 'The kinema [sic] must please the women or die,' said film critic C. A. Lejeune in a hard-to-argue-with 1926 article.[2] Remove women from the equation, and film might have stalled at peep shows.

That's because attracting single men on rowdy nights out was not going to be enough for film to achieve its potential; these early cinema showmen needed the entire family to turn up. Women are often credited by historians with turning the novel into a phenom-enon in the 1700s and 1800s, to the extent that hysterical men of the day worried that they would ruin their minds and child-bearing bodies with all that unhealthy reading. Same for theatre. Hugo Münsterberg, a German-born Harvard psychologist, lamented in 1901 that 'theatre managers claim that eighty-five per cent of their patrons are women'.[3] He disapproved of this frivolous activity, but for film exhibitors it was a huge opportunity. If women were *that* important to the theatre, they could make or break cinema, too. But spectacular images alone would not be enough; photography was an everyday phenomenon already and even moving pictures would soon become familiar. Cinema needed to tell powerful stories, and communicate emotion. It needed not just to capture but to *hold* the attention of audiences, and that required more ambition and more feeling, and consideration of what women as well as men might want to see.

One odd holdover from the Victorian era was the (wildly patron-ising) belief that women were morally superior to men, by nature. The early cinema pioneers therefore wanted their imprimatur on this new form because it would show that film could be a force for good in the world (with the flip side, as they would soon learn, that women often led censorship and certification efforts). Involving women in filmmaking was a quick way to demonstrate film's moral force. Optimists at the General Federation of Women's Clubs even wondered, in 1907, if the mass appeal of the cinemas might not entirely displace saloons. They linked cinema to the temperance campaign, bless their naive little hearts. Not every campaign against the early cinemas was a moral one: they were often death traps in case of fire (a real threat given the highly flammable celluloid reels of the time). But safety upgrades were easily made as money came in; it was the content of the films that would prey on campaigners' minds far longer, especially as exhibitors succeeded in drawing more and more women and children to the pictures.

So how to channel this moral force that women apparently possessed to shape cinema for good? The presence of actresses on screen was not enough; the world's second oldest profession was always too closely associated with its oldest.* But women could be prominently positioned elsewhere.

Cinema pioneers hired women to work on the box office and play the music that accompanied the silent shows. When cinema began, enterprising widows and couples were among those who bought a projector, and many prospered enough to put down roots in their own small-town nickelodeons.[4] Some even used exhibition receipts to fund their filmmaking. As early as 1903, Fannie Cook was screening films on tour to support her own shoots, and in the 1920s Maria P. Williams, one of the first Black female filmmakers in the US, acted as an assistant cinema manager to her husband Jesse L. Williams' general manager post.

During the desperate push to respectability, female proprietors were seen as a guarantor of middle-class respectability and Victorian virtues of good behaviour and discernment. Some women played into this stereotype, specifically promising uplifting and family-friendly entertainment, making themselves the moral guardians of their customers. They gave interviews emphasising the similarities between running a movie house and a home: both demanded cleanliness and comfort. These exhibitors timetabled shows for housewives, so that there would be something to watch while the washing

---

* Generally, prostitution comes in for a mention among the 'world's oldest profession' jokes, though it has serious competition from tailors, who point out that Adam and Eve sewed their own clothes. 'World's second oldest profession' can refer to actors but also any of a number of fraud-related professions. Sorry, actors.

dried, and for shop girls, to offer respectable entertainment after a long day on their feet.

These women worked hard, assembling a varied selection of short films, adding music and possibly even creating a sort of live commentary on the film. But they couldn't do everything. Even then, women were rarely allowed to work as projectionists. That was a matter of science and ill-suited to female strengths, it was thought; one survey of the trade papers of the day saw mention of 140 female theatre operators but only six female projectionists.

Still, women could shape programming; could write the romances, comedies and adventures that might draw people into the auditorium, and even direct films. That's how, for a brief, glorious period, roughly from 1907 to 1920, some women were able to forge careers in film and earn equal acclaim – and sometimes near-equal pay – to their male colleagues.

It helped that, in the early days of what was not yet Hollywood, filmmaking was a free-for-all. Anyone with a film camera, a few friends and a little patience could make a film; anyone with a projector and a white sheet could distribute it. As the new century brightened the horizon and strange new technologies like cars and aeroplanes gained popularity, it seemed that the sky was the limit – and for a wider group of people than ever before.

The time seemed to promise great advancement for women. They were still fighting for the vote in the US and Europe, but the upswell of activism and optimism that the fight for suffrage had provoked was dizzying. What better way to achieve parity with men than through a new art form, with no rules or traditions yet in place to hold you back? At the very least, women would soon be able to count on cinema as a reliable form of entertainment and escape. Far more than theatre – or even, perhaps, novels – cinema seemed to offer a way to see and step into other people's lives: into other classes, other countries, other worlds. After a day on the factory floor, the modern woman of the 1910s or 1920s could sink into a velvet chair and be whisked away.

A few plucky go-getters like Alice Guy, the young secretary to soon-to-be French cinema mogul Léon Gaumont, took advantage of those heady times. Guy had taken a secretarial job with Gaumont to support her mother after the family was left destitute, and there she learned about these new moving-picture cameras. Just a few months after the Lumières' projection debut, aged just twenty-two, Guy asked to borrow a company camera and M. Gaumont's terrace to try something.[5]

'"It seems like a silly, girlish thing to do, but you can try if you want,"' Guy remembered her boss responding.[6] Guy was a veteran of amateur dramatics, and she shot a fanciful story called *La Fée Aux Chou*, or *The Cabbage Fairy*. It was barely thirty seconds long and simply saw a fairy retrieve a baby from a cabbage patch. Despite the flat, cardboard cabbages, it opened up a world of possibilities. While the Lumières and Gaumont himself had focused on documentary images, Guy – like another French visionary, Georges Méliès – saw the potential for fantasy.

Over the next decade or so, Guy made hundreds of short films, by some estimates over a thousand. She became Gaumont's head of production, which meant that she could learn and develop revolutionary techniques, including new-fangled tricks like semi-close-ups and even early trials with colour, like *Danse Des Papillons* in 1897. She made more than one hundred short films with Gaumont's 'Chronophone', an early sound system using a wax cylinder. Her job was not just to make entertaining shorts but to showcase everything that Gaumont technology could deliver. It wouldn't be unreasonable to compare her work to Pixar Animation's early short films. There, tech pioneer Ed Catmull pushed the art of computer graphics as far as it could go and Disney-trained animator John Lasseter created stories to show them off, while in turn pushing Catmull to solve new

9

problems that arose as their ambition grew (Curves! Irregular shapes! Organic surfaces!).

Unfortunately, that analogy falls apart when you compare how the two filmmakers were treated. While Pixar sheltered Lasseter and rewarded him richly, Guy fought battle after battle at Gaumont. There had been no particular prestige attached to directing films when she started. The roles of writer, director and producer would not be solidified for decades, and she essentially did all three roles for most of her career. There was no threat in letting a woman do it, no credits to fight for or awards to win. But after Guy's department became profitable, attempts were made to replace her with a man. She took her case to the board and impressed the Chairman, Gustave Eiffel (yes, the one who built the Tower), enough that she kept her post by unanimous vote. But it was a sign of things to come. As the company became less experimental and more professional, having a woman in such a senior position came to seem like an anomaly and caused resentment among her subordinates. While filming the ambitious *La Vie du Christ* (*The Life of Christ*), her biggest French film and, at a bum-numbing thirty-five minutes, an epic for its time, the head of the studio workshop actually removed one of her completed sets and chopped it up for firewood because, Guy believed, of personal animosity. 'That was one example,' she shrugged years later, filing this among many more aggressions.[7]

By the time she left Gaumont, Guy had completed huge, ambitious projects, like that *Life of Christ* and an adaptation of Victor Hugo's *The Hunchback of Notre Dame*. The latter had three hundred extras and twenty-five sets: equivalent in terms of scale and spectacle to eight months of VFX and a whole mess of *Transformers* today. These were also, by the standards of the time, prestige films, the sort of thing to convince snobby middle-class art lovers to check out this new cinema trend. If there had been Oscars back then, they might have been called Oscar bait. Guy was at the very forefront of her art.

She wasn't alone. In 1907, scattered entrepreneurs began to find their own sunny, sheltered spots and create their own films, from Méliès' long-standing studio making fanciful science-fiction films in France to England's George Albert Smith, who developed techniques like double exposure and reverse film. Perhaps it was their example that spurred Guy to leave Gaumont. More likely it was her new marriage to cameraman Herbert Blaché, with whom she moved to the US. There, in Fort Lee, New Jersey, in 1910, Madame Guy-Blaché founded the Solax Company studio, becoming its artistic director and director of much of its output. She seemed to have found her niche, producing a regular supply of films and a steady stream of profit.

In a 1914 issue of *Moving Picture World*, Guy wrote:

It has long been a source of wonder to me that more women have not seized upon the wonderful opportunities offered to them by the motion picture art to make their way to fame and fortune ... Of all the arts there is probably none in which they can make such splendid use of talents so much more natural to a woman than to a man and so necessary to its perfection.

There is no doubt in my mind that a woman's success in many lines of endeavour is still made very difficult by a strong prejudice against one of her sex doing work that has been done only by men for hundreds of years. Of course this prejudice is fast disappearing ... [8]

Most of Guy's surviving films come from her time at Solax, where she was neighbours with other future studio behemoths like Biograph, Metro, Goldwyn and Selznick Pictures. Solax was a custom-built facility that handled everything from shooting to editing, and there Guy made films that are remarkably modern compared to many of her contemporaries'. There's considerably less over-acting than in some films of the day; Guy painted the motto 'Be natural' on her wall and drew relatively understated performances from her casts.

In particular, she got good work from children. Check out the very sweet *Falling Leaves*, like many of these early silent films available on YouTube, where a little girl – told that her ailing sister will be dead before the last leaf falls – ties autumn leaves back on to trees to save her sister's life. A passing doctor asks the child what she's doing and, wouldn't you know it, is working on an experimental treatment that saves the day.

Guy also tackled feminist issues. In 1912's *Making an American Citizen*, an Eastern European immigrant learns, through a series of vignettes, that he must treat his wife respectfully in order to assimilate into his new culture. It's a forward-thinking and idealistic notion, as well as an effective comedy, but one that few male directors would have considered.

By some distance her most shockingly feminist work was a 1906 effort called *The Consequences of Feminism*, remade in 1912 for the American market under the title *In The Year 2000*. The 1906 film (the remake, like many silent-era films, is lost) imagined a world where boisterous, dominant women rule and sexually harass small, simpering men who fret about their hats. It's funny and silly and gloriously pointed: the men are trapped in meaningless busy-work and the women strut about as if they own the place. Eventually the men rebel and throw the women out of a bar. The metaphor is pretty clear: in the real world, men risk provoking the same resistance if they don't change their ways. Nor was that her only radical piece. In 1912 she made *A Fool and His Money*, thought to be the first film with an all-African-American cast. It's not at all progressive to modern eyes, but even to make it was remarkable in those times.

Guy's career eventually foundered on a double blow: Herbert Blaché left her to work in Hollywood in 1918, and in 1919 she almost died in the Spanish influenza epidemic. She recovered her health but her career lagged: it was harder to manage the business side without her husband as front man to deal with male investors. Guy made her last film in 1919, and by 1921 had to sell what remained of Solax to pay off debts. In 1922, following her divorce from Blaché, she returned to France, where despite repeated attempts she was never to make another feature.

In the official history of Gaumont's early days, Guy's role was excised by her former boss. But Guy herself never gave up. She hunted down her surviving films, and in 1953 was awarded the Légion d'honneur in recognition of her work. It was a belated accolade for her extraordinary role in film history, but cold comfort for all the years she was barred from working.

2

From Pioneers to Pariahs
How women fell silent before sound

G UY MIGHT have been the first female director, but soon she
was one among many. As the American industry mushroomed –
first around New York and then in its forever home of Los Angeles
– other women found space to work and, for a while, to thrive.

The most powerful of those early Hollywood women was Lois
Weber, who would become the most successful female director of the
silent era, and arguably of the twentieth century, given her clout and
prestige in her day. She was also one of the few whose career would
survive – just about – into the talkies.

Weber started out in theatre and actually worked as an actress for
Guy in a Solax film before she and husband Phillips Smalley set up
on their own. After she took up directing as well as writing and starring, Weber became known as a social filmmaker, tackling issues
from gossip to sexual assault to poverty to abortion and birth control
(though not always successfully to modern eyes: birth control
campaigner Marie Stopes was so appalled by her film on abortion
that she asked for it to be banned[1]). But far more than that, Weber
became a sort of first lady of filmmaking throughout the 1910s, even
becoming mayor of the newly built 'Universal City' in 1914. That
seems fitting for the first American woman to direct a full-length
feature (1914's *The Merchant of Venice*) – so why was she, too, largely
written out of the silent-era histories?

It's extraordinary because Weber was a *really* big deal in her day. She was already established on the East coast when she moved out West and became part of the new Universal Studios. Cecil B. DeMille's directorial debut, *The Squaw Man*, was the first film shot in Hollywood, in 1913, but within a few short months the entire industry followed him. They found a vast desert bowl between the hills and the sea, where they could take advantage of the bright natural light and warm climate. That landscape, and the distance from the money men in New York, would shape American filmmaking for decades.

Carl Laemmle's Universal occupied a huge tract and claimed to have found a new way of living and working (though few people actually lived there), 'electing' officials from among its stars and filmmakers. In this unincorporated town, Weber ran for mayor on a suffrage ticket, at a time when women did not even have the vote nationally. She lost the election by fifteen votes, but 'business changes' demanded that winner Isadore Bernstein resign, and Weber was appointed to the vacancy. Call it a publicity stunt (it was) but it also spoke to Weber's reputation as a woman of substance.

At work, Universal's regime initially allowed Weber to push the boundaries of the art form via what historian Shelley Stamp calls her 'living newspaper' films. Weber argued that cinema had the potential to spark discussion about important social issues, to be a tool of education and improvement, and that women had the potential to bring that power to fruition. She spoke at women's clubs frequently to make that case, wrote articles about it, and by all accounts presented a personal case for the power of cinema in her demeanour as well as her work. Weber didn't challenge the status quo with a wild lifestyle, outrageous displays of wealth or even loud support for suffrage: she presented herself as a respectable married woman, inviting journalists into her home with Smalley and showing them a vision of collaboration – though it was always clear who led their creative endeavours.

After her career ended Weber was portrayed in Hollywood histories – if she was remembered at all – as a star maker, plucking silent star Claire Windsor out of the lunch queue in the Universal canteen, for example. But in her day she was among the foremost directors in the industry. *Universal Weekly* dubbed her the 'Greatest Woman Director in the World' and claimed that some would suggest dropping the modifier 'to make it really fit her'.[2] Laemmle, who was not known for his spending, said that he would trust Weber with 'any sum of money that she needed'. While she did find future stars, she also networked with, encouraged and mentored an entire generation of women across Hollywood.

Aside from the blatant unfairness of her historical portrayal, it's frustrating to think of the films she and her followers might still have made. Although D. W. Griffith and Cecil B. DeMille are credited with developing a majority of visual tricks and film grammar in the early years, Weber actually used some of those styles before her male contemporaries. She was an early adopter of split-screen with her 1913 home-invasion thriller *Suspense*, showing the creeping danger alongside the terrified victim, and she was a proponent of shooting on location and, where possible, in sequence. On films like *Hypocrites* and *Where Are My Children?*, she used multiple exposure, and she was chosen to shoot world-famous ballerina Anna Pavlova's only film, *The Dumb Girl Of Portici*. While Weber technically shared a directing credit with her actor husband Phillips Smalley at first, it was always clear from contemporary accounts that she was the driving creative force as both writer and director. She even started displaying her signature on her films, hoping that this would stand as a guarantee of quality. After their divorce Smalley never gained another directing credit while Weber, for a few years at least, continued to rank among Hollywood's top names.

During the mid-1910s, Universal entrusted Weber with more quality features than any other director on their roster,[3] to the extent that she dominated their 'Bluebird' offshoot. While she always pushed to make films of social substance, she also had huge successes with *Hypocrites* (a religious allegory set in two parallel timelines). She became Universal's highest paid director, on $5,000 per week (adjusted for inflation, about $127,000; Premiership footballer money, in other words), and enjoyed almost total creative control. Films like *Shoes* and *The Blot*, both of which deal with poverty, still stand up remarkably well: the latter's plea for fair pay for academics feels all too current.

There was a lively community of female filmmakers around Weber at Universal, including Ida May Park, Ruth Ann Baldwin, Cleo Madison and Ruth Stonehouse. By the count in historian Mark Garrett Cooper's book *Universal Women*, women directed 170 films at Universal during the 1910s. That wasn't just because studio head Carl Laemmle hired cheap talent, though he did. So did other studios that barely employed any women. Actress Ruth Clifford put the studio's particular openness to women down to acceptance. 'The other directors, the men, were very cooperative. And the actors . . . took direction just the same as if it were a man directing. Everyone cooperated. It was like a big happy family at that studio.'[4] Universal sold itself as a place of 'play', as studio advertising of the time put it, and what better way to show novelty than to have women working in senior roles? Weber was the Beyoncé of the group. But Park was also a force to be reckoned with. She wrote forty-four films between 1914 and 1919, directing eleven between 1917 and 1919. Baldwin, meanwhile, directed thirteen films for Universal and a further six for Fox before her career finished in 1921.

By 1921, a lot of careers were finishing. Weber had set up her own studio, Lois Weber Productions, under Universal's auspices in 1917, but within two years she was struggling. While she made one film at a time, the big studios were engaged in industrial-style production. Weber contracted herself out to Louis B. Mayer and then to Paramount in an effort to keep her career alive, but by April 1921 Paramount turned down her fourth film under their agreement, a film called *What Do Men Want?*. It portrayed the abandonment of a pregnant, unmarried woman and her subsequent suicide, and the studio considered it too risky, crippled by two opposing forces: censorship was increasing around the country, while at the same time the Jazz Age made such moralistic tales seem passé to the nation's youth.

It became harder for Weber to find steady work. Through the '20s she was still working with Universal but at a lower level: as a talent scout, a script doctor and just one more time as director. She shot her only sound effort and last film, *White Heat*, in Kauai in 1934, taking a ship full of equipment and generators with her to get authentic surroundings. The film 'was not a hit but will not lose any money', according to Weber.[5] But it wasn't enough to relaunch her career. She died five years later, trying until her final days to get back behind the camera. Her screenwriter protégée and friend, Frances Marion, paid for her funeral.

Universal's women were not the only female directors working: the Women Film Pioneers Project at Columbia University, which researches women in every role in the first decades of the industry, has documented at least 121. Lillian Gish, the star of D. W. Griffith's racist milestone *Birth of a Nation*, turned her hand to directing in 1919 with a mid-budget, five-reel film called *Remodeling Her Husband*. The film is lost, so we can't judge if Griffith was right when he complimented Gish on the result. It had been an ambitious under-taking. Gish set out to make it as female as possible, writing the script with her sister and star Dorothy Gish, and hiring Dorothy Parker to write the inter-titles at the suggestion of Weber and screenwriter Anita Loos. The one role she couldn't find a woman to cover was cameraman (then, as now, camera departments were heavily male-dominated), and the man she hired, George Hill, caused problems when he became, she said, 'hysterical' because a set was slightly too small for the master shot he wanted. Her rented studio space was another nightmare: the furnace broke, the set froze and the actors had to hold their breath while the camera rolled so that the mist wouldn't be visible. Gish wrote to a friend later that, 'It was almost too much for me. Would never do it again, however it was a good experience and I am not sorry. Am cutting and editing (is that the way you spell it) it now.'[6]

The reviews were not all glowing ('Lillian does not qualify as a particularly strong directress,' sniffed *Variety*, reserving all praise for Dorothy), and in the immediate aftermath a bitter Gish said that women should not direct. 'I am not strong enough,' she told *Photoplay*. 'I doubt if any woman is. I understand now why Lois Weber was always ill after a picture.' But Gish came around, pointing out to film historian Anthony Slide in 1977 that the film took ten times its cost: a rare achievement in any age.

Outside the Hollywood bubble, we know that Marion E. Wong set up the Mandarin Film Company in Oakland and made a film called *The Curse of the Quon Gwon*, casting her family as her stars and playing the villain herself.[7] That film survives only partially, though 1917 accounts describe its plot as concerning 'the curse of a Chinese god that follows his people because of the influence of western civilization'.[8] It was turned down for wide distribution. A few Asian stars like Tsuru Aoki were able to make a career without relying on exoticised stereotypes, but it may have helped that Aoki was married to heart-throb Sessue Hayakawa (he later starred in *The Bridge on the River Kwai*). Yet such roles were few and far between.

African-American filmmakers Tressie Souders and Maria P. Williams both directed films that are now lost, 1922's *A Woman's Error* and 1923's *The Flames of Wrath* respectively. Williams' film seems to have grown out of her work as a cinema manager and social campaigner, into which roles she apparently retreated, but Souders moved to Hollywood at some point before 1936, so she may have tried to make a career in film and run up against a wall of racism. Hollywood was not immune to the racism that afflicted, well, everywhere, and Black people were largely confined to servant roles and certainly barred from directing. Alice Guy had been able to make her film with an all-Black cast because she was white, but no Black women were able to follow her lead in the studio system.

A parallel African-American cinema did develop, but as far as we know none of its major directors or producers were women. That said, there *were* notable characters like Anita Thompson, a Black Los Angeles-raised star of 1921's *By Right of Birth* for the Lincoln Motion Picture Company.[9] The film portrayed Black people more positively than most movies at the time, part of the company's riposte to the horrific success of *Birth of a Nation* – but it was Thompson's later life that stands out. Her politically active mother (Booker T. Washington and W. E. B. Du Bois were family friends; Langston Hughes was a cousin) gave her money to go to college in Wellesley but instead she headed to Paris and hung out with the likes of Picasso, Hemingway, James Joyce and Coco Chanel. Thompson had more fun than practically anyone, though in screen terms her legacy was brief. Evelyn Preer, leading lady to Black filmmaker Oscar Micheaux, had a far more significant impact. She was known in Black communities as the 'First Lady of the Screen', appearing in sixteen films, on stage and in cabaret (backed on occasion by Duke Ellington). She steadfastly rejected roles that were demeaning or racist, but was not stodgily moralistic: her last role before her sadly early death from pneumonia was as a prostitute opposite Marlene Dietrich in *Blonde Venus*.

Other marginalised groups managed some firsts. Alla Nazimova played the exotic vamp on screen, carefully cultivating her real-life image to match, but she was also one of Hollywood's foremost lesbians. She developed, produced and starred in 1923's *Salomé*, an adaptation of the Oscar Wilde play, though it was officially directed by her 'lavender' husband Charles Bryant ('lavender' or fake marriages were relatively common in Hollywood as a cover for gay men and women). *Hollywood Babylon* author Kenneth Anger claims that the film was the first to feature an entirely gay cast. It's certainly one of the most stylish and stylised efforts of the silent era, however, thanks in part to the set design of Natacha Rambova, the future Mrs Rudolph Valentino.

Lule Warrenton was described by *Motion Picture News* in 1917 as 'one of the best known directors on the Pacific Coast', and became an independent director and producer.[10] She had developed a reputation at Universal as a gifted director of children, so her studio was designed to cater exclusively to 'juvenile' films. Warrenton came from the stage, and was older than Weber and the rest, so it's possible that she simply retired in the mid-1920s, but certainly her planned 1923 all-female studio in San Diego, a world first, does not appear to have made an impact.[11] Ruth Ann Baldwin, another Universal Woman, became the first woman to make a Western feature with '49–'17 in 1917 – and there her directing career ended, though she continued to write.

But the Western genre gave us one of the most intrepid of the directors of that era, male or female: Nell Shipman. She literally went further than her contemporaries and journeyed into the Northern wilderness to make her films, outdoing even Alejandro González Iñárritu's *The Revenant* in her capacity to endure remote locations and harsh conditions. Shipman started off as a star, became a writer and producer and finally turned to directing too.[12] Her breakthrough as an actress was with 1915's *God's Country and the Woman*, based on a story by Jack London-alike author James Curwood. Having thereby gained some clout, she wrote and produced a sequel, based on Curwood's story *Back to God's Country*, in 1919.

Curwood was apparently not happy with her decision to transform his tale so that the heroine was a woman called Dolores rather than a

Great Dane called Tao (showing that great roles for women have always been thin on the ground, and that purists have always objected to rewrites to create female leads. Take heart, 2016 *Ghostbusters.*). Perhaps that's why Curwood insisted, as permitted by his contract, on a filming location at Slave Lake in Canada, just south of the Arctic Circle.

If he hoped to force Shipman to drop the idea, he was disappointed. Shipman and her crew bundled up against the shocking cold and went into the heart of the Canadian winter, facing temperatures of -40 degrees (Curwood went home). Shipman's cameraman, Joseph Walker (a camera pioneer and later a legend of the studio era), recalled lenses freezing open in the cold and the constant danger of death in the frigid conditions. Frostbite nearly claimed director Bert Van Tuyle's foot and made him delusional with pain. Original leading man Ronald Byram, after going outside without his coat and breathing too deeply in the icy air – despite warnings to take shallow breaths – apparently 'froze the tips of his lungs' and died of pneumonia.

Shipman soldiered on: writing, producing and starring in several more wilderness epics. Her final two efforts as director were less successful: the taste for such adventures seemed to have passed. Still, she deserves to be remembered for her toughness. While Leonardo DiCaprio and Iñárritu resorted to a CG grizzly, Shipman had a pet bear that she brought on shoots, as well as a full complement of other wild animals. Making 1923's *The Grub-Stake* turned rough when hostile locals killed many of her animals and Shipman and Van Tuyle were left stranded in the wilderness for two days. Her last production company finally went bust in 1925 and she left Hollywood to set up an animal sanctuary. For the rest of her life she pitched screenplays, but she was left in the cold by Hollywood. When she applied for benefits from the Motion Picture Relief Fund in the 1960s, they could find no record of her film credits and denied her claim.

Shipman followed a decade-long vogue for action-packed thrillers, giving lie to the long-standing Hollywood claim that female-led action films don't sell (unless we've gone backwards in the last hundred years?). Long before *Captain Marvel*, there were hit action serials led by extraordinary stuntwomen – extraordinary because they benefited from almost none of the safety precautions used today. Take, for example, the 'Peerless Fearless Girl' Pearl White. She starred in serials like *The Perils of Pauline* and *The Exploits of Elaine*, and was the most popular film star of 1916. White and her fellow action stars – Grace Cunard, Helen Holmes, Rose 'Helen' Gibson (rechristened when she took over *The Hazards of Helen* series from Holmes), Cleo Madison, Kathlyn Williams – were spiritual ancestors to Tom Cruise. White learned to fly, threw herself off moving cars and swam across rivers. She dangled off a Manhattan skyscraper as a publicity stunt. Holmes jumped from a moving train to a moving car, and saved her character's father, boyfriend and employer from disaster. Gibson leapt from a railway-station roof on to a moving train, and when the train's motion caused her to almost roll off the other side she grabbed an air vent and held on like a true Indiana Jones, nailing the take. Williams' speciality in 1913's *The Adventures of Kathlyn* was working with wild animals, though that serial was most notable as the first to use cliffhanger endings. Madison had to survive a car crash and a forest fire for her films, and if Cunard did less in the way of stunt work, she played jewel thieves and reporters so she still packed in the thrills. She and Madison were also credited directors and screenwriters.

Of course, some stunts *did* go horribly wrong. Spinal injuries left White in persistent pain and she became too valuable to risk on her own stunts. That became public knowledge when a stuntman in a wig, John Stevenson, was killed during her last serial, *Plunder*, in 1923. White had been savvy with her money and lived in comfort for the rest of her life – though that was shortened by the alcoholism that numbed the pain of her injuries. Gibson was replaced by the Spencer Production Company in 1921 after a ruptured appendix left her hospitalised. For a few years she retired from Hollywood to become a trick rider in the circus, because that seemed safe, before returning to spend a decade doubling for other stars.

Like the stunt stars, some female pioneers were almost immediately written out of the history books. That girl from the train tracks, Mabel Normand, was one of the leading lights of comedy studio Keystone Pictures.[13] Normand was often the object of desire for a big lug played by Mack Sennett or Fatty Arbuckle, but behind the scenes she was a writer, director and producer, creating and controlling her own work. Her co-star and boss Sennett said that it was Normand who taught Chaplin to direct, though Chaplin (of course) denied that in his own accounts, saying that he had complained about her competence and directed himself from the start. Keystone's own records show that Normand was directing in 1914 and Normand told *Picture Play* that she directed her own pictures 'for a long time'.

Normand finished her career as an actress, her filmmaking largely forgotten. A series of scandals involving men around her also diminished her public appeal, and through the '20s she was dogged by stories about her drinking and drug use. She died in 1930 of tuberculosis, aged just thirty-seven, and never had the chance to write her own self-aggrandising story like her male colleagues.

By then, women were already being written out of film history. Shipman and Guy would write their own memoirs but find no takers in their lifetimes (they have since been published).[14] It's only recently that projects like Columbia's Women Film Pioneers Project are beginning to uncover the buried stories of the silent-era women. 'I would never have done this project if I'd known how they'd come out of the woodwork,' jokes Professor Jane Gaines[15], one of the leaders of the Project. 'Every time I go to the Library of Congress, I find a new name. It might be in the credits, or we look at a Chinese film and discover that White Rose Woo, who was the Chinese [equivalent of action heroine] Pearl White, has a screenwriting credit on another film.' Families still find troves of movie memorabilia in attics courtesy of great-grandmothers, and pass them on. Much of what was lost is being reconstructed, and recent funding for the American Film Institute to work with the WFPP will mean that the credits for those women are now added to their catalogue of movie history.

Back then, if you wanted to assure your legacy, the best option was to tie your story to a man. Dorothy Davenport did just that when she turned a drug-related tragedy into a crusade. Davenport was a star and occasional director, but also part of a dream couple with fellow actor Wallace Reid. He was a major heartthrob, a genial and handsome sort with a lighter screen presence than the brooding likes of Valentino or Hayakawa: think Tom Hiddleston. But Reid was injured in a train crash and given a huge dose of morphine so he could keep shooting. He became addicted and died while trying to get clean with the 'help' of quack physicians. The *New York Times* genteelly reported his condition as a 'nervous breakdown', but fans knew better. Davenport – now billing herself as Mrs Wallace Reid – responded with drug drama *Human Wreckage* the following year, which finishes with a direct-to-camera plea to fight narcotics pushers. Her story inspired the many versions of *A Star is Born*, with the famous wife adopting her husband's name to protect his legacy.

Reid's tragedy was part of the dark side of Hollywood stardom from its outset. People literally worked themselves to death on hundreds of shorts in a year, took risks that no sane person would countenance and accepted whatever substances they were offered to keep doing it, chasing that movie-stardom high. It quickly became clear, by the early 1910s, that there was too much money at stake to slow down, not when the outfit next door was going to shoot on regardless. Money began to shape the industry in unhealthy ways.

If that environment was bad for adults, it was significantly worse for child stars. Take one of the longest surviving, Baby Peggy, aka Diana Serra Cary, who died in February 2020.[16] She earned millions of dollars – *not* adjusted for inflation – as a child star before most kids have learned to spell. She worked eight hours a day, six days a week, playing adorable tomboys off on mini adventures, often with 'Brownie the Wonder Dog', who, she noted later, was the same age she was. Cary did her own stunts, because who else was small enough? She was hit by a bicycle in one film, nearly drowned in a water scene with a large dog, and bucked from a speeding truck for her art. Her expressiveness and willingness won her praise but stemmed from absolute obedience to her domineering father, a woodsman-turned-stuntman-turned-alcoholic who ruled his family with an iron fist. He spent her money like water, and ended her career when he argued with the wrong studio executive and got her blacklisted.

Cary would later campaign for the passing of the 1939 'Coogan Act', aka the California Child Actor's Bill. Named after her contemporary Jackie Coogan, the law safeguards a portion of child actors' salaries even today and guarantees them school time and breaks. It came too late for its sponsors. By the time Cary reached adulthood her film money was long frittered away, and as recently as 2014 she was denied medical assistance from the Motion Picture and Television Fund because they could not establish her film credits. This came despite the fact that Cary said she 'stood next to Mary Pickford when the fund was established', and despite her many decades of work preserving the history of silent film.

The problem for the legacy of Baby Peggy and so many others of the silent era was how Hollywood changed when sound came in. As part of the campaign to convince theatre owners to switch to sound, studio heads actively ridiculed silent movies. Lois Weber's *Shoes*, a socio-realist portrayal of a girl who's so desperate for new shoes that she sells herself to buy them, was re-released with a comic voice-over.

'*Shoes* was an incredibly female-led, feminine film,' says film historian Pamela Hutchinson, 'but one of the reasons it survives is that they made a mocking sound version with a sarcastic narration. It's so callous! But it's interesting. At the same time we're saying, "Oh, look at these silly silent films" we're also saying, "Look at these silly films for women."'[17]

But it wasn't sound that killed women's careers. Most female directors were long gone by the time *The Jazz Singer* launched the talkies in 1929, and the tiny few who remained had already seen their autonomy diminished. In the late 1920s, a high-ranking studio executive said that he didn't feel that women were suited to be film directors. Lois Weber responded with a two-part newspaper column saying that not only are women suited to directing, but more women should direct. Yet she knew she was fighting against the tide. In the same piece she admitted that men were now reluctant to accept her authority as director, whereas ten years earlier she had been judged on her merits. Ruth Clifford's claim that men were willing to work with women was no longer true.

As those filmmakers left the pictures, the most important remaining way that women could shape cinema was as audience members. Irving Thalberg, as gifted a movie executive as ever lived, said in 1924 that, 'Pictures should be made primarily for the feminine mind.'[18] Cinema became a mass art form *because* it attracted women, and succeeded to the extent that more women than men made up its audiences in those early decades. The nascent Hollywood created a hunger for its product, its own addicts. Exhibitors expected to show four new short films every day, twenty-eight a week, in the earliest days. Long after feature films became the norm they would be accompanied by a short, as well as perhaps a newsreel or travelogue. Cinema enthusiasts were already reading fan magazines in the 1910s and sitting through entire programmes to get one look at a favourite star.

Before stars were named in credits or marketing, viewers – especially women – had taken them to their hearts and invested their hopes in them.

Perhaps it's because women are discouraged from taking up space in the real world that there was something magical about sitting in a dark room and seeing your image reflected back, ten times bigger than life. Perhaps, at a time when women were encouraged to marry young and devote their lives to husband and children, it was transporting to see pure desire played out on screen. Weber's social films dared to discuss real issues that women faced, and treat them seriously, but there was the other sort of film too, the pure fantasies of romance and drama. A male star who *really* hit the mark with straight female audiences could rocket to superstardom, as heartthrobs Fairbanks, Hayakawa, Reid and especially Rudolph Valentino would find out. And Valentino, the biggest sex symbol of them all, was spotted by a woman and supported by women, even as he became the most hated and envied man in America.

June Mathis, a hugely successful MGM screenwriter and executive ('the most responsible job ever held by a woman', according to the *New York Times*), spotted Valentino's potential and pressured the studio to give this unknown a lead role in 1921's *The Four Horsemen of the Apocalypse*. She then counselled him through his first few features, even bailing him out of jail when he was arrested for bigamy (you know how it is, one divorce isn't *entirely* finalised when you marry the next woman in line – *Salomé* designer Natacha Rambova in this case). It's hard to overstate how successful Mathis was. A contemporary studio puff piece described her as having, 'supervisory responsibility for the expenditure of millions of dollars a year', and said, 'her salary will be the largest ever paid by a motion picture company to any woman, except two or three of the foremost stars'. Such bumph was designed to make the studio look wise and progressive in the mid-1920s, sure, but it also wasn't untrue.

Mathis fought for Valentino's role in *Horsemen* and played peace-maker between the star and a director who hated him. Practically all men *hated* Valentino; they saw him, and the frenzied admiration he inspired, as a threat to all-American manhood. Never mind that it was the 1920s and every dandy in the world was living it up in the Jazz Age; the tradition of blaming it all on movie stars started early, and women loved Valentino too much for him to be trustworthy. There's a long old tradition of men getting hysterical when women show a preference for a man who doesn't meet their definition of masculinity. Few men object to women fancying, say, Chris Hemsworth or Douglas Fairbanks – big, bluff men who seem virile and muscly – but the ardour for a Harry Styles, Edward-from-*Twilight* or Valentino is treated with far more suspicion. There's a certain type of man who believes, deep down, that with a bit of time in the gym he could become a Fairbanks or a Hemsworth, but he knows he could never have been Valentino. One would feel sorry for them, except that such men are so often sexist, too, that it's hard to have sympathy for their fragile sense of selves.

The problem for women was the increasingly masculine character of the film business. When film was essentially a cottage industry, something hand-crafted in small workshops around the country, women could take their place among its makers. But an industry on a national (and international) scale was a different matter. It had happened before in whisky[19] and in wool spinning,[20] and it would happen later with computing. Women were allowed to flourish to a certain point and no further. Men controlled industry, men made business decisions, and there was no place for women there, not even if they did stand on the verge of winning the vote. Much of the longevity of Weber and Guy's careers owed to the fact that their husbands were, essentially, their front men. Actresses had to hide their husbands and children from public view, but for directors they could be helpful. Other businessmen could pretend that they were dealing with Phillips Smalley or Herbert Blaché when they went to Universal or Solax; once those marriages failed, so did that façade.

There was also a shift that still hampers women today, and that was the cementing image, in the public mind and in particular among executives, of what a director looks like. If there is someone with control and authority over a film, someone whose word is law on set, then it felt instinctively right to people in the 1920s (and often in the 2020s) that that person should be a big strong man. The towering D. W. Griffith and his long, patrician face fitted the bill; so did Cecil B. DeMille with his jodhpurs and riding crop (who's he going to whip?). But Lois Weber, with her old-fashioned, matronly ways? Not so much.

If female directors and producers had trouble with their crews, that was a drop in the ocean compared to the trouble they had with financiers. The money that poured into the Hollywood studios at the dawn of the 1920s came from Wall Street investors who liked known quantities. 'We have this all the time now where you hire people who look like you,' says Pamela Hutchinson. 'If you think the director is the person who's going to protect your investment in a film, [you're looking for] the same guys, all very corporate. The kind of women who had the ambition and drive to do something like this, in what was even then a very male-dominated space, were maybe the kind of person who didn't want to make the kind of films that would appeal to the corporate line.' It's always been easier for the people who look like they belong to smuggle in nonconformist ideas, after all. For women, even slight deviations were now suspicious.

As women were pushed out of directing, the female producer followed. Early stars like Clara Kimball Young, Mary Pickford and Gene Gauntier essentially produced their work. Actresses set up self-titled companies to protect the profit share they were due, although some only lasted for one or two pictures. Giving stars their own producing credit when trying to keep them at your studio was a Hollywood technique that started early; there would be literally hundreds of such deals in the 1990s when they came back into vogue, and they're still common now, as we'll see. But as the studio system began to solidify, individual production deals died away and were replaced by studio contracts assuring stars of a steady income rather than a profit share.

The genius of the big studios was to seize control of not just the means of production but also the means of distribution. The biggest studios of the 1920s and '30s controlled chains of cinemas as well as making the content that filled them. MGM's dominance would rely not only on the talent of Irving Thalberg and its stable of star names, but also on its ability to supply a country-wide network of big screens.

That was bad news for the women who worked in exhibition too. As the studios tightened their grip, the barriers to opening your own cinema rose. Studio-owned theatres came to dominate the markets in cities and large towns, and the price of setting up a cinema climbed to $100,000 in the sound era – far more than most could afford. At the time women were almost always unable to get business loans in their own right; the Equal Credit Opportunity Act, guaranteeing women the right to apply for a loan without a man to co-sign, only passed in 1974. Yes, the right to get a loan without a man is younger than Kate Beckinsale or Rose McGowan. Some women were able to hang on in exhibition, just as a few – as we'll see – hung on in directing. But the studio era ended most female careers in exhibition as well.

It was about who was allowed to exercise authority. If films are a lark, like amateur dramatics almost, then you – a strapping young Jazz Age fellow – might well take orders from a woman and treat it as a novelty. When it becomes your job and she expects you to continue to do what she tells you, suddenly it seems like an imposition. That's why Weber and others reported crews becoming more difficult to work with over time, why Guy had trouble with her studio team at

Gaumont towards the end of her decade there. Increasingly the experience and knowledge these women had counted for less than what they could not change, the fact that the men around them would no longer admit that women even belonged in that space.

Worst of all, as Gaines points out, 'They didn't have any words or language for discrimination. So they had to fight against prejudice [with] no name for it. They might have been angry, and frustrated, and exhausted, but they didn't have feminism to explain it. Now, we understand what the forces [at play] are.'[21]

When film was a novelty, a way of telling stories that was all possibility and little profit, women made space for themselves and in some cases made history. They could tell stories about underrepresented groups, including themselves; they could make big-budget spectacles for mass audiences. But with such abilities came money, independence and authority, and none of those consequences were so appealing to men. When film became industrialised by big money investors, women were pushed out because allowing them to stay would suggest they were equal to their male peers. We see it now in tech: women can thrive as influencers and advertisers, but face higher barriers in launching their own start-ups.

That's what Weber complained of towards the end of her career. Studio bosses didn't want thoughtful drama that might engage female audiences; they wanted starlets. Weber and Guy were out of step with the times because they thought cinema could change the world. They were not militant feminists; both were wary of identifying too closely with the suffragist cause. But their art was a challenge because it took women's concerns seriously and suggested that they mattered. Even if the guy still got the girl in the end, even if they tended to emphasise the importance of respectable marriage and traditional values, even though they were overwhelmingly white and socially conservative, it wasn't enough to reassure the new studio bosses that they were trustworthy.

The sort of subject that Weber tackled in the 1910s was beyond the pale a decade later. 'Important' films from now on would be those that dealt with issues coded as male: war, politics, law and serious (male-led) journalism. Women's films would be considered niche, domestic, melodramas of little consequence. The sphere of female directors was more and more narrowly defined, until almost all the women at Universal – by then virtually the only studio with significant numbers of female directors – were making films about how to marry well, and only that.

By the end of the silent era, only a tiny handful of women still hung on in directing and producing roles: Weber among them, with the rising Dorothy Arzner and Dorothy Davenport Reid. All but Arzner would be gone in another decade. Writers like Frances Marion were able to continue work, since even then writing was considered a secondary skill to directing and one better suited to women.

There's no evidence that these female directors had significantly more flops than their male contemporaries, incidentally, or that they were incapable of hitting the same box-office heights from the same budgets. Weber was very highly paid precisely because her films made a huge amount of money. Executives like June Mathis had at least as many hits as any male contemporary: if she was implicated in the disastrous budget overruns of the 1924 *Ben-Hur*, she rebounded with a string of further hits. This wasn't a performance issue or a lack of enthusiasm. It was a slow, steady closing of the doors, to the white women who had briefly been able to prosper and certainly to the women of colour who had fought to make independent films.

Filmmaking was a mature industry, and the days of women standing alongside male peers and pushing the art form forward were over, for now. Meet the new boss, same as the old boss.

3

The Factory
Putting the industry in film industry

THE HOLLYWOOD studio system lasted from the early 1920s until the end of the 1940s. Many of the studios had come into existence earlier, in the 1910s, or are still going, but the 'system' in place during those short decades was a particular one, and it shaped film history in peculiar ways. It was designed to treat film as a factory product, a way to feed the insatiable demand of early audiences. The priority was to make as many films as possible, as fast as possible. Initially, with short films of one or two reels, filmmakers might churn out literally hundreds per year; even in the early feature era some stars and directors would make dozens of films back to back (and you thought Steven Soderbergh was productive[1].)

Output was key. Up to two-thirds of the US population attended the cinema every week and many went more often. No cinema owner wanted people to turn away because the programme of shorts contained something they had seen before. They needed new product, all the time; the public was hooked and the studios wanted to keep them that way. That's why Irving Thalberg at MGM, Adolph Zukor at Paramount, and the rest, began to build a system that would be cost-effective, efficient and, above all, fast. That's why stars (and writers, directors and other crew members) were not signed up film by film, as they are nowadays, but hired on studio contracts that paid a certain amount per week whether they were working or not.

The effects of the studio system linger even now, more than half a century after it fell to pieces. We still talk in ways prescribed by the studio myth-makers and propagandists, about stars and the fabulous lives they lead. We still buy into the awards system that the studios endorsed, and the behind-the-scenes stories they 'leak'. The genius of the system is to make us think that it was inevitable, that it is natural, when – as the previous chapters show – it was the result of choices that put men in charge of major movie-making for a century.

These choices didn't leave *all* women out in the cold. There were women who did very well out of the studio system, becoming extremely rich stars and forging careers that lasted for decades. Bette Davis, for all her fretting over money and fighting for roles, would live very comfortably into her eighties. When she first collapsed with the cancer that would kill her, she was at an awards ceremony – and after a short stay in hospital she travelled to Spain to receive another prize. Ingrid Bergman, too, would live to see herself become a grande dame of Hollywood, living well to the end on chocolates regularly sent to her in return for long-ago voice-over work. Rosalind Russell escaped Hollywood for a second career on Broadway; Lucille Ball also bailed and became a significant TV producer and star of her own legendary show. Smart and beautiful women did well by Hollywood, and some of them came out the other side happy and wealthy. But that's only fair, because the glamour of the movies was due in huge part to its female stars and the women who hung on in key roles behind the scenes. Some of those women realised that they had more leverage than the studios publicly admitted, and were eventually able to create the first major cracks that would transform the system into something (at least theoretically) more open.

This term 'studio system' implies a level of premeditation and strict codification that isn't quite accurate. In fact the 'studios' had quite distinct identities and histories. Metro-Goldwyn-Mayer took a few years to gather 'more stars than there are in heaven', its signature boast, but from the off it billed itself as a powerhouse for high-quality, high-budget fare. Warner Bros began as a scrappy outsider that built a reputation on gangster movies and was notably hostile to female-led stories. But it grew steadily, and came to rival MGM for its talent roster. Fox Films, which became 20th Century Fox, was often a launching pad for new, young stars, and would become enormously profitable by the war years. RKO Radio Pictures made big, splashy musicals and, of course, ambitious classics like *King Kong* and *Citizen Kane*. Paramount Pictures (born from the silent stable Famous Players-Lasky, itself the result of a merger) was another star-driven concern in the early years, but was notably business-forward: the first studio to sell its films nationwide rather than state by state.

Columbia Pictures began as a penny pincher, barely above the 'Poverty Row' B-movie producers, but became home to the screwball comedy and Frank Capra. Universal Pictures, the oldest American studio, dominated Hollywood from the mid-1910s to the mid '20s. After those remarkably female-friendly early years and a series of disastrous big-budget gambles on the likes of Erich von Stroheim, it re-established its footing with monster movies and a run of award-winning prestige hits.

Not all the studios functioned identically. The first five above owned chains of theatres (technically MGM was owned *by* the chain, Loew's Incorporated) and were therefore better positioned to set up labyrinthine accounting systems so, even today, no one knows how much some hit films of the period made.

All, however, put in place a system that was essentially designed to industrialise movie making. The studio would hire promising directors, stars and the rest on regular salaries. Then they tried to keep these people working as long and as hard as possible, slotting them into each new film in production with barely a break.

Based to a greater or lesser extent on Irving Thalberg's model at MGM, the studios quickly oriented themselves under a small cadre of almost entirely male executives (June Mathis was an early exception; there would be almost none after her). These guys headed 'production units' charged with making A-pictures (big budgets, big stars, prestige material like adaptations of successful plays and novels) and B-pictures (smaller budgets and stars, quick production schedules, stories largely written by in-house screenwriters). The aim was to manage the studio's resources as efficiently as possible. If Greta Garbo was about to finish one picture, what would be her next job? If the studio needed a B-list title to shore up the release schedule, who was free in a week's time?

Human needs were not really supposed to enter in to it – though of course they sometimes did, because people don't work like car parts on assembly lines. And because the producers were also human, sometimes artistic ambition got a look-in. Prestige pictures had a business case: they burnished a studio's image and helped it attract valuable talent. After the Academy Awards began in 1927 that prestige became quantifiable – a way of keeping score beyond mere commerce. On a wider scale, too, literary or artistic visions helped to protect the industry as a whole against government censorship (on which more later) and gave it a defence against charges of sensationalism or immorality. Art had value, to a point, but that was by no means the main aim.

This set-up put producers and executives firmly in charge, not directors or even the small producer-director-studio-owners like Lois Weber or Alice Guy-Blaché. Henceforth, studio bosses would all be men until 1980, and the executive level almost entirely male until the 1970s. That had a trickle-down effect on directors. Universal employed not a single female director from the dawn of the sound era until Amy Heckerling for 1982's *Fast Times at Ridgemont High*. That's nearly sixty years without a woman – and the other studios were not much better.

Where once there had been female directors and executives, there were now, at best, female-*friendly* directors and executives. The enormously successful David O. Selznick, a producing titan first at MGM and then independently, was known to have a knack for 'women's pictures' – something cemented when he made *Gone with the Wind*, still the highest-grossing film ever if you adjust for inflation (adjusting for inflation is disrespectful to *Avengers: Endgame* but it's permissible this once, for context). George Cukor made his reputation as a woman's director with the deliciously soapy, all-female *The Women* in 1939, but also with his input on *Gone with the Wind* and *The Wizard of Oz*, both of which he worked on for a time that year. He was, by the standards of his time, openly gay, which is to say that by the standards of our time the closet door was slightly ajar. He also stood as the informal centre of Hollywood's gay community, helping them to network and work with each other.

But friendly to women or not, men ran the show. The studios would shape and mould you into whatever they needed and expect loyalty and obedience in return. If you proved your worth they'd protect you from the law itself: witness a young John Huston causing a fatal hit-and-run accident while drunk in 1933, covered up after his father Walter called in some favours,[2] or Clark Gable killing a pedestrian in a traffic accident the following year.[3] The studios offered pay that was astronomical. Moderately big stars could earn more in a week than a factory worker would take home in a year, and there was incredible extravagance, like Mae West's jewellery collection and her claim that her pet monkey, Bad Boy, had eaten a 4-carat diamond.[4] But if the stars lived like royalty, the studio demanded its pound of flesh in return.

The set-up had some advantages over the modern system, in theory. Stars had a steady pay cheque, often an extravagant one. They had the studio's help in crafting a persona that would connect with the public. That personality might give them a certain amount of distance from themselves, which might or might not be a comfort. Joan Crawford seemed content to leave her early life behind, but others were more conflicted about their hard-to-live-up-to images. 'Even I wish I was Cary Grant,' sighed Cary Grant famously. Marilyn Monroe later expressed a similar feeling: 'I'm not so important! Who does he think I am, Marilyn Monroe or something?'[5] But would Archibald Leach or Norma Jeane Mortenson ever have gone so far?

As a new star you'd be given dancing lessons and elocution; you might learn to ride horses or sail a boat. The contract at its best could give actors room to fail: if the first film or two didn't hit, the studio might reassess and find something better for you (although if you failed *really* big, the contract could be cancelled). Stars were sometimes better off with a few failures or minor hits: an early success could see them typecast for years. It's the difference between Olivia de Havilland and Bette Davis. The former hit big instantly opposite Errol Flynn and was stuck as his love interest for seven films. The latter didn't quite fit in as a love interest or sidekick, until she fought her way into more complicated roles and became a superstar.

It wasn't all fur coats and roses, in other words. The system significantly limited star freedom, far beyond the ability to work elsewhere. Actors would be cast in roles chosen by the studio, whatever their own preference – and while certain hard men managed to write their own story to a significant degree (James Cagney, top of the world, Ma!), the majority of actors were moved around like pawns by all-powerful studio heads. If they weren't needed at their home studio, they could be loaned out to other studios at will, often at a much higher rate than their contracted salary. The studio, naturally, would pocket the difference. Joan Fontaine recalled being loaned out by David O. Selznick at a cost of $150,000 for ten weeks, while he paid her $2,000 per week.[6] That's a profit of some $130,000, entirely on someone else's work, in less than three months.

*   *   *

If you're wondering how far the studios' control of their stars went, the answer is *really* far. Will Hays, the first chairman of the Motion Picture Producers and Distributors of America (MPPDA) and Hollywood's studio-head-appointed moral guardian, pressured the studios to include morality clauses in stars' contracts from the early 1920s. This gave bosses control over more than a star's working day; it's no exaggeration to say that those clauses would twist people's lives for ever. Morality clauses are common even now, of course; they're a way for businesses to ensure that their reputation won't be damaged by an employee. They're standard in sports, where a shoe company signing a million-dollar sponsorship deal wants to be pretty sure that the all-American, apple-pie-eating superstar they're signing won't be revealed as a cocaine-abusing sex addict. Such revelations are traditionally bad news for the prospect of sales of shoes to children, after all. But in a time of Prohibition and much more stringent moral standards than today, very human behaviour could be career-ending.

The cry for morality clauses began in 1921, and reached a fever pitch during the trial of Roscoe 'Fatty' Arbuckle, at that point second only to Charlie Chaplin as a worldwide comedy draw. With his big belly and high-waisted trousers Arbuckle played ordinary Joes and likeable lugs, often opposite his friend and co-star Mabel Normand. But after a wild weekend party at a hotel in San Francisco in the summer of 1921, Fatty was accused of raping and accidentally crushing to death the starlet and 'best dressed woman in Hollywood' Virginia Rappe. Modern experts believe that Rappe was not raped, and that she died of a combination of an undiagnosed bladder issue and a weekend of heavy drinking. Both Arbuckle's account of her death and her previous medical history support this, and the only person who accused him of rape was a third party who wasn't present in the room. What happened was therefore a tragedy for Rappe but also for Arbuckle, because neither his career nor his life would ever recover.

By the time Arbuckle was acquitted of Rappe's death after two mistrials, with the third jury going so far as to apologise to him for the 'great injustice' done to him, it was too late. The court case had revealed the drug use, hard drinking and casual sex that were common among Hollywood's elite. The papers, especially the reactionary Hearst titles, bayed for blood. They thundered that Hollywood must reform its ways or be federally censored. That was a nightmarish prospect for studio bosses, so they took the capitalist way out: trumpet the organisation's virtue and blame the individual. Hays and the studio bosses hit the stars where it hurt: their wallet. They had a model to use. What's believed to be the first morality clause was an addendum to baseball player Babe Ruth's contract in 1922, stating that he would refrain from hard liquor and would not stay up after 1 a.m. without permission during the playing and training season.

Soon similar provisions were in use all over Tinseltown – though not for everyone. Flapper girl Clara Bow, the original 'It girl' (she starred in a film called *It*, not to be confused with the Stephen King horror), was the biggest box-office star of the late 1920s and refused a morality clause. As a compromise the studio put aside $25,000, due at the end of her contract if she behaved.[7] In 1929, she was named as co-respondent in a divorce case and lost the lot – but at least her contract wasn't cancelled outright. Others were not so lucky.

A typical morality clause prohibited hard liquor, and often any alcohol, completely. Drugs were right out – unless administered by studio doctors, on which more below. These clauses were frequently ignored, and as long as you weren't arrested (and sometimes if you were) the studio would turn a blind eye, or get the charges dismissed by shadowy fixers. One was Eddie Mannix, played by Josh Brolin in the Coen Brothers' *Hail, Caesar!*. (The real Mannix was a domestic abuser. That was also covered up.) Think *LA Confidential* and the seedy business of selling or burying star secrets, for an idea of what could go wrong.

The system could be ruthless to those who threatened it. *Vanity Fair*'s David Stenn reported in 2003 on the case of Patricia Douglas, who was put through hell by MGM in 1937.[8] Douglas was only twenty years old when she was hired for what she thought was a regular chorus line, but it turned out that she was to be a hostess at a wild party for MGM executives visiting from all over the country for an annual retreat. Among the attendees was a regional salesman, David Ross. As the 300 men present got deeper into the 500 cases of liquor provided, they began molesting the girls. When Douglas slipped away from Ross's harassment and hid out in the ladies' room, he took offence, and retaliated when she emerged by holding her down and forcing alcohol down her throat while others stood around and laughed. After she vomited and stepped outside to recover, he followed her, dragged her to a parked car and raped her.

Unlike most survivors of the time, who were so ashamed to be 'ruined' that they hid their attacks, Douglas was determined to seek justice. The district attorney was a close friend of studio boss Louis B. Mayer and did nothing, until her attorney took the story to the press. MGM paid off or threatened the witnesses while studio detectives smeared Douglas, desperately trying to dig up dirt on the teetotal virgin. Still, Ross was not indicted. When Douglas brought a civil suit against the studio it was dismissed. She tried again in the US district court, making a case that the rape violated her civil rights. This time, to be safe, the studio paid off *her* lawyer as well, and he failed to appear in court three consecutive times. Douglas was left without redress, and said the attack ruined her life. But her courage shone a light on the grubby underside of the studio system. This would be the only rape case on record that would implicate a studio, so Douglas achieved that much. But it's impossible to believe that her case was the only time that a studio ruthlessly suppressed such a claim. If lives were ruined as a result, well, they were only women – and Douglas wasn't even a big-name star.

Divorces, sex scandals, drinking and drugs were inevitable, despite the morality clauses. When else in history had such a concentration of gorgeous, charismatic young things been gathered together for so long? What other group had been given so much money and so many exciting new ways to spend it? Louis XIV wishes he were so blessed. Even as the Depression devastated the country in the 1930s, Hollywood seemed immune (it was not, entirely, but the studios would get through). Those struggling escaped their circumstances by diving into the vicarious pleasures of film. As the Depression deepened, the films got more lavish, the songs lighter and the dances more graceful. People who had almost nothing would spare a few cents to see a screwball comedy set among the upper classes, or a grand musical, or a giant ape taking Manhattan. The fan culture around cinema mushroomed too, with magazines that followed stars' lives obsessively. Audiences wanted to know every detail, and studio publicists quickly rose to meet those demands, filling the columns with fashion tips and titbits from the stars. Better to feed the beast than let the real news leak out.

Where morality clauses got unduly difficult for women was that they prohibited sex outside of marriage. In an age where birth control was still in its infancy, the consequences of extramarital sex weighed harder on women than men. Even sex within marriage could be problematic when studios objected to their leading lady's parenthood, because the image of a perpetually available and unfailingly glamorous *femme fatale* was not compatible with the realities of motherhood. Ava Gardner was forced to choose between suspension and giving birth at a time when she and husband Frank Sinatra had no other income than her studio fees; she chose to work.

The studios not only facilitated abortions for stars who wanted one (Bette Davis among them, allowing her to take the role in *Of Human Bondage* that made her a star), at a time when they were illegal in the US, but pressured stars to have abortions where they were *not*

43

wanted. One star, cast in a big movie, discovered she was pregnant shortly before shooting was due to start.[9] She asked if the schedule could be changed and was told that they would fit the work around her abortion, no problem (that star ended up having the baby and not the role).

According to 1930s blonde bombshell Joan Blondell, Carole Lombard had to drop out of *The Greeks Had a Word for Them* (aka *Three Broadway Girls*) after a botched abortion left her too ill to continue. Blondell got the role instead at the last minute. Lana Turner had several abortions to meet the demands of her contract.[10] One, in 1941, was carried out in a hotel room during a publicity tour of Hawaii. Turner was given no anaesthetic, and the doctor's $500 fee was deducted from her next pay cheque.

Gloria Swanson, a silent-era star who survived into the talkies, was also forced into an abortion when she became pregnant by her lover and soon-to-be husband, the fantastically named Henry de La Falaise, Marquis de la Coudraye, a minor French nobleman who worked as her translator while she shot 1925's *Madame Sans-Gêne*. Try as she might there was no way to hide the child's illegitimacy from anyone with a calendar. So she chose the abortion, but the illegal operation in her Parisian hotel was botched and she almost died. She later claimed in her memoir, *Swanson on Swanson*, that even her struggle for her life was turned into valuable publicity for the studio, as fans waited for regular updates on her health.[11] Swanson herself battled depression for months after her physical recovery. When the time came to renew her contract, she signed a new, less restrictive deal with Paramount. Swanson held her old boss personally responsible for her trauma. The new contract had no morality clause, and if she made fewer films thereafter, she got to choose her roles.

A few actresses managed to juggle both family and work: star Jeanne Crain, who appeared in *A Letter To Three Wives* and *Pinky*, sustained a career through the 1940s and 1950s while also giving birth seven times (after the first baby was born, she reluctantly gave away her pet lion though).[12] She lost the Anne Baxter role in *All About Eve* as a result of pregnancy, but Crain took a role from Baxter in *People Will Talk* a year later when Baxter became pregnant in turn, so it evened out numerically if not in terms of quality.

Actresses pregnant outside wedlock who refused an abortion could be blacklisted. Anita Björk was hired by Alfred Hitchcock to star in *I Confess* after he was blown away by her performance in the Cannes-garlanded 1951 *Miss Julie*. But Björk arrived in Hollywood with her lover Stig Dagerman and their daughter Lo, and studio head Jack Warner refused to allow her to work, much to Hitchcock's displeasure.[13] Instead, Anne Baxter was shipped up to Canada for the shoot, again the beneficiary of another woman's uterine complications.

That wasn't the only star that Hitchcock, or Hollywood, lost. Ingrid Bergman was an established draw, but she too became a victim of Hollywood morality. She started an affair with director Roberto Rossellini in 1951, though she was already married with a young daughter. Their relationship caused a sensation: Bergman had twice played a nun and even *Joan of Arc* herself, so the public tended to see her as a saint – an impression that her conscientious working style did not dispel. She was denounced in the US Senate and barred from *The Ed Sullivan Show*, and when it became clear how damaged her reputation was in the US she went to Italy with Rossellini and stayed there for five years.

Perhaps the most elegant solution to the odious double standard came from Loretta Young. She became pregnant by her co-star Clark Gable during 1935's *The Call of the Wild*, following what she came in her later years to understand was a date rape (she had considered the attack her own fault until learning about the concept).[14] Opposed to abortion for religious reasons, Young had the baby in secret while claiming an ill-defined illness, and later announced that she was adopting a young girl called Judy. While not everyone was fooled, she kept up appearances and avoided blacklisting.

Marriage could also land stars in hot water. Jean Harlow was reportedly barred from marrying William Powell because marriage would be incompatible with her bombshell image, and therefore had an abortion when she got pregnant from their affair. Judy Garland, a woman raised in the studio system and horribly scarred by her experiences there, also ran into marriage trouble. Desperate to get away, she married musician David Rose when she was nineteen. She did not have studio permission, and was peremptorily ordered back to work a day later. When Garland became pregnant, her mother and the studio arranged an abortion. Two years later, when an affair with Tyrone Power (also the man responsible for Lana Turner's Hawaiian termination) made her pregnant again, they reportedly arranged another. MGM believed that audiences were still in love with the fifteen-year-old Dorothy Gale and had no desire to see young Garland as a mother.

So neither bombshells nor ingénues could marry, and ideally no one would get pregnant. If women were haunted by these incidents – as Swanson was, and Garland – so be it. Incidentally, Mayer also stepped in to cancel psychiatrist appointments Garland booked in 1944 to deal with her traumas, worried that analysis would distract her from work on *Meet Me in St Louis*.

Those were all white women; actresses of colour faced extra burdens. Dorothy Dandridge, the stunning star of *Carmen Jones* and the first African-American nominee for a Best Actress Oscar, became pregnant in 1955 by the film's director, Otto Preminger. The studio demanded an abortion, and Preminger left her no cover when he refused to divorce his wife and marry her. The studio supported their director because interracial marriage was still against the law in many US states (though not California) and their union could have sparked boycotts in Southern states. The pregnancy would not just have undermined Dandridge's status as the sexy Carmen Jones but also put her in breach of racist laws across half the country.

Dandridge's experiences should leave a bitter taste in anyone's mouth. Hollywood may claim to be at the liberal end of the US political spectrum, but inequality has a way of creeping in anyway, via its wallet. There's a direct line from Dandridge's treatment (because of the South!) to the way that modern films tiptoe around gay characters and pay only lip service to representation (because of China! Or wherever is the latest scapegoat). Saying 'We're OK with it but we worry that other people might not be' just ensures that the least inclusive people still control the agenda.

It's therefore no surprise that morality clauses caught some LGBTQ+ stars. All such stars lived in fear of exposure by one of the scandal rags of the time like *Eyewitness* and *Confidential*. Bette Davis told a story about Kay Francis, once a huge star on the Warners lot, that suggests how rumours of sexual nonconformity could damage a career. Francis worked with William Powell several times, who, Davis said, 'went around telling anyone who would listen that she *must* be a good actress, because she played convincing love scenes with men'.[15] Davis saw those rumours as the reason that Francis suddenly shifted from starring in A-pictures, the top-paid star in the studio, to B-pictures and supporting roles. Francis's private journals make it clear that she was bi, and while there were other reasons that the studio might have cooled on her – she openly threatened a lawsuit at one point if she didn't get better scripts – the difficulty Francis had finding work at other major studios at the end of her Warners contract supports the notion that a whispering campaign played a part in her career's end.

Other LGBTQ+ stars were encouraged into 'lavender' marriages. Actor William Haines refused one in 1934 and his MGM contract was immediately cancelled (happily, he and his partner Jimmie Shields set up a successful furniture business and sold to his previous co-stars). Faced with the same choice, Rock Hudson married his agent's secretary and created a façade of straightness. How many Hollywood marriages were similarly fake still isn't clear. Many claims about the LGBTQ+ members of the 1930s and 1940s A-list are traceable back to self-described Hollywood pimp Scotty Bowers. By his account – and contemporaries vouched for his honesty – stars including Cary Grant and Spencer Tracy were gay or bi, while Katharine Hepburn was a lesbian. The relationship between Hepburn and Tracy was therefore a lavender affair for both.

Even if your private life was sufficiently locked down to survive, you still had to endure working conditions that were far from glamorous. Those studio-created personae could become stifling: much of Marilyn Monroe's unhappiness stemmed from the limited 'sexpot' role she was expected to inhabit, and the difficulty of persuading anyone to see past it. Stars worked hard for their salaries: like theatre actors in repertory companies, they often went straight from one production to the next, sometimes even overlapping, in an era when fourteen-hour days were the norm and weekends were for wimps. Los Angeles was not initially a big union town – that was one of its attractions for the early moguls – and they fought limits on working hours as long as they could.

Nor were the studios understanding of human frailties. When young Judy Garland faltered at the pace of filming, her mother, with the connivance of studio doctors and executives, administered pills to control her energy levels. They would pep her up for work and bring her down to sleep. After puberty hit, they tried to control her weight with amphetamines. The resulting drug dependencies would haunt Garland for life, and significantly shorten it. Louis B. Mayer's daughter Irene told historian David Thomson that the studio would deliberately give some stars worms in order to keep them slim (at least that's an organic solution, right? It's a wonder the modern wellness gurus haven't promoted it).[16]

The studio managed everything, in other words. They'd change your hair colour, your history, your name. They didn't even hide it: everyone knew that Ava Gardner had electrolysis to lift her hairline to the studio-approved shape; it was discussed in fan magazines. Studios ran competitions to decide star names, so it was no secret that your favourite star had been born with a more prosaic moniker – and by taking part in such a competition you could seize a tiny part of their success. When Lucille LeSueur got some attention in 1925 silent movies, the studio called on the public to decide her stage name. Joan Crawford, as she became, wasn't impressed with the result (it smacked too much of crawfish to be glamorous) but accepted it as a step towards world domination, striding along in the shoes she famously described as 'fuck-me pumps'.[17] Unlike the studios, Crawford did not hesitate to call a spade a spade.

It's not surprising that stars bucked their confines, because temperamental artistes rarely love it when others try to dictate their behaviour. Once their first contracts had established their image, some made a bid for freedom by going freelance: Cary Grant, Rosalind Russell and Irene Dunne among them. But freelancing worked best for stars who had been under contract long enough to prove their box-office appeal, so it never fundamentally threatened the system. Even with a good agent, freelancers faced the perennial worry that the studios would save money and rely on in-house talent instead – which they did, where possible. It's a dilemma familiar to millions today in the gig economy.

Not that in-house talent always made life easy. Bette Davis had a famously tempestuous relationship with Warner Bros throughout her long career. Davis came from a well-to-do family and had grown up with every reason to be self-assured: if she never considered herself quite as straightforwardly beautiful as her peers, she knew she was more talented than almost any of them. She tried to get out of her contract in 1937 after being offered a series of roles she considered disappointing or unsuitable. Ironically, one of them was in a remake of *God's Country and the Woman*, considerably changed from the Nell Shipman wilderness film and refocused far more on the male lead. Davis refused the role and fled to England. 'I was unhappy, unfulfilled and further compliance would only have destroyed the career I had so far built,' she wrote years later in her autobiography, *The Lonely Life*. '. . . I couldn't and wouldn't play this part. This time it was final. The very contract system that once offered me such security had become stultifying.'[18]

In London, Warner Bros took out an injunction against Davis when she tried to work for someone else and the star counter-sued to break her contract. Warner Bros' barrister opened the case in magnificently patronising form by calling Davis 'rather a naughty young lady' and dismissively claiming that she just wanted 'more money' on her already high salary. The newspapers were initially hostile, but her case – that her contract required her to play roles that were 'cheap', politically odious or 'distasteful' and that the studio could use her image however it liked – gradually won public support, especially after Jack Warner admitted on the stand that he could order her to appear in whatever he wanted. The law came down against her, but if Davis lost the battle she won the war. Warner Bros took her back, covered her court costs and cast her in considerably better roles. She made most of her classics in the next ten years, including *Jezebel*, *Dark Victory* and *Now, Voyager*.

The more lethal blow to the contract system came from someone considered less militant – at least until she was pushed past breaking point. Olivia de Havilland is best remembered as Melanie in *Gone with the Wind*, though she had enormous range: look at *The Snake Pit* or *The Heiress*, never mind her scarier turn in *Hush . . . Hush, Sweet*

Charlotte. 'I have utter admiration for the career of Olivia de Havilland,' wrote Davis of her friend. 'She had a big hurdle, in the beginning, which I did not have. Physically she was beautiful. Warner Brothers only cared that she was beautiful and therefore cast her, not as an actress, but as a leading lady opposite male stars as their love interest.'[19] Yet de Havilland's boss Jack Warner would later describe her as having 'a brain like a computer behind those fawnlike brown eyes'. De Havilland's biggest contribution to studio history was to fatally undermine the contract system: she turned out to be less a Melanie and more a Scarlett O'Hara.

No one saw it coming. De Havilland was recruited to Hollywood while still a teenager, reluctantly putting her original plans to train as a teacher on hold. She had landed her first professional acting job in an extraordinary way. After performing in *A Midsummer Night's Dream* in community theatre, she was spotted by an assistant to the actor/director Max Reinhardt and made second understudy to Hermia in his Hollywood Bowl production of the same play – only for both the women above de Havilland to leave the production suddenly (they got movie offers; she didn't poison them or anything). When Warner Bros hired Reinhardt to film the play soon after, he brought de Havilland along. She signed with Warner Bros on the director's advice. Once in the studio system, she was cast, as Davis described, as a love interest, often opposite Errol Flynn. She and Flynn looked so good together that audiences fell instantly in love, and Warner Bros figured, *Eh, why try harder?* They just recast her in the same thankless role, over and over. Eventually, she rebelled, refusing roles and taking suspension for months at a time.

Those suspensions became the lynchpin of her court case. The studios could not physically compel stars to act, certainly not to act well, so if an actor adamantly refused a role, they were placed on unpaid suspension and prevented from taking other work. That created a stalemate: usually the offending role would be recast and another opportunity would come along that was more acceptable to both parties, or impending bills would force the recalcitrant star back to work. But if the problem proved intractable, the studio reserved the right to add time on suspension to the end of a star's contract. If you had a three-year contract, but spent a year of that suspended, you could be tied to the studio for four years as they tried to recoup the lost time. And if you still refused roles during that fourth year and beyond, you could be prevented from working more or less for ever.

De Havilland had spent months on suspension after balking at the endless ingénue roles she was given by Jack Warner. Nor was she rewarded for success: while her co-star Errol Flynn got a salary bump to $2,250 per week after their *Captain Blood* and *The Charge of the Light Brigade*, de Havilland remained on $500.[20] But it was the lack of roles that rankled most, with de Havilland doing virtually all her best work while on loan (to MGM for *Gone with the Wind*, for instance), and sitting on suspension at home.

When, at the end of her seven-year term, the studio informed her that they were adding six months to cover her suspensions, de Havilland sued. Her case argued that the studios were in breach of a previously obscure California law, Labor Code Section 2855, which stated that no employment contract could last more than seven years. By adding those extra months, the studio went into breach, and in August 1943 de Havilland sought a declaratory judgement that she was no longer bound by her contract. In November the California Superior Court found in her favour. Warner Bros appealed, and lost again.

'Olivia should be thanked by every actor today,' said Davis.[21] The case fundamentally changed the balance of power between studios and stars. From then on, stars *could* sit out their contracts if they were careful with their money, and studios couldn't stop them. At least, not officially. After the case, Jack Warner wrote a letter to his rival studio chiefs that saw de Havilland unofficially blacklisted from all studio films for two years. But if she worked less after her Warner Bros contract, her films were, on average, significantly better. Her next studio film was *To Each His Own* in 1946, which landed her Best Actress at the Oscars. Now that's a comeback.

A later attack on the contract system came from a similarly unlikely source. Marilyn Monroe is remembered as a sex goddess, just as she was portrayed in her lifetime. But Monroe was far more than that, and only people who don't know much about her would confuse her with the 'dumb blondes' she played so beautifully. Monroe was a life-long student of anyone who would teach her, especially acting, and an avid reader (of intellectual stuff, too: her personal library included Albert Camus and James Joyce. Her first LA charge account was at a bookstore).[22]

She was deeply frustrated under her contract at 20th Century Fox, where studio head Darryl F. Zanuck seemed determined to keep her in musicals and comedies as a 'sexy ornament',[23] as she called it, rather than give her the more dramatic roles she wanted. Her discontent grew, leading her co-star Jane Russell – who, as a veteran of Howard Hughes contracts, knew a thing or two about working with overly controlling men – to predict in 1953 that, '[Marilyn] doesn't like what the studio is doing to her and she doesn't know how to say no. One of these days she will . . . start swinging axes.'[24]

Towards the end of her Fox contract, in the mid-1950s, Monroe had become a huge box-office draw with *Gentlemen Prefer Blondes*, *How to Marry a Millionaire* and *Niagara* (a really powerful drama, proving she could do more than Zanuck liked to allow her). Yet her contract did not let her choose projects and denied her the sort of salary bump that usually accompanied such success. She earned only $1,500 per week on the delightful *Gentlemen . . .* , for a total of about $18,000, while her freelance co-star Russell earned $100,000. So Monroe turned down Fox's next offer, *The Girl in Pink Tights* (a film worth refusing for the title alone) and departed on a USO tour of the Far East with her new husband, baseball legend Joe DiMaggio. The troops greeted her like the Second Coming, and her own fragile self-image received a much-needed boost. That tour confirmed her A-list status; the celebrity marriage only enhanced her fame (the modern portmanteau might be 'DiMonroe').

Monroe reluctantly took a small role in *There's No Business Like Show Business* in return for a promise that she could star in *The Seven Year Itch* afterwards. Fox finally negotiated a new contract, with a $100,000 bonus. But after she finished shooting on *Itch* and the promised bonus had not materialised, Monroe declared the studio in breach of contract and set up her own company, Marilyn Monroe Productions (MMP). 'I am tired of the same old sex roles,' she said. 'I want to do better things. People have scope, you know.'[25]

Initially she was ridiculed. Conservative columnist Hedda Hopper suggested that Monroe was, essentially, aiming too high; others blamed the 'disturbing influence' of her business partner. But Monroe saw herself trapped in an existential struggle. 'I realized that, just as I had once fought to get into the movies and become an actress, I would now have to fight to become myself and be able to use my talents. If I didn't fight I would become a piece of merchandise to be sold off the movie pushcart.'[26] Monroe's fears weren't unfounded; other stars like Mae West and Dolores del Rio had seen their Hollywood careers evaporate when audiences got tired of the same old thing. Only reinvention assures career longevity, and Monroe wanted 'a long-term program'.[27]

When Monroe's determination became clear, Fox made a new deal with MMP: $400,000 for four films, with the right to make a project of her choosing after each completed Fox film. She would also have the right to approve the subject of her Fox films, as well as her director and cinematographer. This was a far cry from the old contract model; from now on Monroe would be in control of her own career. In the modern era, she'd probably earn an 'executive producer' credit for that work. *Time* magazine hailed Monroe's skills as a businesswoman, but she won by doing nothing. In 1955, while the negotiations dragged, Monroe studied theatre in New York with Method guru Lee Strasberg, and started an affair with intellectual playwright Arthur Miller. Still the media coverage rolled on, and the public fascination with her only increased. With her celebrity at its peak, it was Monroe's willingness to walk away from Hollywood that gave her the leverage she needed. She would go on to more daring projects: *Some Like It Hot*, *The Misfits* and *Bus Stop* among them. But her battles show how profoundly stars were disadvantaged in the studio era. If someone with Marilyn Monroe's gifts – fame, fans, A-list husband – struggled for fair treatment, how would less visible talent fare?

4

The Underdogs
How marginalised women fought the odds

E VEN WITH their many limitations, at least actresses were visible enough to sometimes challenge the system. For those below the line, or from marginalised groups, it was *much* harder to fight your corner. The further you stood from the glamorous centre of white, straight stardom, the harder it got. For people of colour, roles were thinly drawn and few in number. For women who wanted to write or, particularly, direct, it was almost impossible. With the exception of Lois Weber's lone sound film, Dorothy Arzner was almost unique during her directing career from 1927 to 1943.[1]

After a successful start as an editor at Paramount (not yet so called when she worked there), in 1926 Arzner wanted to direct, and was offered her chance at Columbia. But before she left Paramount she wanted her departure to be acknowledged. It had, after all, been almost a decade of often high-profile work, like the Valentino-starring *Blood and Sand*. Arzner wandered the studio's executive suite until she found Walter Wanger, head of the New York office, and figured that he was senior enough to stand as a proxy for the company and hear her farewell. Wanger, however, was horrified to learn she was going. He called the head of production, B. P. Schulberg, and they promised to let Arzner write and direct an A-picture in order to keep her.

She wound up staying for six more years, surviving the turn to talkies, and then went freelance. Arzner directed twenty films and invented the boom mic that proved such a boon for sound recording when she tied a microphone to a fishing pole, the better to capture Clara Bow's dialogue on *The Wild Party*. She didn't patent the idea, any more than several male peers who would also claim the invention later, but she did pull it together on the fly (no pun intended).

Most of Arzner's films were financially successful and critically acclaimed. Those include *Christopher Strong* in 1933, the film that established Katharine Hepburn's stardom, and *Dance, Girl, Dance* in 1940, with Maureen O'Hara and Lucille Ball as best friends struggling to make it in show business. The latter is famous for a speech when serious ballet dancer Judy (O'Hara – no relation), working in a burlesque club because she can't find a job elsewhere, berates the baying audience.

'I know you want me to tear my clothes off so you can look your fifty cents' worth,' says Judy, crossing her arms defiantly. 'Fifty cents for the privilege of staring at a girl the way your wives won't let you! What do you suppose we think of you up here, and your silly smirks your mothers would be ashamed of? We know it's the thing of the moment for the dress suits to come and laugh at us too. We laugh right back at the lot of you, only we're paid to let you sit there and roll your eyes and make your screamingly clever remarks. What's it for? So as you can go home when the show's over and strut before your wives and sweethearts and play at being the stronger sex for a minute? I'm sure they see through you just like we do.'

It's a literal showstopper of a scene and remarkably prescient in its description of what would come to be called the 'male gaze' (see Chapter 7), and it speaks to the cinema audience as well as the crowd in Judy's theatre. A lot of feminist film theory would be built around it in the decades ahead, but it's also a significant moment for the character, with her dream employer (unbeknownst to her) sitting in the audience, watching her go off. A male director might not have played it with as much force, because he wouldn't necessarily see the truth in what Judy says.

Looking back, Arzner's films are interesting because of these small moments where she added depth and interest to her female characters, and avoided lazy stereotypes that pit women against one another. Judy and Bubbles (Ball) in *Dance, Girl, Dance* are friends rather than rivals for most of the running time, and their conflicts are professional rather than romantic. Her 1936 film version of *Craig's Wife* took a play about a straight-up bitch and made her a nuanced and sympathetic character, played by Rosalind '*His Girl Friday*' Russell. Arzner said she told the story faithfully, but 'from a different point of view', and added, 'When I told [playwright George] Kelly this, he rose to his six-foot height, and said, "That is not my play. Walter Craig was a sweet guy and Mrs Craig was an SOB." He left. That was the only contact I had with Kelly.'[2] That change of viewpoint was consistent with Arzner's approach as a writer and director: she gave interesting characters interesting dilemmas. She wasn't strictly a feminist, by modern standards, but if there is a common theme to her work, it's a deep suspicion of heterosexual relationships, which tend to end in unhappiness and disaster.

Pictures of Arzner show her with her hair slicked back, in tailored jackets and often the jodhpur-and-boot combo that was already standard thanks to DeMille and Griffith. Maybe it helped that she presented herself like one of the guys; certainly Ida Lupino, two decades later, was sometimes pictured in similar clothes for her directing work. Arzner was fairly openly lesbian (again, by the standards of the day) and lived with her partner, choreographer Marion Morgan. Perhaps her sexuality helped the men around her to see her as something other than a potential conquest, or perhaps she kept just enough plausible deniability that they were unaware of it. It must have been some balancing act. Almost alone, she was able to keep working after every other female director fell away.

There's a dark side to that longevity, however. Film historian and professor Karen Ward Mahar has suggested that Arzner was so concerned with proving her competence that she never dared to innovate – or certainly not as much as traces in her films suggested she might have done, all things being equal. If you are the lone representative of your social group in a highly competitive, high-risk profession like film directing, how far can you really swing for the fences? Better to stick to what works and be sure that you can direct another film down the line. Yet such caution means that we lose not only the films of the women who never have the chance to direct; we also limit the full potential of those who do.

Arzner's reasons for retiring in 1943 have never been entirely clear: she had suffered a near-fatal bout of pneumonia, which might be reason enough, and she'd long been financially independent of Hollywood. In the 1960s, Arzner taught film at UCLA for four years, mentoring the young Francis Ford Coppola (*The Godfather*) among others, so film never entirely left her blood. But it shows again that behind every great man is a woman hardly anyone has ever heard of.

The major studios were without a female director for more than a decade after Arzner left, until an actress managed to slide into a new role. Ida Lupino had a different path to directing and, in some ways, a more modern one. Like Jodie Foster, she became a star in her teens. The wide-eyed, button-nosed Lupino came from generations of English stage actors and had already appeared in two British films before leaving for Hollywood.[3] Ickily, both cast her as a young girl intent on seducing a *much* older man; her co-star in one, *I Lived with You*, was also her godfather, Ivor Novello, who was forty at the time (imagine the awkward family get-togethers).

Paramount signed Lupino in 1933, hoping that she would play their Alice in Wonderland – but decided she looked too old. Instead, Lupino worked in forgettable ingénue roles after a battle with polio in 1934 saw her released from her contract early (she'd already been on suspension for refusing a small part in the Claudette Colbert *Cleopatra*). In 1939 she finally made a splash in *The Light that Failed*, after lobbying director William Wellman for the role of a Cockney painter's model. She followed that with *They Drive by Night* in 1940 for Raoul Walsh, and her early promise seemed to have been fulfilled. Lupino was offered a standard seven-year contract by Warner Bros but, burned by her Paramount experience, she refused, signing only for one year with freelance rights. She sometimes called herself 'the poor man's Bette Davis', since she often got the bigger Warner Bros star's rejects, but even Davis' rejects pile offered dramatic roles.

Then again, the bad roles kept coming too, and Lupino was suspended when she refused them, or when she rewrote scripts to make them more interesting. She was already spending her downtime observing her directors, cameramen and editors; when suspended, she had more time to educate herself in filmmaking. Since she had worked with directors like Wellman, Walsh, Michael *'Casablanca'* Curtiz and Charles Vidor, as well as Hitchcock editor William Ziegler, she gave herself quite an apprenticeship.

Yet despite that preparation, her directing career still began as a Trojan horse. She was producing a film about an unplanned pregnancy, 1949's *Not Wanted*, when director Elmer Clifton suffered a heart attack days before production was due to start. Whether for practical reasons, ambition, or both, Lupino took over and delivered the eight-day shoot on budget ($153,000). The film was a financial success. Lupino kept Clifton's name on the film publicly, out of respect for his work, but the fact that she directed it was widely known in the industry and gave her proof of her competence. She might never have been able to get a start without that stroke of tragedy.

Later that year, Lupino set up The Filmmakers with then-husband Collier Young and Oscar-nominated screenwriter Malvin Wald. Their idea was for an independent production company to 'explore new themes, try new ideas, discover new creative talents'.[4] Wald told the *New York Herald Tribune* that, 'We are trying to make pictures of a sociological nature to appeal to older people who usually stay away from theatres. We are out to tackle serious themes and problem dramas.' For Lupino, it was a chance to continue working in film, which she loved, but to move away from acting, which she was less keen on. She told Hedda Hopper that, 'I've never really liked acting. It's a tortuous profession, and it plays havoc with your private life.'[5] In 1950 she was the sole female member of the Directors Guild of America; meetings began with the greeting, 'Gentlemen and Madam'.

Like Lois Weber, Lupino saw the potential of cinema to tackle big social issues. She addressed the debilitating effects of polio in the Filmmakers' first outing, 1949's *Never Fear* (a topic Lupino knew from personal experience, of course); and rape in 1950's *Outrage*. She wasn't above making genre films either. Lupino had had experience on otherwise all-male sets, like *The Sea Wolf*. That prepared her for her own foray into all-male filmmaking, and film noir, with *The Hitch-Hiker*, probably still her best work. In it she didn't bother with the usual femme fatale role: it's just two fishing buddies who unwittingly and unwisely pick up a convicted murderer, and the drama that plays out between the trio.

Still, it was not easy to forge a career as Hollywood's sole female director. The big studios weren't interested, so Lupino relied on her partners in The Filmmakers. Yet Young never seemed to raise as much money as he promised, and Wald's prediction that *Never Fear* would meet a cold shoulder from distributors proved correct. Howard Hughes' RKO seemed to offer a lifeline when they came in with a partnership – but it was, naturally, a deeply uneven deal that gave RKO complete control of their films, and allowed the bigger company to charge all promotional expenses to the Filmmakers, limiting their long-term viability (the company would make its last film in 1955, though Lupino continued to direct on film and TV).

Lupino also had to innovate in order to get her cast and crew to do what she needed. She had quickly acquired the nickname 'Mother' from the teenage cast of her first two films, and played that image to the hilt on set from then on. In 1967 she described her tactics: 'You do not tell a man; you suggest to him. "Darlings, Mother has a problem. I'd love to do this. Can you do it? It sounds kooky but I want to do it. Now, can you do it for me?" And they do it – they just do it.'[6] Given the long history of female directors facing recalcitrance from their male cast and crew, and indeed the present-day problems that female directors can encounter, Lupino's tactic was understandable and apparently effective. It allowed her to sidestep criticisms of being too 'strident' without giving in on every point. But the wheedling tone is not something that you can imagine many male directors having to adopt.

In terms of trailblazing for other women, Lupino said that, 'I never thought of myself as a crusader' and was wary of too much talk about her unique status. There was no way, at that time, to combine activism with a career in film and not lose the fragile foothold she had gained. Yet merely by existing she proved that women *could* direct, if given the chance.

The studios continued to employ women as writers, though in smaller numbers than before and often alongside a male partner. Established names like Frances Marion and Anita Loos flourished initially, with Marion winning her two writing Oscars (the first person of any sex to do so) in 1931 and 1932. Marion was a fascinating figure. Early in her career, producer William Fox asked Marion if she was sure she wanted to write and not act, saying, 'If you're smart you'll gamble on yourself. Easy, just like tossing a coin!' Marion claims to have snapped back, 'A coin, Mr Fox, can only fall heads or tails. And I'll gamble on heads; they last longer.'[7] She turned down Fox's offer of $80 a week for her screenwriting and landed herself a better position with William A. Grant.

Through the 1920s and into the 1930s, Marion hosted 'cat parties' every Friday for other women in the film business. It's an idea that's been revived in the last few years with organisations like Film Fatales and Cinesisters, and through the less formalised networking that followed the revelations of #MeToo. Marion encouraged the women around her to act like collaborators rather than competitors, even as the films were becoming more reductive of female roles, and placing women in opposition on the rare occasions they shared the screen ('bad' girl vs 'good' girl stories were rife; one 1936 offering was *Wife vs. Secretary*, with Clark Gable the innocent, misunderstood schmo in the middle). Marion's networking was a continuation of Lois Weber's efforts in the silent era, and Weber was one of her cats at first, advising younger women and striving to get back to directing. The writer was also key in getting Weber her final directing job, 1934's *White Heat*, though it did not lead to the career renaissance for which they both hoped.

Unlike many of her peers, Marion left Hollywood on her own terms in 1946, retiring to write plays and novels. The death of her great supporter, Irving Thalberg, had left her sidelined at the studio and out of favour after nearly thirty years. Decades later, director Mimi Leder (*Deep Impact, On the Basis of Sex*) tried to adapt Marion's story for the screen but found no takers. Women's stories are often a harder sell to male executives, of course, but in this case the erasure of both women's history and the silent era must have contributed. Even such a towering figure was deemed too niche and not sufficiently interesting – though surely her profile cannot be much lower than *Ed Wood* was, or *Trumbo*.

The tiny, elfin Anita Loos was another story. One of the wittiest women who ever lived (read her masterpiece, *Gentlemen Prefer Blondes*, and its almost equally good sequel *But Gentlemen Marry Brunettes* if you want proof), Loos was professionally gifted but personally held back. After a brief early marriage to get her out from under her parents' roof, Loos settled down with, or settled for, director John Emerson. He was eleven years her senior, and spectacularly ill-equipped to deal with a successful wife.[8] As Loos' star rose through the 1920s and his lagged behind, he developed hypochondria, losing his voice entirely following her massive success with the novel of *Gentlemen Prefer Blondes*. When Emerson was brought to a leading psychiatrist after no physical cause could be found, Loos was told: 'The only cure for your husband is for you to give up your career.'[9] Yet both wanted to live large on Loos' income, so that was no solution either. Loos was one of the most in-demand screenwriters of her day: with the arrival of sound her fast-talking style came into its own. She rewrote *Red-Headed Woman* for Jean Harlow, replacing a fired F. Scott Fitzgerald, which gives you some idea of her place in the pecking order. She would also script Cukor's *The Women* and then rewrite it repeatedly after a whopping eighty lines initially fell foul of the censor, who felt they were overly risqué.

Even as her star rose, Loos frequently put her career on hold to cater to Emerson's whims and often gave him co-billing on her scripts. Years later, after his real diagnosis of schizophrenia and a period in hospital, Loos finally asked for a divorce. She never got it, but the pair separated at last. She paid for his nursing care for the rest of his life, but it's tempting to wonder what she might have accomplished with a supportive and less troubled partner.

Lenore Coffee was another writer who made it work. She had been a troubleshooter for both Irving Thalberg and Louis B. Mayer; had collaborated with Cecil B. DeMille and earned $1,000 per script during the silent era. But by the time she started at Warner Bros in 1938 she was the only woman writing there. Those that remained were mostly husband-and-wife teams, like Garson Kanin and Ruth Gordon, who wrote some of the Katharine Hepburn–Spencer Tracy comedies (Gordon later starred in cult classic *Harold and Maude*).

Even though a writer famously has little authority or status in the filmmaking pecking order, what scraps of power they had were often too much to leave to women.

As tough as things were for white women who wanted to work behind the camera, they were exponentially tougher for those who faced more than one form of prejudice breaking into Hollywood. Disabled roles were few and far between, as is the case today, and were generally cast with able-bodied actors. When the story of deaf–blind author Helen Keller was told in 1962's *The Miracle Worker*, for example, the sighted, hearing Patty Duke took the role. Harold Russell, who lost both hands in the Second World War, won two Oscars for his role in William Wyler's *The Best Years of Our Lives* but could find no follow-up work. Actress Susan Peters did a little better: she was a stunning ingénue signed with MGM when she was left paraplegic in a shooting accident in 1945. She managed to land a role as a villain in *The Sign of the Ram* in 1948 and had success onstage, but suffered clinical depression – partly because of her limited career options – and died in 1952, aged just thirty-one.

The odds were also stacked against Black people. As African-American entertainment journalist Geraldyn Dismond had noted as early as a 1929 article, most Black actors landed their first film role by playing maids or servants.[10] Sometimes, they really *were* a maid or man servant: Libby Taylor worked for Mae West, who cast her in *I'm No Angel* in 1933. Taylor would go on to make dozens more films, but was often uncredited and usually still cast as a maid. Louise Beavers, who is heartbreakingly good in the original adaptation of race drama *Imitation of Life* in 1934, also worked as a maid – for silent star Leatrice Joy – before starting her own acting career. Ironically, Joy's career took a hit in the sound era because of her thick Southern accent, while the Cincinnati-born Beavers had to learn a Southern twang for many of her roles.

Even the biggest African-American stars were confined to servant roles. Stepin Fetchit, born Lincoln Theodore Monroe Andrew Perry, was a vaudeville star who became famous on film for a series of roles as 'the laziest man in the world'. He was usually a servant who so exasperated his bosses that they did his job themselves. This portrayal of laziness made him an embarrassment to civil rights activists, though more recently fans have argued that this character is a trickster archetype rather than just a grotesque stereotype of sloth. In real life Perry was extremely literate (though also a domestic abuser), and was the first Black man to become a millionaire through his film work.[11] He fought, unsuccessfully, for equal billing and equal pay with white co-stars, while the nascent NAACP campaigned against him as an unhelpful and racist stereotype. Perry retired in 1940 and was broke within a few years, leaving only his character's name as a term of derision.

His contemporary Hattie McDaniel famously played a house slave in *Gone with the Wind*. McDaniel appeared in over three hundred films, was credited in eighty-three, and became the first Black actress to win an Oscar, for her Supporting role in *Wind*. Even there the indignities continued: the ceremony was segregated, so McDaniel and her escort were not allowed to sit with the rest of the cast. Selznick had had to protest for the hotel to allow her into the venue, and she had been barred from the film's Atlanta premiere because of the state's Jim Crow laws. In her acceptance speech McDaniel said of her Oscar, 'It has made me feel very, very humble; and I shall always hold it as a beacon for anything that I may be able to do in the future. I sincerely hope I shall always be a credit to my race and to the motion picture industry.'

McDaniel *was* a credit to the industry, though it would never extend her the same courtesy. Even with an Oscar on her mantel, she was cast almost exclusively as maids. In her personal life she had to fight attempts by white homeowners to have her and other wealthy

66

Black people evicted from their homes in Los Angeles' West Adams Heights (now Sugar Hill), and won a court case that declared such neighbourhood race laws unconstitutional.

McDaniel also faced criticism from the NAACP, who considered her roles backward and her comic touches undignified, and who were disappointed by her failure to fight for independent Black film production. Her standard response was that she could either earn $7 per week as a maid or $700 a week playing one.[12]

Louise Beavers, her contemporary and successor in the role of *Beulah*, would eventually speak more openly in support of civil rights and better treatment for African Americans in the film industry. Perhaps McDaniel would have done so too had she not died in 1952. Even in death, her wish to be buried at Hollywood Forever Cemetery was refused by the racist owners at the time. She eventually received redress for that final insult, at least. The cemetery's current management offered to pay for McDaniel to be reburied there in 1999. When her family elected to leave her where she lay, the cemetery (with their permission) erected a cenotaph instead. It now stands in pride of place by the picturesque lake at the heart of the grounds, surrounded by flowers.

Aside from maids and servants and slaves, there weren't many options for ambitious Black actors who wanted to provide more encouraging role models. A 1927 production of *Uncle Tom's Cabin* was seen as a big step forward (Beavers appeared in a tiny role), but not all the Black characters were played by Black actors. The talkies began to change the picture: the late 1920s had seen white audiences learn to appreciate African-American music (they don't call it the Jazz Age for nothing) and with that came a chance for Black stars. The white Al Jolson 'blacking up' in *The Jazz Singer* was a practice criticised even then, and it quickly became clear that mass audiences were not going to be fobbed off with gross imitations. Dismond wrote that such performances were 'indifferent imitations of their dark brothers' but was intrigued by the promise of King Vidor's *Hallelujah* in 1929, set to be the first major studio film with an all-Black cast.[13]

Hallelujah was seen as a huge risk for MGM: Vidor had been pushing to make such a film for years with no luck, until the advent of sound allowed him to include spirituals that the studio hoped would give the film the same appeal as Broadway hits of the day. He still had to waive his own salary to get it made, and if the result is, perhaps inevitably, a racist mess of stereotypes, it also has moments of grace. Vidor was given virtually all the credit, with some reviews reading like he had miraculously extracted good performances from thin air. He was more generous, saying of leading lady Nina Mae McKinney, 'It took no great effort to bring it out. She just had it. Whatever you wanted, whatever you visualized, she could do it.'[14]

The film was hugely profitable and led to other studios hiring Black stars, though they were not necessarily welcomed into Hollywood society. When society girl Pepi Lederer, Marion Davies' niece, invited McKinney and some of the *Hallelujah* cast to her Hearst-owned house for a three-day rave, the neighbours kicked up such a storm of complaints that Davies sent emissaries to end the affair.[15] She could not afford to be associated with such revelry, as the long-term mistress of conservative newspaper mogul William Randolph Hearst.

Nor were *Hallelujah*'s stars able to build on its success, since the studios essentially dismissed Black stars as a 'fad' rather than seeing an appetite for non-white content. As another African-American critic, Ruby Berkley Goodwin, put it, 'The Nordic [white] draws its entertainment from every group. One season they go wild over everything Italian, another season the French have the spotlight, another season everybody is strumming a uke and hula dancing is the vogue . . . it's a fad now, this color craze. Or is it a cloud the size of a man's hand that will grow and grow until color equality covers the universe . . .?'[16] In

1939, the Screen Actors Guild's 'colored official' Jesse A. Graves was still pointing out the unreality of having only white faces in street scenes and crowds and saying, 'We are entitled to more employment and realism in pictures. Not just some far-fetched ideas thrust upon the American people. We spend enough money to warrant employment of colored actors in all pictures, and many should be stars.'[17]

McKinney had been hired straight from Broadway and hailed as the 'Black Garbo' for her beauty (photos suggest that, if anything, that was *under*selling it). She signed a five-year contract with MGM in 1929, the first African-American actor to land a long-term contract with a major studio, but once there no one seemed to know what to do with her. *Hallelujah* did not cause the studio to suddenly start making more Black-led films, and, given the paucity of female roles *and* the Production Code's rules against interracial romance (more on which later), there were few opportunities to cast her.

McKinney's next feature would be two years later, as a hotel manager in *Safe in Hell*. She didn't have another credited feature role until leaving MGM and making *Sanders of the River* in the UK in 1935, playing the exoticised wife of Nigerian chieftain Bosambo (star and campaigner Paul Robeson). Robeson had made it a condition of his involvement that the Nigerians under colonial rule be portrayed positively, but it was re-edited after the two stars finished work and without their knowledge to emphasise the 'greatness' of the British Empire, which was then entering its dying days. When Robeson discovered the switch, he was so furious that he tried to buy back all copies of the film to destroy them.[18] In 1938 Robeson said, 'It is the only film of mine that can be shown in Italy or Germany, for it shows the negro as Fascist states desire him – savage and childish.'[19]

After McKinney left for Europe in search of work, another Black woman would make a bigger impact in Hollywood, but also find her potential stymied. Lena Horne was signed to MGM in 1942, immediately becoming an iconic pin-up for African-American GIs. Soon she was barred from even segregated USO shows, however, after complaining about the treatment of Black troops. She managed to make far more films than McKinney despite refusing to play maids or prostitutes (the default roles for Black women at the time), but almost always in a discrete musical number unconnected to the film's plot, the better to snip her out before the film was sent to the southern US states. This was common practice, the same way gay kisses are cut from Hollywood films now before release in China or the Middle East. It was Hollywood's craven solution to the obvious fact of Black excellence: hire them for their jazz, let them sing or play up a storm, and then ignore them once again. 'The only time I ever said a word to another actor who was white was Kathryn Grayson in a little segment of [the musical] *Show Boat* included in *Till the Clouds Roll By*,' said Horne in a 1990 interview.[20]

Like McDaniel, Horne faced prejudice at home, too. After a white friend, Felix Young, signed the lease on her house because Black people were not allowed to live in Hollywood at the time, the neighbours tried to have her evicted. Only Humphrey Bogart, who lived across the street, threatened those responsible for the racist outcry and sent Horne word that if anyone bothered her, she should let him know.[21] 'I didn't have any more problems,' she said simply about the incident. Even with stardom and the wealth that her singing career brought her, Horne never got her due in Hollywood. Despite having sung music from *Show Boat* in that 1946 film, she wasn't even considered for the role in its 1951 film adaptation. The part went to Ava Gardner, a close friend of Horne's. To add insult to injury, Gardner, a non-singer, was told to practise her singing to Horne's recordings, which Horne said offended both actresses (Annette Warren would dub Gardner in the end).[22]

After 1956 Horne largely quit film, partly due to disenchantment and partly because she was briefly blacklisted as a suspected Communist for her work in activist groups supporting civil rights.

This was part of the long-running McCarthyite witch-hunts that threatened Hollywood's liberal wing in the late 1940s and early 1950s – even Bogart had to make clear that he was no Commie. While the blacklisted but white-skinned 'Hollywood Ten' screenwriters were the most talked-about victims of that era, prevented from working for decades, the House Un-American Activities Committee (HUAC) also cast aspersions on the activism of high-profile Black entertainers like Horne. To save her TV career, Horne wrote a series of letters denouncing Communism, but she never quit the civil rights work. She would return to the big screen as Glinda in Sidney Lumet's *The Wiz* in 1978 (Horne was Lumet's mother-in-law at the time), but it was a rare outing. Ultimately the world of TV variety shows and musical performance was far more welcoming than Tinseltown, and her civil rights activism was too important to compromise.

Other actresses of colour suffered similar fates. Dona Drake was Black and Latina and presented herself as Mexican, presumably on the basis that it offered better roles. She had to be *very* racially flexible to work regularly: she was cast as a Native American maid to Bette Davis in *Beyond the Forest* and a North African Arab in *Road to Morocco*, opposite Bob Hope and Bing Crosby. Drake too ultimately found touring with a band more productive than the screen.

Hazel Scott, like Horne, was recruited to Hollywood for her phenomenal musical talent (she was a piano prodigy and singer) and again found limited options. Also like Horne, she was cast in single musical numbers that could be excised for release in the South. Eventually she clashed with Columbia studio head Harry Cohn over a costume she felt 'stereotyped blacks'.[23] 'I had antagonized the head of Columbia Pictures,' she wrote in her journal. 'In short, committed suicide.'[24] She was then caught up by Joseph McCarthy's HUAC, also for her civil rights activism. It was enough to end her tenure as the first Black woman with her own TV show, which was cancelled a week later.

People of colour were locked out of almost all roles: even in *The Wizard of Oz*, with casting agents desperate to find enough little people to fill Munchkinland, the colour barrier remained and seasoned performers like African-American tap dancer Crawford Price were overlooked.[25] When a decent role *did* come up, there was an appalling tendency to cast white actors instead. Myrna Loy played a half-Javanese woman hell-bent on revenge in *Thirteen Women* in 1932, while Jeanne Crain played a slightly more sympathetic mixed-race girl passing as white in Elia Kazan's *Pinky* in 1949. Both Horne and Dorothy Dandridge had hoped for a chance at that role, but censorship rules ruled them out because of Pinky's boyfriend: an actress of colour could not be seen kissing a white man. Incidentally, original director John Ford was fired after a week on *Pinky* because of his clashes with veteran supporting actress Ethel Waters (who played Pinky's Black grandmother) and because his Black characters were, according to producer Darryl Zanuck, 'like Aunt Jemima. Caricatures'.[26]

Luise Rainer won an Oscar playing a Chinese farm worker in *The Good Earth* in 1937, a role that Chinese-American star Anna May Wong was not even allowed to audition for – despite fans of Pearl Buck's book favouring her for the role. The problem for Wong was the same law against 'miscegenation', or interracial romance. She could only play opposite an Asian actor, and Paul Muni was already lined up to star in *The Good Earth*. That was that for what should have been Wong's best role (as it is, seek her out in 1929 silent film *Piccadilly*). She was instead offered the role of the villainess but turned it down. Wong knew it was censorship that destroyed her career:

I can't for the life of me understand why a white man couldn't fall in love with me on the screen . . . without breaking some terrible censorship law. What is the difference between a white girl playing an Oriental and a real Oriental, like myself, playing them? The only difference I can see is that in most cases, I would at least look the part, where the white girls definitely do not. If it were possible to overcome this terrible censorship barrier, a new field would open for me, giving endless chances to act in good parts. I don't want to play white girls, but I do think I should have the chance to play the roles that are mine by rights.[27]

As it was, refusing to play an endless stream of offensive stereotypes and treacherous villains, her career was limited to the tragic and the doomed. 'When I die, my epitaph should be: "I died a thousand deaths",' she said in 1959. 'That was the story of my film career . . . They didn't know what to do with me at the end, so they killed me off.'[28]

Dorothy Lamour, these days best known as the alluring third leg of the Bob Hope and Bing Crosby *Road To . . .* movies, started her career playing a succession of 'exotic' women from jungles and South Pacific islands, to the extent that wearing a sarong became her signature style. When Lamour took a cruise to Polynesia years later, she was surprised to learn that the women there wore the sarong as a skirt rather than the sort of mini-dress that studio costume designers had concocted for her.[29] An authentic Oceanic star, of course, could have told them that.

This bad habit of race-bending good roles went on far too long. Mickey Rooney's horrific portrayal of a Japanese businessman in *Breakfast at Tiffany's* makes parts of that film unwatchable. Fisher Stevens was cast as an Indian student in 1988 in *Short Circuit 2*, and Rooney Mara and Johnny Depp have been cast as Native American characters in the last decade, in *Pan* and *The Lone Ranger* respectively (Depp claims some 'Cherokee or maybe Creek' ancestry).[30] Native Americans, of course, are arguably the most stereotyped group in Hollywood history, thanks to all those Westerns painting them as either savages or noble savages. It was notable, as recently as *Dances with Wolves*, to try to portray the daily lives of the Plains peoples without sensationalism, and to hire exclusively Native American actors for those roles. In Cameron Crowe's film *Aloha* Emma Stone played a woman of native Hawaiian and Chinese ancestry who is frustrated that neither bloodline is visible in her appearance – a joke that might have been felt less insulting had non-white people played any significant role in the film's story elsewhere. It may be relevant to this continuing picture to note that, in 2013, 94 per cent of studio executives were white.[31]

Things improved, a little, after Dandridge and Horne's time, given that Sidney Poitier was able to win Best Actor for *Lilies of the Field* in 1963. But for Black women such a breakthrough took a lot longer: Halle Berry would be the first Black actress to win an Oscar in a leading role, in 2002. Hollywood simply seemed uninterested in their humanity. It's depressing to think of the women who were born to be stars and never even got their foot in the door, never mind to wonder what a Nina Mae McKinney, Lena Horne, Dorothy Dandridge or Hattie McDaniel might have become in a more inclusive time.

The system kept women, and especially women of colour, down, but it could not last for ever. In the end, it was the US Supreme Court that struck the fatal blow. An anti-trust case that Hollywood had successfully resisted for decades finally came to an end in 1948 with the decision in *United States V Paramount Pictures, Inc.* (the other studios were also named in the suit, along with various subsidiaries). The 'Paramount Decree', as it was called, forced these huge companies to split up their movie production and exhibition arms, ending the practices that had enabled them to dominate the film landscape like the 'block booking' of their films, sight-unseen by theatre managers.

While the largest companies, like Paramount, simply split into production and exhibition arms and became two new, big companies, the result allowed independent cinema to rise up, which in turn led to new opportunities for foreign and independent filmmakers. The Paramount Decree lasted until 2020, when the US Justice Department decided it was no longer needed, with many of the studios affected no longer in existence.

The studio era sometimes produced great movies – it could hardly fail to, with the talent that flocked to Los Angeles and the money being spent – as well as endless formulaic dross. That much is true of most art. Its real failing was how limited its view of humanity was, how shallow the stories it told, and how much that has shaped what is made even today. Almost all films were about white people, almost all able-bodied, almost all straight, definitely all cis, reined in by good old American values. It's still the big-budget default setting, and it was baked into American (and English-speaking) film very early on by a layer of bankers and financiers who weren't willing to risk anything else – despite the silent pioneers showing that audiences were far more daring than they were given credit for.

The studio system propped up the social status quo. When there was adventuring to be done, brave men would do it and women would swoon in their arms. When crime was rife, tough men would fight it and women would swoon in *their* arms – though scarier, wilder women might temporarily mislead and endanger those guys. The job of most women on screen was fretting about sex, except in a marriage designed for procreation. After the Second World War, when the return of the troops prompted calls for women to patriotically abandon their jobs to make way for these now-unemployed men, there was a marked decline in women's onscreen professional ambitions. As critic Molly Haskell points out, it was vanishingly rare on screen to see a woman choose her career over love and marriage at the end of the film – all the more ironic given that in reality, that was the choice that Hollywood's Golden Age stars made.[32] And there was lots of self-sacrifice, of course. Mothers would sacrifice themselves for their children, or regret it; well-meaning but 'fallen' women would sacrifice themselves for the man they loved, in favour of a more socially acceptable bride; the sick or disabled would sacrifice themselves by trying not to be a 'burden', only to be drawn back into the fold by a compassionate hero or heroine.

But people of colour and their stories did not much figure, and the existence of LGBTQ+ people was rarely acknowledged. Hollywood reflected a world of white supremacy but it also reinforced it, suggesting by its output that only one small segment of society mattered enough to have their stories told, and only a smaller subset of that group mattered enough to drive the stories and control their own destinies. It was a small, limited portrait of humanity, and as the nation's moral guardians realised the impact that films could have, it was about to become even smaller.

Censorship
Or, a great way to screw everyone over

THE 1990s cartoon *Animaniacs*, pound-for-pound the greatest animated show ever made,* did an episode on Hollywood censorship. In *The Girl with the Googily Goop* – no relation to Gwyneth Paltrow – a Betty Boop-style cartoon star is menaced by censor Will Hays, the real-life politician put in charge of Hollywood's clean-up efforts. He decrees Googi Goop's dress 'too skimpy, too suggestive' and orders her to remove it at once – which would unfortunately leave her naked. But whadya know? This Hays is the Big Bad Wolf in disguise, and is secretly obsessed with controlling Goop for himself. As with most things in *Animaniacs*, it's simultaneously very smart and very silly. This Wolf is defeated by a volley of pies, but he also reflects an important piece of movie history and the prurience beneath its high ideals.

The censors of movieland really were out to dictate how women dressed and how much flesh they were allowed to show, and at times their rules resulted in careers being eaten up and spat out wholesale. In theory they worked to prevent people from being exploited, and the tightened moral standards of the Production Code supported better roles for some women in some films, workplace comedies like

---

* I will fight you on this. Per square inch, it has more genius gags than even *The Simpsons* in its heyday.

His Girl Friday or *Adam's Rib*. But at times, there was a sense of slavering hypocrisy and a hungry obsession with the female form that hints at more discriminatory, and more wolfish, effects.

Even today, the US is an oddly puritanical country. You can chop and slice people to your heart's content (unless you show that there will be lots of blood as a result) and still get a PG-13 or even PG rating. But add a scene that shows a woman having an orgasm – even non-explicitly and fully dressed – and you will struggle for an R-rating, which requires children under seventeen to be accompanied by a parent or guardian. You may even be slapped with a commercially prohibitive NC-17, which allows no one under 17 into the theatre, and which many cinema chains will refuse to programme.

Yet sex sells. If you want to catch the eye, and wallet, of a potential punter, what better way than to promise them that they can ogle attractive people? The selling of sex tends to escalate, too. One minute it's the twenty-second long, 1896 film *The Kiss* portraying – well, you can figure it out. Just a few decades later and you have *Deep Throat*. Even in the mainstream you get films like *Basic Instinct* or *Secretary* or *Y Tu Mama Tambien*. Some people feared that, left unchecked, this tendency would result in hardcore porn taking over the big screen and sweeping all before it – but this confuses porn's tendency to be an early adopter of new tech with the fact that people do like other things, honest. Rather charmingly, in the 1900s, they saw that slippery slope starting as soon as a few too many ankles or bellies were flashed. Maybe it did, but in truth porn was always on a separate track, because people don't generally want to watch it in a group.

So Hollywood provided fodder for the morality police. There were calls for censorship almost immediately, fended off with promises of self-regulation and restraint by filmmakers. The Woman's Christian Temperance Union (WCTU) was already trying to reform the five-cent cinemas by 1906, only about a year after they opened.[1] That was part of the same moral movement that had film companies thrusting their female directors front and centre, presenting them as moral guardians of the art form; an early attempt to distance cinemas from the less reputable sort of vaudeville show.

For very different reasons there were calls to ban the film of a boxing match between Jack Johnson, a Black man, and Jim Jeffries, a white man, in 1910, after the former won the match.[2] The visceral nature of boxing films meant that they often sparked controversy at the time – think of the blood and pummelling of *Raging Bull* for an idea of the impact of these early films – but this fight came in for more attacks than most. It would, claimed pressure groups and lawmakers, be 'degrading and dangerous' to show a Black man winning, and might spark race riots. Race would continue to be a major factor in censorship. Those in power feared that cinema might become a subversive, destabilising influence on the society they ruled.

In the 1910s, local censorship boards around the US and abroad caused problems for films like Lois Weber's *Hypocrites*. It did feature female nudity, though of a strictly artistic sort: the nude was literally a statue of Truth brought to life. Worse was to come. The US Supreme Court decided, in 1915's *Mutual v. Ohio*, that screen censorship was entirely constitutional and not in breach of the First Amendment's protection of free speech. Motion pictures were a business, not an art form, and one capable of 'evil' at that, so issues of freedom of expression did not arise. That meant that it was open season in the land of the free. Chicago proved a hotbed of censorship, even snipping at adaptations of literary classics like *The Scarlet Letter* in 1914. A delegation of female viewers asked that the film be shown; the police officer in charge demurred on the basis that he could not face explaining what the scarlet 'A' stood for to his fifteen-year-old daughter.[3]

The desire to censor movies wasn't only driven by what was on screen. There were concerns about film as an industry and, after 1913, Hollywood as a place. Newspapers engaged in endless handwringing over the young women flocking to Los Angeles in the hopes of becoming a star. Young men leaving home in search of adventure was commendable and daring, but women? That was a matter for concern. These girls' hopes were fuelled by endless studio-seeded gossip pieces about stars being 'discovered', plucked from obscurity to greatness. In an era with almost no respectable ways for a young woman to make a good living in her own right, cinema offered an extraordinary opportunity. Never mind that many girls thus 'discovered' actually had a close link to some financier the studios needed to court, or were a girlfriend of some rich executive. The myth was everything.

For a naive young outsider it sounded plausible – even destined. It didn't appear that any particular skills were required to act in silent movies; in those early days there was no guarantee that Broadway stardom would translate into movie success and in fact many theatre transplants bellyflopped badly. If you didn't need to be an actor then presumably you just needed a pretty face – and tens of thousands of genetically blessed hopefuls headed West. Fan magazines gave advice that was designed to be off-putting, advising wannabes to save enough money to keep them for a whole year, but such boring prudence didn't stem the flow. If it were that easy to save a year's salary, after all, they wouldn't need Hollywood.

Once they arrived, a tiny handful found a straightforward break. Maybe a few more landed on a casting couch and managed to parlay that into real work (the likes of Joan Crawford among them). But others found only disappointment and exploitation, the waitressing jobs that would soon become a cliché for failed wannabes, and there were rumours of even worse, of young people spirited across the border to Mexico or sold into what was referred to as 'white slavery'. Universal had had a hit in 1913 with a film on that topic, *Traffic in Souls*, about a girl who goes on a date with an apparently nice guy and wakes up locked in a brothel, and after that there was a mini trend for such stories. They were all presented as cautionary tales, though the censors suspected that they were just another way to smuggle lewd-ness into theatres.[4] But the stories got people worried.

By 1916 Constance Adams DeMille (wife of Cecil) and Mary Pickford were so disturbed by all these desperate young things lining up each day for studio work that they sponsored the creation of the Hollywood Studio Club, a dormitory where hopeful starlets could live in respectable, chaperoned surroundings and attend classes to learn more about the profession. Astonishingly, the institution lasted until 1975, and would house future stars like Marilyn Monroe, Donna Reed, Rita Moreno and Sharon Tate. Yet it was just one building; only so many women could find a spot there.

The gossip about Hollywood venality swirled, and the press took notice. In a 1920 *Photoplay* article, journalist Karl K. Kitchen wrote that, 'There is [a] widespread impression that . . . motion picture studios, while not surfeited with art, are nevertheless "hotbeds of vice".' But when he looked into the stories of casting-couch use he said that, 'Nine-tenths of these stories are downright lies. They are the pitiful excuses of the unsuccessful.'[5] That's coming from an anti-Semitic writer who would call the men who run the movie studios 'foreign-born Jews of the lowest type' in a 1922 article for a Catholic magazine, so Kitchen was presumably not overly friendly with the studio bosses.[6] Yet he *was* sugar coating the situation, portraying the casting couch (not yet so called; that phrase came from the procliv-ities of Broadway's Shubert brothers) as something from the past. According to Kitchen, there was no point in would-be starlets sleep-ing with directors by 1920, because studio heads and casting direct-ors made all the big decisions and 'there is not time to bother with amateurs and incompetents . . . Only the high officials of a producing company have the power to engage or advance a personal favorite. From which it will be seen that favoritism of this kind is consider-ably restricted.' Even recent history would show that this rosy assess-ment is far from accurate.

These sex scandals were one ostensible reason for cracking down on Hollywood, in response to rumours and exposés like *The Sins of Hollywood: An Exposé of Movie Vice*, a sensationalist take on Tinseltown life published in 1922. 'There is something about the pictures which seems to make men and women less human, more animal-like,' said its anonymous author (later revealed as *Photoplay* editor Ed Roberts) before detailing such scandalous activities as strip poker, nude dancing and drug-fuelled parties.[7] Big-name stars of the day were easily identifiable from his descriptions, and his tone was one of moral alarm.

But society has only ever cared so much about young women's real-life safety. There was another, deeper discomfort lurking underneath all the prurient fears for girls' protection in Tinseltown itself. After the relative reserve of the Great War years, films were becoming more risqué, diving into the rising tide of the Jazz Age with gusto. Skirts were getting shorter, the dancing was getting wilder and flapper stars like Clara Bow were burning up the screen. Their activities look tame to modern eyes – silent-era star Patsy Ruth Miller described it, in her 1988 memoir, as 'just a teeny bit more racy than *Sesame Street*' – but it seemed to threaten the very foundation of society.[8] Films like Theda Bara's *The Serpent* in 1916 showed a woman plotting revenge against a man who had wronged her, and that sort of thing could not be encouraged. Bow, meanwhile, specialised in flirtatious flapper girls who didn't give a fig what the older generation thought. What might impressionable young minds make of such examples? Why, girls might not rush to marry, reproduce and keep house for the rest of their lives. The moral guardians of the US (and many other nations) convinced themselves that movies could not just be entertainment; they were creating 'a reckless lack of appreciation of true values', according to one commentator of the time.[9]

Thirty-six US states therefore started to seriously consider film censorship legislation. By 1922, Hollywood had been hit by a triple whammy of scandal: the damaging Arbuckle affair, a 1921 corruption trial in Massachusetts that implicated Paramount executives who had been partying in a brothel, and the unsolved murder of director William Desmond Taylor. Within days of Arbuckle's arrest his films were pulled from screens, and a general drop in middle-class audiences followed as the masses appeared to reject Tinseltown.[10]

As with its morality clauses, Hollywood took inspiration from baseball. That sport had answered the 1919 'Black Sox' cheating scandal by hiring a person of unimpeachable authority to clean house. If Something Had To Be Done, hire a man to do it. No one was quite sure *what* he'd do, not even William Hays himself when the studios decided upon him, but he looked right. Hays was a Presbyterian elder, former Postmaster General and member of Warren Harding's cabinet*. Hays was put in charge of the newly formed Motion Picture Producers and Distributors of America (MPPDA; later the MPAA) and introduced to the press as Hollywood's new sheriff. His greatest early achievement, however, was for the studios, not against them: he persuaded thirty of the thirty-one states debating censorship legislation in 1921 to drop it.

It's unsurprising that Hays was a man, but it was not inevitable. The early efforts towards film censorship had been led by women's groups like the WCTU. In the Victorian mindset, women were the more moral sex and best suited to police such behaviour (think *The Handmaid's Tale*'s Aunts, or the UK's Mary Whitehouse). Particularly mothers: the WCTU campaigned for purity in filmmaking on the basis that children were flocking to the movies. They even made it a matter of US foreign policy: a failure to export 'clean' films might, warned one member in 1926, undermine America's missionaries in 'heathen' nations.[11] But as censorship became a more institutional

---

* At least, apart from his involvement in the Teapot Dome scandal that rocked that government just after he left to take up his new position.

and powerful position, one that involved dealing with studio heads and politicians, there was no question of women leading. Indeed, as of 2020 the MPPDA and MPAA have *never* had a female head (though its ratings board has). The MPPDA was immensely patronising to the female-led efforts that had preceded it. Its industrial relations director Jason Joy wrote to the WCTU in 1928 and, among other things, argued that the WCTU should campaign generally, by all means, but not against specific films. 'Therein lies the greatest obstacle to successful club work with motion pictures – this eternal looking for flaws,' said Joy (who would have done very well as a reply guy on Twitter).[12] The WCTU basically rolled their eyes at that and continued to campaign for a federal censorship bill, convinced that everyone else watching films was a helpless addict and only their own membership could see the danger posed by the movies.

Hays, meanwhile, got to work. Adaptations of 'salacious works' were banned as early as 1924, and in 1925 he boasted that he had prevented 160 plays and books from being filmed simply by identifying offensive content and telling member studios that the film rights should not be purchased.[13] He formed a Committee on Public Relations to draw in the religious and social pressure groups that had pushed for censorship through other avenues, and worked hard to win over the 'Club women', Mrs Thomas G. Winter and her General Federation of Women's Clubs.

But Hays didn't initially do much in the way of censorship. He *looked* like he did, but his office offered reassurances to outsiders without really controlling anything. As the years went by, however, his influence spread. In 1927 he created the Studio Relations Committee to advise on likely problem areas at the script stage, and in 1929, spurred on by the new threat of vulgar language in the talkies, he started work on what would become the Motion Picture Production Code. The Code was written in 1930 but was toothless until 1934. In the interim, Jimmy Cagney still flung bullets and punches in every direction and Mae West littered innuendos in her wake with impunity. And then the rules started to be enforced.

In 1933, the incoming Roosevelt administration hinted that federal film censorship might still be required. The move coincided with social reformers, stung by the repeal of Prohibition that same year, giving up their crusade against saloons and turning to cinema instead. A pseudo-scientific analysis between 1929 and 1932, the Payne Fund study on 'Motion Pictures and Youth', attempted to show the deleterious effects of motion pictures on the young minds of America. If the results lacked scientific rigour (any sort of control, for example) it hardly mattered to pressure groups like the newly founded National Catholic Legion of Decency, which pledged in April 1934 to boycott any films that the Church labelled 'indecent', and forged an unholy alliance with other religious groups. The Legion would be a huge force for censorship for more than thirty years. Weirdly, the studios found it a more convivial adversary than the mainly Protestant groups that had led decency campaigns before. At least the Legion did not push for state or federal action, but only boycotts of non-conforming films – and those the moguls felt more able to handle.

The 'Code', as it was simply known, was, from its inception, sexist, racist and homophobic. It assumed that heterosexual married life was the only legitimate romantic or sexual activity, and shared all the toxic beliefs of white supremacy. Interracial or homosexual relation-ships – both of which the Code called 'sexual perversion' – were entirely forbidden under its seal, and even after the Code loosened enough to allow delicate depictions of both, filmmakers were still counselled against them, on the basis of likely protests in less enlight-ened parts of the world. Southern censorship boards like the one in Atlanta, for example, were particularly vigilant in their attempts to 'protect' white women and children not only from those 'white slav-ery' films of enforced prostitution, but also from depictions of independence.[14] 'Women are responsible for the ever-increasing public taste in sensationalism and sexy stuff,' said *Variety* in 1931, and that was not to be encouraged.[15]

Race was often a flashpoint. The career of Black filmmaker Oscar Micheaux was littered with objections made on racist grounds: in his efforts to critique white supremacy he was accused of having created films that would 'tend to corrupt morals or incite to crime'.[16] He found ways to discuss interracial relationships by having one partner merely 'passing' as white, technically avoiding the law against depicting miscegeny (as inter-race relations were called at the time) but telling a similar story. In treating race as a serious issue, without stereotype, Micheaux was accused of inciting racial unrest. He responded to one such charge in 1923 that, 'There has been but one picture that incited the colored people to riot, and that still does, that picture is *The Birth of a Nation.*'[17] The unease over interracial relationships lasted a long time: in 1957's *Island in the Sun*, Joan Fontaine and Harry Belafonte were in a relationship but could not be depicted even holding hands, never mind kissing. She recalled brushing against his arm one day and being ordered to reshoot the scene.[18]

The rules reflected the times. While we can still get behind the idea that excessive cruelty to children or animals should be discouraged in films for general audiences, there's surely a little more room for 'excessive kissing', swear words as strong as 'hell', and the potentially arousing sight of 'stomach dancing'. Childbirth was also banned. The three men who wrote the Code (one a Jesuit priest) feared that too honest a depiction of what was involved would stop women from wanting children (fair). They also emphasised that nothing on screen should make anyone question the sanctity of marriage (less fair).

There was a general requirement to avoid vulgarity and ensure good taste, nebulous provisions that covered any number of possible objections, and predictable rules against the depiction of crime, prostitution or cruelty. Two separate headings covered dancing: the costumes could not 'permit undue exposure' or 'indecent movements', and the dances themselves should not 'suggest or represent sexual actions or indecent passion'. Apparently no one told these guys what the maypole represents, or quaint folk dances would have been right out.

It was often a smothering set of requirements. The Code repressed honesty in storytelling and stifled daring. Every crime had to result in comeuppance; any deviance had to be condemned; stories could not make drunkenness or adultery look attractive. At one point Katharine Hepburn wanted to star in a film adaptation of Anita Loos' 1946 Broadway hit *Happy Birthday*, but the censors would not accept a story where the heroine, mousy librarian Addie, spends much of the play drunk. By the logic of the Production Code, her drinking meant that Addie couldn't have a happy ending with the bank clerk she adores, so the film was never made. Retellings of true-crime stories were also out. That was a rule that Ida Lupino would struggle with on *The Hitch-Hiker*. Significant fudging of that story's real-life inspiration was necessary to get it past the censors, though echoes of reality remain.

According to the Code's General Principles, 'No picture shall be produced that will lower the moral standards of those who see it' – another catch-all phrase that allowed the censors considerable leeway and audiences no fun. The Code called for respect of other nations – for more commercial than moral reasons, because no one wanted a Hollywood film to cause a diplomatic incident – and banned ministers of religion from being either villainous or comical. Hays argued, in 1932, that, 'Liberty of expression is not imperilled when protest is made against playwrights who glean their plots from the scribblings on latrine walls or search the garbage dumps and sewers of society for situations and characters.' You can practically see him foaming at the mouth in these words, long nose twitching and big eyes bulging at the thought.

To enforce these rules the studios established the Production Code Administration (PCA), and hired Hays' troubleshooter, and prominent Catholic layman, Joseph Breen, to enforce the Code. He would stay in post (with one short break) until 1954. English paper *Film Weekly* called Breen 'the Hitler of Hollywood'. Breen and his team would examine scripts, costumes and song lyrics for objectionable material before release, and the studios agreed that they would not screen films without the PCA's seal of approval, and would be liable for a $25,000 fine if they did. Now there was a system in place, a terribly patriarchal-looking guy in charge, and an easy response to any calls for government censorship. The industry could claim to be policing itself, and the threat of federal censorship vanished.

No sooner was the PCA established than it faced the woman born to test it. The PCA had carefully combed through the script for Mae West's *She Done Him Wrong* in 1932, suggesting ways that Paramount could tone down her character's scandalous backstory (multiple affairs, mostly with gangsters; some sex work) and emphasise the period setting to avoid modern-day comparisons that might offend the delicate sensibilities of cinemagoers. But they reckoned without West herself, able to invest filth in a shopping list. Perhaps it's not the censors' fault, only five years into the talkie era, that they couldn't see her innuendos coming (oo-er!), but she would become a persistent thorn in their side as the Code struggled to clean up her act.

It should not have been a surprise. West came to Paramount after consistently pushing the limits of respectability on Broadway, arrested on obscenity charges for her plays *Sex* and *The Drag* in 1927, and again in 1928 for *Diamond Lil*, which formed the basis for *She Done Him Wrong*. In October 1933 *Variety* called her 'as hot an issue as Hitler', though the censors' reaction suggested that she was considerably more dangerous.[19] West didn't just refuse to be ashamed of her sexuality, she positively weaponised it – and not only behind closed doors, either. She talked openly about friendships with gangsters and gay people, and showed no remorse for her obscenity convictions. 'I didn't discover curves, after all,' she was modestly quoted as saying in 1933, 'I just uncovered them.'[20]

'She believes in the battle of the sexes – and in being well equipped for the fray,' said Cecelia Ager in the same article. The French author and Nobel Prize nominee Colette was a huge fan, precisely because of West's intemperance. Colette hailed the fact that, 'She alone, out of a an enormous and dull catalogue of heroines, does not get married at the end of the film, does not die, does not take the road to exile, does not gaze sadly at her declining youth in a silver-framed mirror in the worst possible taste; and she alone does not experience the bitterness of the abandoned "older" woman. This impudent woman is, in her style, as solitary as Chaplin used to be.'[21]

Her very existence embarrassed Hays and his office. All his talk of cleaning up film was shown up by West's enormous success – because audiences *absolutely* got what she was saying. The head of the rival Fox Film Company complained to Hays that it was 'the worst picture I have seen . . . and they got away with it . . . I cannot understand how your people on the Coast could let this get by.'[22]

She Done Him Wrong required expensive, last-minute cuts from the song 'A Guy What Takes His Time' (also a feature of the delightfully terrible Christina Aguilera classic *Burlesque*) at Hays' insistence. Paramount tried to rein West in for her next film, *I'm No Angel*, with Harlan Thompson writing a slightly cleaner story about an innocent gold-digger who reforms for the love of a good man (Cary Grant; who wouldn't?). Once again, they reckoned without West's ability to inject stank into only mildly risqué lines like, 'When I'm good I'm very good, but when I'm bad I'm better.' This time she seemed to tread the right line: the audience got it, but the censors could claim to have limited her bad behaviour. The film was a mega-hit.

Unease about West was building, however. Somewhat to the studio's shock, her biggest fans were not hordes of baying lads but young women who enjoyed the uninhibited joy she took in her power over men. The prospect of a copycat generation must have terrified them. The PCA took considerable flak for allowing West leeway, and their attitude quickly hardened. Requests for reissues of *She Done Him Wrong* and *I'm No Angel* in 1935 were turned down, with Breen writing to Hays, 'Both pictures are now so thoroughly and so completely in violation of the Code that it is utterly impossible for us to issue a certificate of approval for them.'[23]

West's 1936 film, *Klondike Annie,* therefore caused problems almost at once. Her character, Doll, masquerades as a missionary when she goes on the run after killing her Chinese lover. So that's disrespect of the religious orders, criminal behaviour and interracial romance just in the first reel. 'Difficulty is inherent with a Mae West picture,' complained Breen in a private memo. 'Lines and pieces of business, which in the script seem to be thoroughly innocuous, turn out when shown on screen to be questionable at best, when they are not definitely offensive.'[24]

The endless trouble with the censors meant that the moment West's box-office success dipped, the studio began to cool on her. In 1938 she was among those named 'box office poison' (more on which later) and Paramount dropped her. After turning down a supporting role in *Gone with the Wind* because she wouldn't be allowed to write her own lines, it was almost eighteen months before West worked again, when she turned out another hit opposite W. C. Fields in *My Little Chickadee.* Her dialogue was heavily censored but still gave us, 'Between two evils, I like to pick the one I haven't tried before.' Still, as the censors tightened their grip West's days were numbered. 1943's *The Heat's On* was even more tightly controlled and flopped badly.

*   *   *

For what it's worth, West herself claimed to look back rather philosophically and even fondly on her battles with the censors:

> I *believe* in censorship. If a picture of mine didn't get an 'X' rating, I'd be insulted. Don't forget, dear, I *invented* censorship . . . I had my tricks for handling the censors. I'd write some lines I knew they would take out so others could stay in. You had to let them earn their money. You might say I created the Hays Office. They had to do it because of me . . . I made a fortune out of censorship.
>
> They said censorship was my enemy, but I'm not so sure about that. Maybe censorship was my best friend. You can't get famous for breaking the rules unless you've got some rules to break.[25]

West never saw herself as anyone's patsy, and may have been making the best of a bad situation. But there is a nugget of truth there, and West wasn't alone in seeing censorship as an ally. It's been argued by *The New Yorker*'s critic David Denby and writer and critic Molly Haskell, among others, that roles for women were actually *better* in the Code era, because instead of being scantily clad or openly gold-digging, characters had to rely on flirtatious wit and subtle innuendo. The Code also cut down on the number of female characters explicitly written as prostitutes, which was an excellent result given how disproportionately highly sex workers have always been represented on screen (seriously, we're talking Victorian London numbers here) and how mean-spirited and damaging their portrayal has often been.

Barbara Stanwyck's role in 1933's *Baby Face* presented one such challenge for the censors: she played a small-town girl who unapologetically sleeps her way to the top of a large bank. When she takes up with the heir to the business and he gets into trouble she initially refuses to sell her jewels to save him, only to come around and stand by her man. But the Code required punishment for even momentary cold-bloodedness; the film was recut so that her character loses everything. Rewarding crime was prohibited, of course, but there are hints of the same discomfort that *Hustlers* provoked in 2019: some men find it impossible to sympathise with or forgive women who, in desperate circumstances, prey on men in order to get ahead. They must be punished or the whole moral order is upturned.

Hitchcock had to change the ending of both *Rebecca* and *Suspicion* to ensure that his leading men (Laurence Olivier and Cary Grant) did not turn out to be killers – never mind that that made his leading ladies (both Joan Fontaine) seem paranoid over nothing. Women be crazy, right? Still, Hitchcock enjoyed testing the censors' limits. He got around the ban on long kisses in *Notorious* by having Cary Grant and Ingrid Bergman necking for *ages* but never technically kissing for more than the permitted three seconds. He did it again in *Rear Window*, breaking up the kissing with sweet nothings. 'An actress like Grace, who's also a lady, gives a director certain advantages,' he said. 'He can afford to be more colourful with a love scene played by a lady than with one played by a hussy.'[26]

Code films had to work harder than before to contrive possible situations for their male and female stars to spend time together, transforming many female leads from sex workers or showgirls into working girls of a more respectable sort. Look at Katharine Hepburn's career: she played attorneys, reporters, researchers and an aviator (in Dorothy Arzner's *Christopher Strong*) as well as heiresses and queens. All those Rosalind Russell and, later, Doris Day professional characters might not have existed without the Code. And once those rules fell apart in the late 1960s, it freed up the filmmakers of the '70s to bring us the prostitutes of *Klute* and *Mean Streets* and the victims of *Straw Dogs* and *A Clockwork Orange* – great and powerful films, certainly, but not as progressive in their female roles as they were in their willingness to show violence. Censorship thus had the odd effect of propelling some women into professional roles they might not otherwise have been allowed, at least for a while in the 1930s and during the war: by the late '40s and '50s most were back in domestic settings. And of course that never helped actresses of colour, who were hamstrung by the rules against interracial romance *and* the restrictions on their employment, and the fact that no studio seemed willing to cast two people of colour in leading roles to allow for an all-Black romance.

The Code made room for bad behaviour like adultery or extra-marital sex in accounts of historical figures, but not for modern-day characters, so the risqué 1920s sex comedies were replaced by the screwball farces of the late 1930s and '40s, which were smoothed and sanded further into the Doris Day comedies of the late '50s. Busby Berkeley's musicals, with those endless long legs kicking, were subject to close inspection, replaced by the more thoroughly attired Fred Astaire musicals. The crime film survived but with its extremes of violence watered down, and a tendency for gangster stars like Edward G. Robinson to abruptly reform, or simply play FBI men (particularly ones hunting down Nazis, since Robinson was Jewish, the Second World War was looming and Warner Bros adopted a firm anti-Nazi stance early on).

The censors frequently had their work cut out. Mogul and producer Howard Hughes' *The Outlaw* proved a particular challenge in 1941. Hughes, who was obsessed with his leading lady Jane Russell, took over directing the film from Howard Hawks, more or less to add extra cleavage shots. Hughes even designed a cantilevered underwire bra to highlight Russell's already high curves. She described the contraption as 'uncomfortable and ridiculous' and hauled up the straps on her own underwear for the same effect, trusting that he wouldn't undress her to check once she got to set.[27]

The effect appalled Breen, who noted that her already 'large and prominent' bosom was 'shockingly emphasised'. But Breen resigned from the PCA in 1941 to briefly take up a job at RKO, presumably in part because he was exhausted from arguing with Hughes. Hughes finally got his seal of approval following a few cuts, only to decide that that wasn't enough. He toured state censorship boards with the uncut version to stir up more controversy and publicity – though 20th Century Fox refused to distribute the film uncut, with the risk of that $25,000 fine hovering. The war effort then distracted Hughes for a year or so before the film was finally released in 1943, once again with a campaign designed to provoke outrage (Hughes' slogans asked: 'How would you like to tussle with Russell?'). It was pulled for Code violations after only a week.

The Outlaw was back on screens by 1946, released by United Artists, which never signed up to the Code and which saw the potential in Hughes' appetite for shock. Hughes booked a blimp that read 'Kept off the screen for three years, it's coming at last'. After it finally got past the New York State censorship board in 1947, the film would play around the clock there, eventually making over $20 million by 1968. Russell, as is so often the case with women, bore the brunt of the fallout: she wouldn't make another movie until 1946, keeping herself afloat with a recording career (she went on to success in films like *Gentlemen Prefer Blondes* and as Calamity Jane, opposite Bob Hope, in *The Paleface*).

Jane Russell's bosom challenged but did not single-handedly bring down the system, of course. That would be beyond any one woman – though her cleavage caused more problems for 1953's 3D film *The French Line*, which was refused a rating on the basis, presumably, of dangerous curves. Yet *The Outlaw* began to erode the system's power because it showed that audiences wanted racier material than the Code allowed. A double whammy of James M. Cain adaptations, Billy Wilder's *Double Indemnity* in 1944 and *The Postman Always Rings*

Twice in 1946, then showed ways to get remarkably adult content past the censor, with adultery and crime dominating the plot of both so that even a quick crime-doesn't-pay finale could not balance it out. The Second World War struck another blow. It seemed naive, after that, to ban depictions of violence when the real world provided so many. Instead, the first stirrings of a more flexible ratings system started in 1946, when the League of Decency offered a mixed 'B' rating to films allowed for adult audiences.

Even better, the spectre of federal censorship disappeared when the Supreme Court belatedly acknowledged that films had free speech protection in the 1952 Miracle case. Roberto Rossellini's film *The Miracle* had been judged sacrilegious by the New York Board of Regents, but the Court overturned its 1915 decision in *Mutual v. Ohio* and held that the right to free speech under the First Amendment to the US Constitution applied to film.

A series of confirmatory decisions followed, one dealing with Elia Kazan's race drama *Pinky*. By then the MPAA had largely stopped enforcing the rule against interracial relationships, and there was a mini trend for race dramas around the end of the 1940s. These replaced the African-American servant with the noble, tragic Black person: a small step forward in acknowledging the characters' humanity, but not one that went all the way to a rounded, vibrant portrayal of a people. It's the same way that *Green Book* may be a step up from *The Help*, but it's no *If Beale Street Could Talk*.

The times were changing, and suddenly the studios had far less reason to fear the PCA. Just in time, too. There were cooler, sexier and more downbeat films coming from Europe and a more daring public ready for them. TV offered more and more competition as its reach expanded into almost every home and the ambitions of its storytellers grew. The studios could finally take risks – though they reacted slowly to the new freedom. 1959's career-girl drama *The Best of Everything*, for example, shied away from the word 'abortion' even as

95

one of its three leading ladies headed off to get one. Then the story chickened out again and had her miscarry en route.[28]

Independent films still came in for censorship at a state and city level, and LGBTQ+ themes remained a target. Edward Dmytryk (later one of the Hollywood Ten) was able to tell a story about anti-Semitic prejudice in 1947's *Crossfire*, but only by replacing the gay hate crime that had been at the core of the novel on which it was based. Jack Smith's forty-two-minute-long *Flaming Creatures* (1963) featured drag queens, trans and intersex people (and a vampire Marilyn Monroe rising from the grave). During a Tivoli theatre showing in 1964, police stopped the film and arrested the exhibitors and filmmakers for obscenity. Ironically one of the defendants, Jonas Mekas, tried to raise money for the legal fees with a screening of gay film *Un Chant d'Amour* and was arrested again. LGBTQ+-themed films would continue to meet with major hostility from the authorities for decades to come.

Those trans stars who could 'pass', some of whom had had gender confirmation surgery, also had to fear a hostile media. British model and actress April Ashley landed a small role in the Bing Crosby/Bob Hope film *The Road to Hong Kong* in 1961, only to be cruelly outed by the *Sunday People* newspaper and see her credit removed from the film.[29] Years later, model Caroline 'Tula' Cossey appeared in the Bond film *For Your Eyes Only* in a mere cameo – but the *News of the World* splashed her birth identity across its pages and left her near-suicidal.[30] Both women would live to campaign for the legal rights of transgender people in the UK, however, and prove that living well is the best revenge.

In 1966 Jack Valenti was hired away from Lyndon B. Johnson's administration to take over the MPAA and put in place a theoretically voluntary ratings system: something constitutionally acceptable but protective. With that new wiggle room, Hollywood finally acknowledged the existence of LGBTQ+ people, though in tentative, baby steps. As Vito Russo, author of *The Celluloid Closet*, noted, many stars and directors of films on gay subjects stressed that they were about something else *really*, honest.[31] William Wyler claimed *The Children's Hour* is about 'the power of lies to destroy people's lives'; *Sunday Bloody Sunday* is about 'loneliness' according to John Schlesinger, as is *Staircase* according to Rex Harrison. None of that is untrue, but it leaves out a key, homosexual part of the picture. Many films also saw lesbians 'cured' of their preference, ending the film with men, as in 1967's *The Fox* (originally R-rated; revised to a PG in 1973) or Bernardo Bertolucci's *The Conformist* (1970).

Russo also noted that in thirty-two films with major homosexual characters from 1961 to 1976, thirteen featured the suicide of a gay character and eighteen saw gay characters murdered. The old Code attitudes mandating punishment for anyone who stepped outside social norms lingered on. Even today, gay characters die so often in film and TV shows that it's a storytelling trope known as 'Bury Your Gays': see *Four Weddings and a Funeral*, *Land of the Dead* and *A Single Man* for more recent examples.

By 1968 the MPAA brought in the ratings system that has endured, with tweaks, ever since. For women, it didn't necessarily change much. Straight, white men continued to dominate the ratings system, and continued to apply the same old standards to what was and was not acceptable. That's not the theory, of course, but it looks awfully like that is the practice.

The modern US ratings system is voluntary in theory, but it's hard for a film to get a release without its certification – or with its dreaded NC-17 rating, which signals significant violent or sexual content. Its anonymous ratings committee are all (in theory) parents of school-age children who aim to give 'parents the information they need to decide whether a film is appropriate for their family'.[32] Just like the old days, it's all about concern for the children – but what can damage children is strangely defined.

It's fine, for instance, to have a story chock-full of violence towards women: that will most likely get an R-rating. But you will also attract an R-rating if you say 'fuck' more than once, so full-on torture porn is apparently equivalent to two instances of bad language – even if the bad language is used casually rather than aggressively. *The King's Speech* was slapped with an R-rating because Colin Firth's King George VI releases a torrent of rude words during a speech therapy session: the taboo is what allows him to speak without his habitual stutter. In contrast, the UK's BBFC gave the film a 12 because it took into account that therapeutic context.

Comic sex scenes, and glossy ones, are given far more leeway than dramatic or awkwardly realistic ones. British film *Angels and Insects* got an NC-17 for a brief glimpse of an erection in 1995; in 2000 *Scary Movie* had a prosthetic erection stab a man through the head, and got an R. There's also a difference between studio and independent films: while studio filmmakers report receiving detailed notes from the MPAA on what they must cut to get an R-rating, independent film-makers report, essentially, a shrug (the UK's BBFC is considerably more open).

The MPAA's is a ratings system that reflexively judges female sexuality more strictly than male. For years, even non-graphic depictions of a female orgasm resulted in an NC-17 rating while a male one would attract only an R. Director Kimberley Peirce was informed that Chloë Sevigny's orgasm scene in the Oscar-winning *Boys Don't Cry* was 'too long' and she would have to cut it to land the R-rating that the studio mandated; a scene after Hilary Swank's Brandon Teena goes down on Sevigny's Lana and wipes his mouth on the way up was also 'offensive'.[33] Again, there's nothing graphic, but that gesture implied too much.

On *Love & Basketball*, the studio asked director Gina Prince-Bythewood to tweak the scene where heroine Monica (Sanaa Latham) loses her virginity, because Monica didn't seem to be enjoying the experience. Prince-Bythewood shot extra footage and edited it in – but the MPAA slapped on an R-rating because of the scene. She remembered in 2020:

> I said, 'There's no nudity at all. How can you give this an R?' They said because it's too real. I said, 'That should be a compliment, not given an R, because now girls can't see this.' *Meet Joe Black* had just come out, and in that movie, Brad Pitt loses his virginity and you see everything of his first time on his face. I asked, 'Why is the male point of view OK but mine isn't?' But they would not back down. I didn't want to compromise, but the thought of girls not being able to see it, I hated that. My editor took a shot out; we resubmitted it and got the PG-13.[34]

Ryan Gosling and Michelle Williams' 2010 relationship drama *Blue Valentine* initially got an NC-17 because of brief, non-naked male-on-female oral sex. 'There's plenty of oral sex scenes in a lot of movies, where it's a man receiving it from a woman – and they're R-rated,' Gosling told *Moviefone*. 'Ours is reversed and somehow it's perceived as pornographic. How is it possible that these movies that torture women in a sexual context can have an R-rating but a husband and wife making love is inappropriate?' (In the same article, *Moviefone* described the MPAA as 'a venerable American institution that operates with all the value and rationality of the Taliban'.)[35] The MPAA reversed that decision, and the 'Feminist Ryan Gosling' meme was born.

In 2013, the same year that Martin Scorsese's *The Wolf of Wall Street* got an R-rating despite breathtaking amounts of sex, drugs and drug-fuelled sex, *Transparent* creator Jill Soloway released *Afternoon Delight*, where two sex scenes had to be cut to get an R-rating, both showing female pleasure: one a vocal orgasm and the other a cunnilingus scene. Soloway said, 'It's not just women, it's for anyone who's other

... By their nature, indie films disseminate the voices of people who are not commonly heard: women, queer people, people of color. These are pieces of our culture that attempt to dismantle the straight white male perspective, but because they don't have the political muscle of the studio backing or the consigliere to walk them through the MPAA process – the likelihood that they'll have to cut out what's "uncomfortable" is much higher.' As it is, said Soloway, the system 'is so unevenly applied and it ends up just reinforcing all the sexist, gender-violent, women-hating stuff'.[36]

Bo Burnham's *Eighth Grade* (2018) landed an R-rating for bad language and 'sexual material', putting it out of range of the very age group it portrays. Burnham said, 'There seems to be a strange double standard between sexuality and violence. It's a little weird how much violence you can have in a PG-13 movie.'[37] As of 2006, four times as many films received an NC-17 rating for sex as for violence.

Much of this double standard comes from the fact that censors assume – as Laura Mulvey would discuss in her theories on the 'male gaze', on which more later – that the person looking at the screen is male (and straight). The desire for male bodies is, in this world view, perverse, weird, niche. The desire to watch female bodies is normal and profitable, but should be policed because women's very bodies are responsible for all sin, even that committed by men. It's an ancient double standard, and an inconsistent one, but it still seems to pervade censorial thinking and filmmaking priorities.

So R-rated action movies of the 1980s all seemed to involve a visit to a strip club as a vital step in solving any major criminal case, because some passing titillation (no pun intended) was important in attracting a male audience. Even hugely gifted filmmakers act like any truly 'gritty' film will involve sex workers in some capacity. And if such elements mean that there is a high level of female nudity involved, so be it. It's not like they're going to drape that all over the poster, right? There is nothing wrong with the female body, even in the very limited spectrum of shapes considered acceptable in Hollywood, but the quantities of male and female nudity remain vastly different, and censorship vastly inconsistent.

For all its inequity, the ratings system is mostly uncontroversial these days. The energy that once went into censorship and boycotts was long ago replaced by 'culture wars', a term that came into use in the 1980s. Right-wing and religious groups still campaign against content they consider sacrilegious or offensive, but now feminist groups complain of female exploitation and people of colour are finally making headway as they complain of stereotyped and offensive depictions. As a general rule, the successful cases of actual censorship since the 1980s or so came from the right: think of Scorsese's *The Last Temptation of Christ*, which is still banned in several countries, or the long-standing problems that *Life of Brian* faced in getting a cinema release around the world. But the left-wing groups have arguably been more successful in shaping the conversation and the future of filmmaking, by kicking up such a storm of protest that studios have slowly started to make greater efforts to avoid stereotype and sexism.

This isn't censorship, no matter how much the frothing trolls of the internet would like to decry it as such, and it fulfils a different function to the old Code. Where that tried to enforce an existing social order and mandate only one model of proper living (heterosexual but largely sexless, monogamous and conformist, white Anglo-Saxon and probably protestant), the new calls for greater representation are more about widening the screen to include the whole breadth of humanity. The capacity of the internet to shame studios and filmmakers has shaped the way that films get made, so it's worth a quick look. The test becomes not 'Is it sexy?' but 'Is it sexism?', and less about nudity and more the context for it.

There is increasing pressure on filmmakers and studios to show inclusiveness not only in the characters put on screen but in casting too. The 2019 live-action remake of Disney's *Aladdin* launched a months-long casting search to find stars of Middle-Eastern origin, but faced criticism when Naomi Scott, a woman of south-east Asian background, was cast as Jasmine. Disney representatives explained her casting as a conscious decision to include the many south-east Asian fans of the movie, and wrote in a foreign background on Jasmine's mother's side to explain it – but the question was addressed at least, rather than treating all brown people as one.[38] Some offensive lines from the old songs were removed but the film still caused controversy when it was reported that Disney 'browned up' stunt performers, animal handlers and special-effects artists for the film.[39]

It's not only a matter of race. *Black Widow* actress Scarlett Johansson faced criticism after starring in a remake of anime classic *Ghost in the Shell* where her character was race-swapped from the original's Japanese woman. But that was a mere whisper compared to the storm when she briefly signed up to play Dante 'Tex' Gill, a trans man, in a proposed film called *Rub & Tug*.[40] Race-bending was a well-intentioned plot point in the former film and therefore there's a *possible* argument to be made for its inclusion. Or, there would be if the practice were not almost entirely a one-way street: if white roles were frequently race-bent for big-screen remakes starring people of colour, and if white stars did not so heavily dominate the screen.

But *Rub & Tug* was the last straw, because Johansson seemed to be taking a part from a trans man, a group almost entirely unrepresented on the big screen. Johansson's initial response didn't help, scoffing that critics 'can be directed to Jeffrey Tambor, Jared Leto and Felicity Huffman's reps for comment', all actors who had played trans people without much protest. But if there was a time when that casting was OK, that time had passed, and soon Johansson doubled back and 'respectfully' withdrew.[41] Not everyone learned with her:

Halle Berry faced a similar storm of controversy when she briefly signed on to play a trans man in 2020, misgendering her character as 'a woman' multiple times during an interview about the film. She too bowed out amid a storm of criticism.[42]

'Cis actors playing trans characters is directly harmful in the real world,' says GLAAD Director of Entertainment Research & Analysis Megan Townsend. 'We know that only about 20% of Americans know somebody who is trans, compared to about 90% who knows somebody who's lesbian, gay or bi, [so] the majority of what they're learning about trans people comes from entertainment. That is why it is so critical for trans stories to be not only told, but told in a thoughtful way. Specifically, when a film casts a cisgender man as a trans woman, viewers are getting two wrong messages, one being [that] trans is a performance or a costume, but also that underneath the hair and the clothes is really a man. And, you know, trans women, it's not something that they take off. That's why it's a different level of seriousness when the conversation is about a cis actor playing a trans character versus a straight actor playing an LGBTQ+ character. A cis person playing trans absolutely should not happen.'

Rub & Tug stalled there for two years, before *Transparent* and *Pose* writer Our Lady J signed on to direct a TV series take on Gill's story. The next phase of the fight for representation has to be to convince Hollywood financiers that there is sufficient talent among under-represented groups like trans men to allow them to lead films, and to convince stars like Johansson to take a supporting role and be an ally in that way, because it shouldn't be the case that white, cis, able-bodied stars feel empowered to play anyone and no one else gets a chance even to represent their own identities. There *is* precedent for filmmakers launching previously unknown or little-known stars from under-represented groups. Think of *Children of a Lesser God* casting deaf actress Marlee Matlin (to Oscar-winning effect) or Danny

Boyle giving Dev Patel and Freida Pinto a bigger platform in *Slumdog Millionaire*. What's stardom good for if not to use it to promote people who the studios might otherwise overlook? Look at the work Brad Pitt's Plan B has done for films like 12 *Years a Slave* and *Moonlight*; or Keanu Reeves executive-producing Tourmaline's short art film about trans women through history, *Salacia*; or Angelina Jolie's executive-producing role on Cartoon Saloon's Afghan drama *The Breadwinner*, helping to tell a story that might not otherwise have been told.

There are still unfortunate incidents of filmmaking blindness, but stars and studios are learning and listening – in some cases because it's the right thing to do, and in others because they've seen the PR nightmare that can result from failure. This is a bottom-up change, with social media enabling previously marginalised voices to be amplified and heard by those who make decisions, and most importantly of all ensuring that those in power can be embarrassed by their failings. Cultural norms can change very quickly – those earlier stars in trans roles were even hailed for their efforts at representation – but studios have learned the box-office and reputational value of listening to criticism, at least to a minimum degree. Look at the difference in casting between 2010's *Prince of Persia* (Jake Gyllenhaal and Gemma Arterton) and that *Aladdin* remake (Mena Massoud, Naomi Scott). That's not censorship; that's the business sense that the same libertarians who obsess about (their own) free speech profess to worship. And it is the freedom to say whatever is important to you personally that empowered the next group we're going to look at: the auteurs.

6

Directors Behaving Badly
How the auteur theory twisted film

TOWARDS THE end of the studio era, the director's power began to grow significantly, led by superstar – and self-promoting – figures like Orson Welles and Alfred Hitchcock. A very particular strand of thinking underlay, and seemed to justify, this increase in directorial power, and it has shaped film thought and film practice ever since. It started with the same vexing question that came up as regards censorship: do films qualify as 'art'? In Rudyard Kipling's poem 'The Conundrum of the Workshops', the Devil sidles up to generation after generation of artist and whispers, 'It's pretty, but is it art?' In cinema's early decades, its intellectual and artistic status was similarly unsure. Philosophers and thinkers kept trying to explain what made movies important – or if they were even important at all.

Legally, the Supreme Court in 1915 had answered the art question in the negative. Already, that felt instinctively wrong. It was the same year, after all, as D. W. Griffith's racist epic *Birth of a Nation*, and just before his less racist but even more ambitious *Intolerance*. It was the same year as Lois Weber's highly acclaimed and self-consciously weighty *Hypocrites*, and the same year that poet Vachel Lindsay wrote *The Art of the Moving Picture*, arguing quite the opposite conclusion to SCOTUS. To the extent that its fans thought about such a question in the following few decades, the feeling seemed to be that film *could* be art. But how to define it? And who was the artist?

It was in answer to that thorny second question that the auteur theory arose. Somehow inevitably, it was developed in France. An Italian living in France, Ricciotto Canudo, numbered the art forms: the first art was dance, then music, poetry, painting, sculpture and architecture. Cinema, therefore, became the 'seventh art' (photography, comics and video games would follow), a term still in use in the Institut de France's Academy of Fine Art and throughout parts of Europe where people non-ironically wear berets.

Perhaps no artist is needed to make art: we're fine without knowing the name of any architect of the great Gothic cathedrals, or the megaliths and pyramids that dot the ancient world. Yet there's a certain kind of critic or philosopher, usually male, who finds such a shrug unsatisfying. If collectives can create great art, what room is there for the Great Man model of history? Surely everything comes down to one chap and his inspiration? For many people, and especially those born and raised in the individualist cultures of the West, there has to be a single person we can credit, or the work can't *really* be genius.

Some film lovers were therefore drawn to the idea that the director might be the key figure. 'A real director should be absolute,' said Lois Weber in 1916. 'He (or she in this case) alone knows the effects he wants to produce, and he alone should have authority in the arrangement, cutting, titling or anything else that may seem necessary to do to the finished product . . . We ought to realise that the work of a picture director, worthy of a name, is creative.'[1] As early as 1912 she had said, 'The management that interferes with the good director is in the wrong business.'[2] Then again, Weber was a director (and actor, editor, titler and the rest) so she would say that. The idea needed theorists to be taken seriously, and the process began with German film theorist Walter Julius Bloem in the 1920s, and continued via American playwright James Agee and French critic André Bazin in the 1940s.

It was Bazin's protégé, François Truffaut, who really began to change the profile of directors. Not yet the filmmaker he would become, Truffaut wrote an essay in the January 1954 edition of French film magazine *Cahiers du Cinema* called *Une certaine tendance du cinéma français* (A certain tendency in French cinema). There, he argued that too many French filmmakers just plugged elements like actors and lighting into a script, without exercising much creative control over the results. It's a long essay and includes much criticism of the political leanings of long-forgotten French screenwriters, but it comes to one basic point: the best films are made by those who shape the story they want to tell and don't let themselves get bossed about by anything minor like a screenplay or a studio.

Truffaut identified eight French filmmakers who exemplified this creativity, names like Jean Renoir, Robert Bresson and Jacques Tati (he also specifically criticised Henri-Georges Clouzot's *Wages of Fear*, a film now generally considered a masterpiece, but nobody's perfect). Over the following years, Truffaut and his *Cahiers du Cinema* colleagues turned this basic idea into the '*politique des auteurs*', translated – not quite faithfully – into English as 'auteur theory'.

It was an appealing notion. If auteurs are those who control their films, stamping their own personality on the work, then an auteur is something every creative filmmaker would strive to be. Most of those identified as auteurs are great creative role models, if not great people. Hitchcock, Hawks, John Ford and Orson Welles were held up as Hollywood exemplars of the form – especially Welles, the boy wonder, the man who fought the studio system so hard that he finished barely a handful of the films he began. Another heralded as an auteur was comedy director and star Jerry Lewis, which may seem less obvious. Truffaut was right to acknowledge that comedy is 'by far the most difficult genre', of course, but one suspects his acclaim is partly due to the fact that the French just love Jerry Lewis.[3] It's one of those odd quirks that balances out all the chicness. Satyajit Ray, Luis

Buñuel and Sergei Eisenstein were also cited, because auteurs do not only (or even mostly) exist within the Hollywood studio system.

The original essays were sausage fests bereft of even a single female name. Many still are, though thoughtful souls will tip their cap to great filmmakers like Agnès Varda, Chantal Akerman or (later) Jane Campion. The legacy of cinema's early female directors had been so thoroughly diminished that even her own countrymen did not seem to consider the likes of Alice Guy-Blaché (still alive at the time, and recently the recipient of the Légion d'honneur). With some proponents arguing that a true auteur analysis involved dissection of every example of a filmmaker's work, how could her generation ever be included, with so many early silent films destroyed or decayed? Not that there's much evidence to suggest that any of the theorists searched too hard for female filmmakers to include.

Critic Andrew Sarris, who almost single-handedly popularised it in the English-speaking world, broke the theory down into three criteria.[4] Is the director technically competent? Does the body of work show personality? And does the work betray interior meaning? Match all three and, bingo, you're an auteur. What's valuable about Sarris's search for 'interior meaning' is that it allows critics to analyse filmmakers as artists. That in turn helped establish the case for film preservation and the importance of film heritage.

But one of Sarris's contemporaries, Pauline Kael, was a vociferous opponent of the notion, arguing that his were self-fulfilling criteria, assigning auteur status to those critics already rated. 'Criticism is an art, not a science,' she added, 'and a critic who follows rules will fail in one of his most important functions: perceiving what is original and important in *new* work and helping others to see.'[5]

Kael, of course, helped to build the towering reputations of the New Hollywood directors of the late 1960s and early 1970s. Perhaps that explains her immediate aversion to a theory that relied on examining a body of work. It's ironic, then, that few did more to build up the reputation and importance of directors as artists than Kael, so that even the greatest opponent of the auteur theory spent her career bolstering its effect.

Despite such opposition, the term 'auteur' came into general use in film criticism, especially at the more academic end. Later it came to be used, sometimes indiscriminately, about directors because it was flattering. There are people who describe all directors as auteurs, which is self-evidently not the case. Worse, some people act as if there is an auteur for every film, and as if it's always the director – and that feels wrong.

Gone with the Wind went through three directors during its mammoth shoot: is its auteur George Cukor, who oversaw pre-production and started filming? Cukor played Scarlett opposite Olivia de Havilland for her audition, clutching the curtains and hamming it up. Does that get him bonus points? Or was the film's auteur Victor Fleming, who completed the shoot? Does the fact that Sam Wood briefly replaced Fleming when he took time off for exhaustion erode Fleming's claim?

A glance at Hollywood history will tell you that *if* that film has an auteur it was David O. Selznick, the producer who oversaw script, casting and direction. He found Vivien Leigh; delayed production until he could secure Clark Gable's services; signed off on the finished script and determined to burn the enormous Atlanta set.

More recently you might argue that producer Kevin Feige is the auteur of the Marvel Cinematic Universe; he certainly controls its overall direction and content, though *Thor: Ragnarok* or *Black Panther* also show the hands of their respective directors at work. The theory simply doesn't fit every film (of course it might just support Martin Scorsese's contention that the Marvel films are 'not cinema'* [6]).

---

* Please do not ask for my position on this take. This is not a discussion in which I wish to pick sides.

Sometimes you might think a star is the auteur. The French author and critic Colette called Mae West the auteur of her films, though she did so before the word acquired its current meaning. Still, it's not a ridiculous claim: West was usually her own screenwriter, and shaped the look and plot of her films to fit her style rather than vice versa. In modern times, Tom Cruise takes an outsize role in his movies, and works *very* closely with his directors to fine-tune them. Doug Liman recounted lengthy late-night sessions during the shoot of *American Made*, polishing up the script or conceiving new beats, and Cruise's close collaborator Christopher McQuarrie works hand in glove with him on their shared films.[7] But then McQuarrie also says that Cruise exerts all the sway of his star power on his director's behalf, protecting them from misguided studio interference.[8]

Sometimes the screenwriter is a film's dominant personality: Paddy Chayefsky or Charlie Kaufman had such distinctive styles that they stood out even before Kaufman started to direct as well. Stories written about Aaron Sorkin-penned films tend to give him just as much coverage as the director, even when the director is David Fincher (*The Social Network*) or Danny Boyle (*Steve Jobs*). Most auteur writers become auteur directors eventually, so it may not be a distinction that much matters, but the role of the writer is diminished by this cult-like focus on directors. And it has only become more pronounced.

As the studio system began to decline after the Paramount Decree, it created an odd power vacuum in Hollywood. The decline was not in terms of the ability to finance a film, of course: the studios still had that. They still signed actors to contracts, still negotiated the terms of employment with the crafts unions, still controlled the output on a vast majority of screens even with the rise of independent and foreign distribution. But they were faltering in the 1950s and 1960s, and they knew it. It created an imbalance, and star directors filled the gap.

They lacked the ability, usually, to greenlight films, but their power stemmed from a slightly different dynamic. The director was now an artist, and therefore he implicitly offered to cast that artistic glow on his collaborators. As the stature of directors grew, their power to shape your destiny, and to give creative as well as financial validation, rose. These men asserted control over, particularly, the actresses with whom they worked. There were directors who isolated their leading ladies from the rest of the cast and crew, determined that their stars would be dependent on them for support or advice. Some physically or verbally harassed stars to get the emotional reaction they wanted, rather than trusting them to act. And others tried to take over their stars' lives and mould them to fit an ideal, off screen as well as on it. This was a relationship more personal than the studio contract system, and if it was not always based on sex, that was often at least a possibility.

If directors are artists, that made actors their tools. Not all directors, and not all actors, but the possibility was there. The new philosophy followed the authoritarian steps of masters like Hitchcock, already a legend, and seemed to reflect the new Method acting, where actors tried to tap into emotional experiences in their own lives to fuel their work, with spectacular successes like Marlon Brando revolutionising the profession as a result. But it's an attitude that persists even now, and that creates a real power imbalance because it's not applied evenly across the sexes. Method actors come in all shapes and sizes, but directors still tended to be men, and they remain far more likely to resort to extreme measures against their female stars than the men. Such abuse was never universal, thankfully, but it's another case where actresses can see their real lives undermined in pursuit of art.

It's impossible to talk about directors' relationships with women without talking about Alfred Hitchcock. He was a cinematic genius, someone whose influence still rings throughout the art form, and the vast majority of his films were built around a woman in distress or causing distress to the hapless men around her (or both). He gave women some of their best and most complex roles of the twentieth century, from Ingrid Bergman's tormented spy in *Notorious* to Joan Fontaine's second Mrs de Winter in *Rebecca* to Kim Novak's double role in the stunning *Vertigo*. But he occasionally manipulated his female stars to the point of real harm.

At the lower end of the spectrum was an obsession with how his leading ladies dressed and did their hair – off set as well as on, treating them like dolls. He preferred very slim women for his films, even into the '50s where more buxom blondes began to take over. 'Smallness is definitely an asset,' he had written in a 1931 article, and he held to that.[9] When working with Grace Kelly, he had someone tail her to monitor her behaviour. On *Rebecca* he isolated Joan Fontaine from the rest of the cast to keep her off-balance, like her character. She said he 'wanted total control over me and seemed to relish the cast not liking one another'. On release she described him as 'practically a Svengali to me' – a term she seems to have intended in a complimentary way, though the reality is a little more fraught, as we'll see. 'Your performance was Hitchcock's performance,' said *Foreign Correspondent* star Laraine Day. 'You read the lines the way Hitchcock read the lines . . . You did exactly as he told you . . . You'd bring nothing but [your] body to the set.'[10]

The director didn't do much to dispel the impression that it was all his show, and even in his earliest days believed himself the major draw on his films – which would, of course, eventually be the case. 'Actors come and go,' he said in 1925 after making his first film, *The Pleasure Garden*, 'but the name of the director should stay clearly in the mind of the audiences.'[11]

Hitchcock was the priority, and the women were there to be, well, mistreated. 'I always believe in following the advice of the playwright

[Victorien] Sardou,' said Hitch. 'He said: "Torture the women!" ' . . . The trouble today is that we don't torture women enough.'[12] That was tongue in cheek, of course, a reference to the femmes fatales that peopled his films, the dangerous and desperate women in whom he often trafficked. But Hitch came closer to real-life torture on *The Birds* and *Marnie*.

After signing Tippi Hedren to a personal contract, Hedren claimed that Hitchcock made sexual advances towards her. When she turned him down, he became distant and even vengeful, terrorising her and refusing to warn her what was coming from one scene to the next. Hedren spent a week having live birds thrown at her or tied to her limbs, with one clawing so near her eye that she felt lucky not to lose it. After shooting he sent her daughter, Melanie Griffith, a doll of her mother as she was dressed in the film, in a coffin-shaped box. On *Marnie*, the next film under her contract, Hedren said Hitchcock sexually assaulted her,[13] and that she was not informed in advance that her kleptomaniac character would be raped by Sean Connery's Mark, lest she object (Hitchcock had already fired one writer who tried to cut the scene, saying it was the reason he wanted to do the film).[14] Hedren saw the scene as a punishment for her resistance.

Hedren's case was extreme, but there were hints of Hitch's sometimes troubling control over his stars much earlier. 'Some of us actors have ideas, and then Hitch can become a little truculent,' said Ingrid Bergman shortly before his death. Grace Kelly wrote that, 'Sometimes he merely wears actors down until he gets what he wants.'[15] Bergman and Kelly stayed on friendly terms with the director and he was a fan of both, asking them back for repeat collaborations even when their lives made it impossible. But even these friends saw a need for dominance in his behaviour.

Hitchcock was not alone among self-promoting directors in mistreating his actors. The great German filmmaker Fritz Lang moved to Hollywood before the Second World War and hired Anna

Lee (later a fixture on the soap *General Hospital*) for *Hangmen Also Die!* in 1943. In a scene where she had to smash a pane of glass, he insisted on using the real thing rather than the usual candy glass. When she did the first take perfectly and without injury, he asked for a reshoot – on which she cut herself badly, which seemed to satisfy him. He would stamp on her bare feet with his booted ones, and she came away from the film calling it a 'horror' to make and him a 'sadist'.[16]

Then there were the acknowledged bullies. Joan Crawford called Otto Preminger 'sort of a Jewish Nazi' for his on-set bullying, and she was a relative fan.[17] Preminger once asked Robert Mitchum to do so many takes of a scene where he slapped female lead Jean Simmons that Mitchum finally turned and slapped the director instead.

Director John Farrow stalked Maureen O'Hara on *A Bill of Divorcement*, parking outside her house and turning up uninvited with dinner.[18] When she succeeded in convincing him that she wasn't interested (he was married, incidentally) he told people that 'She must be a lesbian' and badmouthed her abilities around set. Later, director John Ford sent her love letters, and was also turned down. He then said of her, 'That bitch couldn't act her way out of a brick shithouse,' which apart from anything else makes no sense at all.[19]

Others kept their misogyny private, though it sometimes leaked into their work. 'Women are stupid,' said Orson Welles. 'I've known some who are less stupid than others, but they're all stupid.'[20] He described women as 'things', too, and claimed that women were responsible for civilisation because men created it 'to impress their girlfriends'.[21] He couldn't 'bear to look at Bette Davis';[22] he thought Jennifer Jones was 'hopeless', and Norma Shearer 'one of the most minimally talented ladies to appear on the silver screen'. When he worked with his then-wife Rita Hayworth on *The Lady from Shanghai* he took away her signature look and almost destroyed her career. Their marriage broke up soon after. Again, Welles is an inspiration for modern directors, the wunderkind who made *Citizen Kane* at twenty-six. With role models like this, who needs bad examples?

Worse than the stories about moments of fear are the ones that sound more like long-term grooming. There's a strange and sometimes creepy phenomenon that grew out of the theatre and into film, one that perhaps always existed in any sphere where women were allowed to flourish. The studio system was a perfect fit for it, though it continues to exist, to a lesser degree. That is the phenomenon of the svengali, almost always a man who shapes his protégée's career – usually a woman – and who is accordingly given much of the credit for their work.

The term 'svengali' comes from the popular 1895 play *Trilby*, by George du Maurier (grandfather of Daphne and of the kids who inspired *Peter Pan*). In that tale, the insidious Svengali seduces the titular young girl and uses hypnosis to transform her into a great singer. As a result of such machinations she depends on him to perform, and finds herself under his domination. The play was wildly successful and the name Svengali became immediately recognisable, to the extent that most subsequent film adaptations were named after the villain rather than the heroine (four, plus a 1983 TV movie with Peter O'Toole and Jodie Foster). It's even the name of a legal defence, famously used by US lawyer Clarence Darrow, and recently in defence of one of the Boston marathon bombers. It argues that one guilty party is *less* guilty because they were under the sway of their co-accused. Legally speaking, a 'svengali' is someone who makes others into their puppets.

In Hollywood practice, it's usually a director or producer who tries to create an entirely new persona out of someone. There's something about the beauty and charisma required of stars that makes certain men want to claim them not just sexually or romantically but professionally, shaping people to their own model of perfection. In

Hollywood there was a phenomenon of men taking credit for women's talent by claiming to have 'created' them from whole cloth, and it fed into a toxic power imbalance.

It's a phenomenon that's distinct from, say, the husband-and-wife pairings that crop up through the studio era – though there are sometimes overlaps. Joseph M. Schenck and Norma Talmadge, for example, were a producer-star couple who consciously worked together to increase her star power. But Schenck, and other power couples like Irving Thalberg and Norma Shearer, were tailoring roles to the star wives rather than wives to the roles, and with the enthusiastic involvement of the women. Other producer-star couples were less egalitarian: David O. Selznick and Jennifer Jones, say. After becoming obsessed with Jones and breaking up both their marriages so they could be together, Selznick managed her career for the rest of his life, putting her only in the films he approved and often turning down good work (including Preminger's *Laura*) in favour of lesser projects.

As the influence of directors grew, they became another powerful svengali figure, a mentor able to lift you to new heights of artistic achievement – in theory. The price of such glory was submission, which makes a certain twisted sense. If directors are artists, if you believe in their vision and want to help to realise it, you will be disposed to do as they ask. Problems only arise when directors, knowing this, ask far more than any reasonable person would allow: for philosophers, it's when they fall prey to Kant's fundamental moral failing of treating people merely as a means to an end. That's been the troubling, familiar theme throughout film history, even from great directors, and especially for their female stars. These are often men who thought they could control the careers of their female stars, and who expected – at the very least – gratitude in return. Many saw themselves as Pygmalions, shaping stars from mortal clay and taking personal credit for all their subsequent work.

Think of Otto Preminger and Jean Seberg. He made much of the fact that he wanted an unknown to star in his film adaptation of *Saint Joan*, reportedly spending '£50,000 or £60,000' on the search for a fresh new face.[23] He hired a young Iowan, Jean Seberg – only to turn into his usual monstrous, dictatorial self on set and repeatedly humiliate her, acting out every detail of each scene for her to copy. Preminger stayed in an apartment above hers in the Dorchester Hotel in London and put her under strict instructions as to clothing, food and even bedtimes.[24] A picture of the pair together shows him towering over her, holding up her chin like a mother with a messy child. He's grinning; she looks defiant but unable to run. 'It's my belief that Otto wanted Jean to feel and actually to be overwhelmed,' said agent Lionel Larner of the set. 'That was how he saw the part . . . Of course such an interpretation could not work out.'[25]

Sure enough, the film did not turn out well. Seberg said later that she was burnt at the stake twice: once in character (an effects accident had left her really burnt; Preminger crowed of the injury that, 'We got it all on film'),[26] and once by the critics. Said Preminger, 'It's quite true that, if I had chosen Audrey Hepburn instead of Jean Seberg, it would have been less of a risk, but I prefer to take the risk . . . I have faith in her. Sure, she still has things to learn about acting, but so did Kim Novak when she started.'[27] Note here that he puts the blame for any failing on Seberg's inexperience rather than his own direction, and that he implicitly takes credit for Novak's career as well. Novak had won a Golden Globe for *Picnic* before making *The Man with the Golden Arm* with Preminger.

Seberg worked with Preminger again on *Bonjour Tristesse*, because she had signed a seven-year contract with him. That film also flopped in the US and he dropped her 'like a Kleenex', she said. Happily, the two films made her a darling of the French, who adopted her as their own and gave her her best roles in the likes of *Breathless*. She was happier, and did better work, in easier conditions there. 'Every time

I've gone back [to the US] to do a film, I've been Miss Submissive. I've let things be done to me,' she said in 1974.[28] Somewhat to his credit, Preminger, later in life, took the blame for the shortcomings of Seberg's performances in his films and defended her ability as an actress, but it must have been cold comfort after his earlier abuse.

Some svengali relationships became more equal. Director Josef von Sternberg made seven films with '30s mega-star Marlene Dietrich, bringing her to Hollywood and crafting her signature roles in *The Blue Angel*, *Shanghai Express* and *Blonde Venus*. After a screen test of the former cabaret star, Sternberg wrote, 'I then put her into the crucible of my conception, blended her image to correspond with mine, and, pouring lights on her until the alchemy was complete, proceeded with the test. She came to life and responded to my instructions with an ease that I had never before encountered.'[29] In his introduction to the published script of *The Blue Angel* in 1968, Sternberg said that he directed actors by 'a sort of mesmerism' and by 'blotting out their traits and substituting a behaviour alien to them'.[30]

In that case Dietrich became *so* famous, so fast, that the balance of power between star and director was not wildly out of kilter: she would sometimes remind him that theirs was a collaboration rather than a master-and-servant bond. 'To my creator, from his creation,' she wrote to him once, in jest but with some affection.[31]

Some directors were serial svengalis. Howard Hawks, the great director of *Bringing Up Baby* and *His Girl Friday*, tried to take that role throughout his long career. 'Despite all of his great accomplishments,' remembered Lauren Bacall, 'his one ambition was to find a girl and invent her, to create her as his perfect woman. He was my Svengali, and I was to become, under his tutelage, this big star, and he would *own* me. And he would also like to get me into his bed, which, of course, horrors! It was the furthest thing from my mind. I was so frightened of him.'[32]

Hawks told the nineteen-year-old Bacall, on 1944's *The Big Sleep*, that he had tried to help Carole Lombard and Rita Hayworth, and that they would have had bigger careers had they obeyed his directions. He shaped Bacall into his platonic ideal, ordering her to go outside and scream every morning to make her voice lower and huskier and fit her to his fantasy. He supplied her stage name (she was born Betty Joan Perske and remained 'Betty' to friends) and was furious when she struck up a relationship with co-star Humphrey Bogart instead of with her director. Bogart's stardom and protection denied Hawks his chance to manage Bacall's career, though Bogart would himself try to stop Bacall working because he wanted, she said, a wife and not an actress.[33]

Hawks always treated Bacall as the one that got away, and was still trying the same lines decades later. When Jennifer O'Neill and Sherry Lansing worked on 1970's *Rio Lobo*, Hawks ordered both to try the same screaming trick, reminding them that he had discovered Bacall and seeking to remake both in her image. He discouraged them from becoming friends with each other or anyone on the crew, a running feature of controlling behaviour. After O'Neill refused to sign a personal contract with him, she experienced his very public anger. 'In front of the whole crew he said he was going to blackball me from the business and that I would never work again. It was very intimidating,' O'Neill remembered.[34] Hawks took some O'Neill scenes (she had the leading role) and gave them to Lansing, later the first female studio head of production. He trotted her around town on his arm in O'Neill's place. 'Hawks didn't want anyone talking to his leading ladies because that was the fantasy: they were there for him alone,' said Lansing.

Actresses did not always go along with their mentors' plans. Bacall had resisted parts of her Hawks-mandated makeover, keeping her own teeth, eyebrows and hairstyle, and when producer David O. Selznick tried to transform Ingrid Bergman as he had transformed so many before her, she insisted on keeping her name and her eyebrows (skinny eyebrows were the fashion; Bergman and Bacall would begin to change that). Selznick even spun her resistance to his advantage, billing her as the 'first natural actress'. He took credit for not changing a thing.

In the swinging 1960s and '70s, and consciously modelling themselves on the greats, the svengali directors pushed forward. Bob Rafelson, director of *Five Easy Pieces*, cast actress Julia Anne Robinson for a supporting role in *The King of Marvin Gardens*. According to star Bruce Dern, Rafelson's feelings for Robinson were 'open adoration, very definitely the whole syndrome of, I'm making a movie star – a director takes an unknown and she blossoms under his tutelage. It was just the way he touched her, the way he moved her around, like she was a possession.'[35] Alas, Robinson didn't have much acting talent, as less besotted eyes can see on screen, and sadly died in a fire a few years later, aged just twenty-four.

Around the same era Peter Bogdanovich tried to mould Cybill Shepherd, who he started dating after he had cast her in *The Last Picture Show* (he was married to production designer and future producer Polly Platt at the time, a genuine movie talent whose genius would often be credited to the men she worked with). 'Cybill started out as a whim, an instinct, a little voice in my head that I listened to,' Bogdanovich said. 'She's very malleable. You can bend her in any direction. She does what she's told.'[36] Shepherd's later career suggests that this is a terrible misrepresentation of her strong personality, but perhaps she was less sure of herself then.

Bogdanovich would try to star-make again a few years later, with actress and *Playboy* model Dorothy Stratten.[37] That relationship would end tragically, though not through his actions. It turned out that Bogdanovich was not the only man who wanted to guide Stratten's career. She had been married previously to Paul Snider, a sometime-pimp who thought that Stratten could make him a lot of money, and set her up with photographers who shot for *Playboy* magazine. When Stratten was named Playmate of the Month, Snider proposed, determined to hitch his star to her wagon. But as she progressed past his experience and outgrew his limits, the marriage hit the skids and she requested a divorce. She was getting cinema attention – unusual for a Bunny and testament to her potential – and went to New York to shoot *They All Laughed* with Bogdanovich, who was smitten and also saw stardom in her future. Shortly after shooting ended on their film, Stratten was killed by Snider, who then shot himself. It's the darkest possible outcome of the svengali story. Incidentally, Bogdanovich would later marry Stratten's younger sister, twenty-nine years his junior.

Recently, Thandie Newton has spoken out about her experiences as a still-teenage actress with director John Duigan, saying that at an age when she was 'super-vulnerable to predators' she felt 'coerced' into a relationship with the then-thirty-nine-year-old.[38] She described herself then as a 'very shy, very sweet' girl who 'wasn't in control of the situation'.[39] The experience had lasting consequences, making her hesitant to work with many people in the industry who seemed to pose a similar risk. She turned down work because she 'didn't want to be put in a position where I was objectified'. In combination with the already limited options available to Black actresses, it was a further handicap on her career – and it's testament to her ability that she has forged a path despite it.

The svengali dynamic is rarely a relationship that ends happily and healthily for all parties. But even when it works, there's something obscene about anyone taking credit for someone else's talent, or trying to shape a human being like clay. That's not even Wonder Woman's official origin story anymore, guys, and the myth of Galatea is old hat.

*   *   *

As personal exploitation became, perhaps, less openly common, a more professional form of exploitation remained, where directors – leaning on Hitchcock as an example – would treat their stars abysmally instead of trusting them to act. While there have always been abusive, angry or manipulative directors, this specific technique, which might be termed method directing, seems particularly common for women.

On *Bram Stoker's Dracula*, director Francis Ford Coppola was concerned that Winona Ryder's Mina Harker did not appear sufficiently upset in a scene where she was supposed to cry. So he encouraged all the actors present to join him in shouting abuse at Ryder, phrases like, 'You whore' over and over again. Ryder remembered that, 'The more it happened, I was like [she crosses her arms like a sulky teenager and frowns] . . . It just didn't work. I was like, really? It kind of did the opposite.'[40] (Please note that Keanu Reeves and Anthony Hopkins refused the director's demand.) This sort of emotional manipulation does not even necessarily get results. Ryder forgave but did not forget. 'Me and Francis are good now,' she said in 2020.[41]

Then there's *Last Tango in Paris*, the 1972 Bernardo Bertolucci film in which Marlon Brando's older American businessman has an affair with Maria Schneider's free-spirited young woman. One infamous scene sees Brando's Paul anally rape Schneider's Jeanne, using butter as a lubricant. It was a last-minute addition that Schneider was not warned about and that traumatised her. 'When they told me, I had a burst of anger,' Schneider remembered years later. 'Woo! I threw everything. And nobody can force someone to do something not in the script. But I didn't know that. I was too young. So I did the scene and I cried. I cried real tears during that scene. I was feeling humiliation.'[42] Bertolucci later claimed that he didn't tell her so as 'to have a more realistic reaction' – apparently forgetting he'd hired her to act.[43]

According to Schneider, Brando himself felt 'raped' and 'manipulated' during filming and did not talk to the director for years afterwards, though she also said that the infamous butter scene was Brando's idea. She remembered the film as 'a lot of suffering, a lot of compromising'. Bertolucci was unrepentant (if inconsistent) to the end, claiming variously that the scene was in the script except for the butter and that, 'The girl wasn't mature enough to understand what was going on' – a magnificently patronising response that demonstrates his failure to obtain informed consent (something only now being addressed, as we'll see in Chapter 10).[44] He felt 'guilty' but not regretful, according to one talk late in his life, and also waved the incident away as the product of a different time.[45]

Such sexually charged material often proved a flashpoint. On 9 1/2 *Weeks*, director Adrian Lyne hired Kim Basinger as his heroine, an artworld professional involved in a sadomasochistic affair with Mickey Rourke's stockbroker. Lyne seemed instantly to trust Rourke with his role, but Basinger was another story. The director deliberately isolated her from decisions and whispered secret instructions to Rourke before each shot. 'She doesn't actually act, she reacts,' claimed Lyne after the film came out, and so he would shout and rage at Basinger if he needed her to appear upset, or instruct Rourke to be friendly if a scene needed to be softened.

'I was like an exposed nerve throughout the filming,' said Basinger at the time.[46] One scene involved the lovers entering a phony suicide pact, and Lyne instructed Rourke before shooting started to grab Basinger's arm tightly and slap her across the face, because 'Kim needed to be broken down'. That scene was eventually cut because, said Lyne, it made the audience hate Rourke's John too much.

After release, Basinger came to forgive her director for his manipulation, saying that she felt she had done some of her best work on the film. But couldn't the result have been achieved without abuse? The ability is there. Basinger was already a Golden Globe nominee for

The Natural and would win an Oscar for *LA Confidential* in 1998. Rourke was nominated for one Oscar for *The Wrestler*, but is yet to win.

Outside the studio system, it could be even worse. Actress Susan George wanted to use a body double for the rape scenes in *Straw Dogs*, but director Sam Peckinpah threatened to sue her if she didn't do it herself. George was so scared of him that she worried about really being raped on camera if she did not give in. 'The way he was talking, it seemed to me that he was intending on this being an actual thing, that was really going to take place on the set.' After a stand-off and those legal threats, she agreed to shoot the scene.

'I did get beaten up, quite badly, during the shooting of the siege,' she said, 'but almost all the violent acts in the movie were done on the first take. We would do something horrific, something violent, something unbelievably dangerous, and then we would move on.'[47]

Recently, in France, there was a blow-up between the director and stars of *Blue is the Warmest Colour*, a critically lauded Palme d'Or winner at Cannes. The Festival's top prize was (unusually) awarded to the two stars along with director and co-writer Abdellatif Kechiche, and both women spoke out afterwards about the 'horrible' shooting conditions and 'a kind of manipulation' by the director.[48] Kechiche called the women's complaints 'indecent'[49] and implied that Seydoux had been somehow manipulated into saying what she did. Later, speaking to *The New Yorker*, he claimed that, 'I certainly have never made anyone suffer. The suffering of an actor is something I can only laugh at . . . The job of an actor, it's one of a spoiled child.'[50] Exarchopoulos talked about 'greed' in the filmmaking of *Blue*. It's a perfect word for this sense that some directors are not happy until they drain their cast of every possibility and speck of energy, especially these young women with whom they are sometimes obsessed (remember Grace Kelly's line about Hitchcock wearing actors down?). On one hand, of course, a director wants to control his work. On the other, when your paints and oils are human beings, how much exploitation is too much?

So the shade of the svengali has not entirely disappeared, and there are sometimes hints that it continues. David Fincher's relationship with Rooney Mara on *The Girl with the Dragon Tattoo* raised some eyebrows while memorably shaving hers. Co-star Daniel Craig called their bond 'fucking weird'. Although Mara claimed that she chose to go on an extreme diet for the role without Fincher's request, and Fincher said that the 'mythology of my sadism' had been overblown,[51] there were odd hints in a *Vogue* cover story that he did at least approve of her extreme makeover for the film.

Then there are the directors who treat women like perks of the job. Horror director Eli Roth, in a 2013 interview,[52] talked about the importance of getting 'beautiful stand-ins' because 'crew members are horny', 'movie sets are still kind of fair game' and 'they've learned not to go after cast members because they'll get in trouble with the producers or a jealous director (ahem)'. He also advocated hiring attractive crew members so there are 'more possibilities for hookups . . . Even if they're not so good at their jobs, somehow their presence gets others to work harder'. This is an attitude that very much assumes women's chief contribution to film sets comes as sexual objects rather than because of their skills – and that actresses are there for the director's pleasure.

The deference due to a director may not come to an end when shooting does either. Actress Megan Fox first worked for director Michael Bay when she was fifteen, on *Bad Boys II*. She was too young to be filmed drinking in a club scene but it was A-OK for her to dance around in a bikini.[53] She later starred in his first two *Transformers* films to general enthusiasm, and was attached to appear in the third when she gave an interview describing Bay as a 'Hitler' and 'tyrant' on set and 'hopelessly awkward' off it – a combination she found 'endearing'.[54] An open letter apparently written by 'loyal crew' of the movie appeared in response, calling Fox 'the queen of talking trailer trash and posing like a porn star' and lambasting her as 'dumb-as-a-rock' (her interview appearances suggest that she's bright and funny).[55] Fox did not appear in the third *Transformers* film. Her representatives maintained this was at her own request. Bay later said that fellow producer Steven Spielberg ordered him to fire Fox, though Spielberg denied that.[56] Eventually Bay and Fox made up, and she worked on the *Teenage Mutant Ninja Turtle* films he produced.

It's hard to read the whole farrago as anything other than a massive overreaction to an actress's comment, and a sense that young, female stars are not allowed to critique their older, male directors. Look at Katherine Heigl, who correctly called *Knocked Up*, in which she starred, 'a little bit sexist'.[57] Director Judd Apatow said a year later that he was still waiting for an apology, while co-star Seth Rogen called her remarks 'batshit crazy'.[58] In 2016 he added that, 'Perhaps she realises that it has hurt her career and I don't want that to have happened to her because . . . I really like her.'[59] It *did* hurt her career, because in Hollywood a mild criticism of a movie that *is* a little bit sexist really can.

Directorial manipulation often attempts to perpetuate this power imbalance, to make women into men's instruments. There are still those who claim to have seen something that no one else could in a raw, untried talent, and to be owed something as a result. And there are still some relationships that feel both intense and uneven in a way that rings alarm bells.

Of course, people are messy, and so are many power dynamics. An ambitious young actress may allow herself to be moulded for the good of the film, which might then coincide with the good of her career. But it's worth examining the way that we lionise these direct-ors, and ascribe them godlike power over a film at the expense of everyone else's input.

That's because the central weakness of the auteur theory is reality. Filmmaking is a collaborative medium: while we talk a lot about directors, they are not the only figures who matter. It is almost impossible to make a great film from a bad script. It is extremely difficult to make a great film with an incompetent producer. You probably need talented actors – whether professional or not – and you must cast them in the right roles with the help of a great casting director. Your cinematographer and their team must ensure that the film's look supports the story it's trying to tell, and so on and so on. Figures like Walter Murch, Ben Burtt, Roger Deakins, Gordon Willis, Sandy Powell or Colleen Atwood are great artists, geniuses in their own right. To credit the work of hundreds like them to one dude with a megaphone is downright disrespectful, however theoretically elegant.

The filmmakers generally accepted as 'auteurs' are also the filmmakers most likely to work with exceptional teams. Editor Thelma Schoonmaker has edited all of Martin Scorsese's films since *Raging Bull* (she also did his first film, *Who's That Knocking at My Door?* and some uncredited work on *Taxi Driver*), to the point that we barely know what his work would look like without her. Orson Welles, the genius behind *Citizen Kane*, worked from an inspired script by Herman J. Mankiewicz and with groundbreaking cinematography by Gregg Toland. Steven Spielberg collaborates with John Williams so often that one can only assume the composer scores the director's alarm to get him out of bed in the morning. Great directors tend to have a deep bench behind them. To quote Spike Lee, 'Game respects game.'[60] Those of enormous ability value the same in others.

That's one of the ways auteurism helps those directors to whom the label is attached, so it becomes a self-fulfilling prophecy. Lee said that in answer to a question about how Adam Driver had come to work with so many greats. Since breaking through in TV's *Girls*, Driver has worked with auteurs including Scorsese, Spielberg, Ang Lee, Noah Baumbach, Jim Jarmusch, Steven Soderbergh, Terry Gilliam and Leos Carax. What ambitious, artistically engaged actor would turn those filmmakers down? Being an auteur means that gifted stars like Driver, who are financially secure due to, say, a role in *Star Wars*, will queue up to work with you between blockbusters, the better to burnish their reputations, to restore their credibility and – less cynically – to do really good work. Auteur status helps you get stars, sometimes at a discount. Both Brad Pitt and Leonardo DiCaprio are said to have worked for only half their normal wage (a destitution-threatening $10 million each) on *Once Upon a Time in Hollywood* because they wanted to work with Tarantino.[61]

Auteur status also helps get your films made, and at a higher budget, because studios and streaming services come to you in search of art. The glow of your auteurism reflects on them, bleaching out their more inane programming and attracting other talent. Look at Netflix, splashing a reported $160 million to make Scorsese's *The Irishman*, a CGI-heavy, 210-minute-long gangster epic that had no realistic prospect of covering that cost at the commercial box office.[62] In 2020 Apple TV agreed to co-finance Scorsese's next film with Paramount, *Killers of the Flower Moon*. That budget is reportedly a huge $200 million, a bananas amount for a story about an FBI investigation, even a period piece, even with Leonardo DiCaprio and Robert De Niro aboard (star and director salaries only account for about 25 per cent of that figure).[63] Both streaming services surely expect to lose money on these propositions, but they want to be in the Martin Scorsese business and share in the prestige he has accumulated over a lifetime of making good movies.

Auteurism can be great for those who claim it. But the picture gets trickier when you consider who is allowed to be an auteur, because the term sometimes seems jealously guarded by critics and the industry. Very few women or non-white American or British directors are hailed as auteurs even now, and when they *are* recognised by critics they don't always reap the same benefits of bigger budgets, more freedom or bigger stars. Female directors – as we'll see in a later chapter – face higher levels of interference from studios, and are rarely treated with the deference and authority of their male counterparts.

The prominence of the auteur theory hasn't helped female directors gain respect, and has arguably held them back. As a society, we're not entirely comfortable in conferring the status of genius, of visionary, of auteur, on women – and maybe until we are, we shouldn't confer it on anyone. 'The auteur theory is an attempt by adult males to justify staying inside the small range of experience of their boyhood and adolescence, that period when masculinity looked so great and important,' said Pauline Kael. If auteurism – as it sometimes appears – is only for the boys, with a few token women to deflect criticism, then it needs to be dismantled.

Too often, auteurism seems like the cinema equivalent of the 'great men' model of history, another way of boiling down years of work by huge numbers of people into a testament to the genius of a few dudes. If a Katharine Hepburn or Rosalind Russell did great work, why, it was only because they were directed by a Cukor or a Hawks. If Anita Loos or Frances Marion wrote a great script, you can still hand credit to the man who directed its adaptation. Screenwriters, editors, costume, make-up, producer, star – all these roles where women could still thrive even during the studio era and some where they still dominate – are diminished in favour of handing credit to a singular auteur.

In this book I've often used auteurist shorthand. Lots of films have similar names; adding a director's credit is a quick way to let you know which one we're talking about. Years of release might work too, but then how do we distinguish Michael Rowe's *Leap Year*, 2010, from Anand Tucker's *Leap Year*, also 2010? And it's *really* important that we do: the former is a tough, sexual drama from Mexico and the other is a dreadful cod-Irish rom-com wasting two talented stars and a number of excellent woolly jumpers.

There's nothing inherently wrong with using a director's name. Auteur theory or not, directors play a major role in shaping films: if it's difficult to make a great film from a bad script, it's nearly impossible to sneak a great film past a bad director. There are rumours, of course, of switched-off but big-name directors who barely engage with shooting and rely on gifted editors to pull the resulting mess together. The results are rarely great. In any case, that director still shapes a film by their absence or incompetence.

But the idea has limits, assigning credit unjustly, promoting a level of hero-worship that can be abused, and denying the basic truth that there are no one-man movies. As we'll see looking at the New Hollywood, auteurism briefly placed an enormous amount of power into the hands of untried men who were not always terribly adept in handling it, resulting in spectacular failures as well as some of the best films of the last fifty years. Naming someone an auteur does not guarantee success. Nothing guarantees success in Hollywood, not even the presence of Tom Cruise, or Iron Man, and attempting to cut your risks by relying on someone hailed as an auteur is often just another way of focusing power in the hands of those who have always, to one degree or another, had it. If we keep anointing the same old white men as auteurs and downplaying the efforts of everyone else in comparison, isn't the auteur theory just a highfalutin cover for the same old attitudes? And the tragedy is that it was meant to be so different, to usher in a new era where new voices were heard. For its early proponents, it was meant to build a New Hollywood.

7

The Revolution
Movie brats and the male gaze

IN THE late 1960s Hollywood faced the same existential crisis it does today: a struggle to survive against growing competition. Television was a challenge back then too, and the whole landscape seemed to be shifting away from the same old Code-approved Hollywood films. There was social unrest and rebellion against the Vietnam War, challenges to old certainties about gender, sexuality and identity. The civil rights movement was, finally, getting somewhere. Yet Hollywood remained stale and out of touch – until a band of white knights appeared, carefully disguised as vaguely hippy-ish youngsters, promising a way to reconnect with the kids. They built a New Hollywood in their own image, and for a short time they created marvels: gangsters and drag racers, taxi-driving psychos and exorcists.

These men catered to a more thoughtful audience, one that was open to new attitudes and experiences. Alas, there was no room in their ranks for women. They could take supporting roles, certainly – editing and production design and soon studio executive – but they weren't allowed to truly shine. Even as Hollywood took risks on untried men, female filmmakers remained confined to lower budget work – on documentary efforts like Barbara Kopple's *Harlan County USA*, or actor-turned-director Barbara Loden's independent *Wanda*.

Yet something was changing. The second-wave feminism of 'women's lib' was exploding the old social contract and women were agitating for equal space in the world, with the US fighting over the Equal Rights Amendment to the Constitution and Ruth Bader Ginsburg's Women's Rights Project litigating key cases for the ACLU. If Hollywood largely tried to ignore that energy or play it for laughs, it still burst through in the form of an upswell in women's voices, a push for better opportunities. It's not that men did all the ground-breaking work of 1970s cinema; it's that women, barred from direct-ing films, laid the foundations for a change that would come later.

Feminist film criticism was born in this fervid mix, as women's lib met the auteur theory and found it lacking. While the New Hollywood giants reshaped what was possible onscreen, women like Molly Haskell, Marjorie Rosen, Laura Mulvey and Black intellectual and capital-letter refusenik bell hooks began to change how women *thought* about film – and to challenge a male-centric cinema that even their male contemporaries took for granted.

The men's impact was more immediate, reshaping what is still seen as important cinema, popular cinema and weighty cinema. But the women's influence is still felt, too. It gave a foundation for our own generation to fight for the films we want to see, and helped put into words the feeling of alienation that many women felt with mainstream movies.

Onscreen, the picture got worse in this bold new era, with the number of female leads dropping to a fraction of what they had been. Even when Hollywood tried to make a women's lib movie, 1972's *Stand Up and Be Counted*, they hired a man to direct it (Jackie Cooper, now best remembered as the Christopher Reeve Superman's Perry White) and made it a comedy. As the 1970s gave way to the bombast and high concepts of 1980s cinema, and the New Hollywood was replaced by the 'movie brats', women were still marginalised – onscreen and off. So how did the revolution fall so short?

It started in a moment of panic much like our own times. Television challenged movies for the market in popular light entertainment, just as streaming services do today. Hollywood executives wondered if the audience would ever come back, like today, and when high-profile, big-budget films like *Hello, Dolly!* and *Tora! Tora! Tora!* flopped, it only increased their angst. The movie-going population had declined from a high of ninety million people a week in the mid-1930s to forty-five million in the mid-60s, and showed no sign of recovering.[1] Some studios in the late '60s were still run by the men who had founded them: Jack Warner officially left Warner Bros in 1969 and Darryl F. Zanuck was not forced out of 20th Century Fox until 1971. Even their successors were mostly older men, the guys who had waited in the shadows for their turn, and they were baffled as the old favourites – big-budget musicals, war movies, even dependable ol' Westerns – fell from favour.

The 1960s had been an era of showy producers, men like Sam Spiegel, Charles Feldman and Walter Mirisch: big personalities who made huge, sprawling films with huge, sprawling casts. These could be great, like David Lean's *Lawrence of Arabia* and *Doctor Zhivago* (for all the problematic whitewashing of the former's cast). But not every filmmaker was a Lean. Efforts like *The Longest Day* in 1962 and *It's a Mad, Mad, Mad, Mad World* in 1963 crossed continents and packed in more celebrity cameos than a *Muppets* movie, but like *Avatar* sequels they cost so much that each threatened their studio's bottom line if they underperformed.

The situation prefigured the predictions of Steven Spielberg and George Lucas in 2013, warning that the failure of even a few $200-million blockbusters could topple studios.[2] That has not yet come to pass – but their wariness makes sense judged against what happened in the late 1960s. The crashing failure of 1967's *Doctor Dolittle* was a particular shock: its $17 million production budget turned into a painful $9 million at the box office. Hard work by the studio miraculously landed it a Best Picture Oscar nomination, but it was clear that the spectacle and Technicolor dazzle that had carried

Hollywood through since the late '40s wouldn't be enough any more. The Boomers – that large generation born between 1945 and 1960 – were coming of age, and they demanded something different. The stolid, stifling, white-American consensus of the 1950s was breaking apart under pressure for freedom, whether that was civil rights or free love or women's liberation or, ideally, all of the above.

The cinema audience was now younger and often college-educated, and they had more adventurous taste than their parents. They flocked to see racier foreign films that challenged the newly liberalised censorship laws with provocative new content, like boobs. The Italian neo-realists had given way to the French New Wave and modernists like Michelangelo Antonioni. Now those willing to put up with subtitles and a lack of traditional elements, like plot, could devour masterpieces in the country's artier cinemas.

In New York and Los Angeles, a generation weaned on movies were entering film schools, fascinated by these new flavours of cinema and the possibilities of what could be done if you were unconstrained by the shackles of the Production Code and old commercial imperatives. These 'movie brats', as producer Linda Myles and cinema historian Michael Pye called them, graduated from childhood diets of Hollywood fare into a wider world of experimentation, and swore that they would combine the two. Everyone who was anyone was keen to push the boundaries – at least in some directions.

That energy bled into Hollywood and went, stunningly quickly, from novelty to new normal. 1967's *Bonnie and Clyde* is generally cited as the first major crack in the old studio ramparts. Screenwriters David Newman and Robert Benton had set out to write an American film that felt European, with unlikeable protagonists and no real hero, just Faye Dunaway and Warren Beatty's unrepentant bank robbers. It would never have been possible under the Code, with criminals at its heart, impotence as a plot point and bloody violence throughout but especially at its end (history spoiler: Bonnie and

Clyde die in a hail of bullets). Beatty, also a producer, largely supported the screenwriters' vision and, after rewrites from future screenwriting legend Robert '*Chinatown*' Towne, shepherded a remarkably bleak story to the screen under director Arthur Penn. Against all studio expectations, it was a huge hit. The same year, Mike Nichols' *The Graduate*, a quasi-love story about a guy, a girl and her mother, proved that you could be cynical even in an ostensible romance, craft an ending that was not entirely happy, and strike a chord with audiences.

'The industry is blooming with potential Orson Welleses, film prodigies wearing flowered shirts, beards and bell bottoms,' wrote journalist Mel Gussow in the *New York Times* in 1970. 'The young are adored, and the younger they are, the better.'[3]

As the new blood proved its worth, studios around town started to meet with untested filmmakers like Robert Altman, William Friedkin and Francis Ford Coppola. Dennis Hopper and Peter Fonda made *Easy Rider*, on a tumultuous, drug- and drink-fuelled cross-country shoot.[4] That success *really* shook the old guard: if such a blatantly disgraceful, improvisational-feeling film could do so well, what was next?

These directors challenged Hollywood's whole image of itself. Somehow this unruly bunch were achieving success that eluded the old guard, an impression only reinforced by films like *The Last Picture Show* and *The Wild Bunch* and, especially, 1972's *The Godfather*. Francis Ford Coppola landed *The Godfather* only after at least seven better-known directors had turned it down, and almost rejected it himself because he thought the novel was 'pretty cheap stuff'.[5] That he turned it into one of the greatest films ever made is testament to his talent, and to the risks he was willing to take to reinvent the gangster movie.

It was a generational shift, with storied directors who had been born around the same time as the cinema itself retiring or declining at last (Hawks, Wilder, Preminger, Hitchcock). The studios also shifted, with younger executives rising alongside the directors they championed, and marketing executives and former agents beginning to influence production decisions. The search was on for new voices who could connect to the vast, disaffected youth of America and keep people going to the cinema.

The New Hollywood was, immediately, extremely male, with more significant figures called Robert than women in its directorial ranks. That wasn't much of a change, of course, but it shows the fundamental gaps in the imagination of the men challenging the system: they wanted to shake up Hollywood, but not *that* much.

There was at least as significant a change onscreen. These new men sometimes seemed so caught up in talking to and impressing one another that they forgot to include women at *all*. Romantic love was out of fashion, replaced by free love, so the sort of will-they-won't-they affairs of years gone by seemed dreadfully passé. It was a time for criminals, rebels without a cause and disaffected drifters, and the idea that women could be any of those things didn't seem to occur. Women were sex objects to be won or shrews to be avoided – or, possibly, both.

Take Robert Altman's *M*A*S*H*: it was an influential smash, but also a film that revels in misogyny and goes out of its way to punish a female character (Maj. O'Houlihan, played by Sally Kellerman) for daring not to want to shag its leading men. If you're looking for a relatable female character in *Easy Rider* well, you'll be looking for a while, and for all its towering greatness *The Godfather* isn't exactly overflowing with rich female roles, much as we all love Diane Keaton. Nor are *The French Connection* or *Mean Streets* or *Chinatown*.

There were exceptions, of course. 'Women may take comfort,' wrote Marjorie Rosen in *Popcorn Venus* in 1973, 'for every dozen or two woman-less or woman-humiliating movies, there are one or two deserving portraits.'[6] The female roles that do stand out – Ellen Burstyn in *Alice*

Doesn't Live Here Anymore, Meryl Streep in *Kramer vs. Kramer* or *The Deer Hunter* – were often those where a determined star set out to make her own material, whether by putting the project together (Burstyn) or amping up a thin role on the page (Streep, a woman who critic Molly Haskell described as being 'typecast as an actress that can't be type-cast'). Burstyn was sent multiple scripts after the success of *The Exorcist*. 'In every one, the woman was either the victim, running from a pursuer, or she was a prostitute,' she told film historian Peter Biskind.[7] Instead her agent found her a script called *Alice Doesn't Live Here Anymore*, by Robert Getchell, and she brought Scorsese in to make that. She took only an acting credit but arguably would have been a producer if she'd been a man. Gena Rowlands did great work during the '70s, in creative partnership with her husband, director John Cassavetes (*A Woman Under the Influence, Gloria*). Jane Fonda, too, proved consistently able to add texture and depth to her roles, in films from *They Shoot Horses, Don't They?* to *Coming Home* and *On Golden Pond* – but then she and Barbra Streisand were among the decade's biggest box-office draws and had first pick of what roles there were.

What's telling, however, is how little overlap there is between the best films of the '70s and the best films with lead roles for women. The cinema of the '70s was not just male but macho. It revelled in a new freedom to show violence, crime or vice, and dispensed with male–female romantic relationships in favour of sex or simply male buddy dynamics. Some filmmakers took their new freedom as a licence to make every significant female character a prostitute, and sex workers represented a chunk of the roles for women in the decade (*Klute, Taxi Driver, Saint Jack, The Owl and the Pussycat* – the latter of which did away with the interracial element of the play on which it was based because Hollywood was still awfully white). This portrayal of women was considered more gritty, more realistic and weightier than the Doris Day career girls of a generation before. Maybe so, but few of these films did much to advance the depiction of sex workers, though Jane Fonda's magnificently matter-of-fact performance in *Klute* presented a more nuanced image than previously.

Shirley MacLaine had an explanation:

The women's movement has intimidated the writers. So when a writer who's a really nice man – sensitive, intelligent – sits down to his typewriter to write a story for me and Paul Newman, and he knows I don't want to play any more prostitutes, and he doesn't want to make me anybody's housewife, what's he going to do? He doesn't know anybody but prostitutes and housewives. He's afraid his chauvinism will show on the page so he says, 'Screw that, why don't we make this with Robert Redford and Paul Newman? That'll be easier.' And that's what happened.[8]

Maybe it was that fear of appearing chauvinistic, but writers and directors sometimes revelled in victimising women. 'It seems women are always getting killed or raped,' said screenwriter Eleanor Perry at the time. 'Those are men's fantasies we're seeing, right?'[9]

Perry had had screenwriting success in the '60s alongside husband Frank Perry with films like *The Swimmer* and *Diary of a Mad Housewife*, but her film career hit trouble after their divorce. Like the silent era women, she found the big screen unwelcoming to single women – though she would go on to win another Emmy for her TV work. Perry was an outspoken feminist, dishing the dirt on studio sexism in her thinly disguised roman-à-clef *Blue Book* and leading a Cannes protest against Fellini's *Roma* and its bizarre she-wolf poster in 1972. Perry perched atop a ladder, trying to paint over the poster, as police tried to shake her off it. You'd struggle to find a better metaphor for the women trying to break into film at the time: reaching precariously upwards, surrounded by men trying to pull them down.

* * *

As the men of the New Hollywood went from maverick outsiders to the giants of the cinema, they wrote their own myths. They sold themselves as the people who could speak to and for the youth of America, who could sell films to the beatniks, Vietnam War protesters and counter-culture weirdos. But they could also reinvigorate classic genres, as with *The Godfather, The Graduate, Annie Hall* or *The French Connection*. Their myths were based on the same auteur theory of their French film heroes and an intensely male model of success: one man, one genius, allowed to go out and create Art. For a few brief years they convinced the Hollywood studios to invest, sometimes heavily, in director-driven, often challenging films. The execs were so disoriented by the failure of their own system that they threw in their fortunes, and a fortune in percentages of the gross box office, with these newcomers who seemed to know what the people wanted. Sometimes it paid off big-time, in films like *The Godfather* or *What's Up, Doc?* or, later in the decade, with *Jaws* and *Star Wars*. Sometimes it flopped painfully, like Dennis Hopper's *The Last Movie* or Friedkin's *Sorcerer*.

But what's striking in retrospect is what *didn't* change. Women trying to break in to film met with less willingness to shake things up. Although a few women were beginning to join the ranks of executives and agents, the number of female studio directors could still be counted on one hand in most years; often only on your thumbs.

'Everyone is ready to listen to wilder forms and concepts,' Warner Bros executive John Calley told the *New York Times* in 1970.[10] 'We're inclined to take enlightened gambles on young people.' But Calley – one of the most forward-thinking executives of the era, and a man who greenlit films as daring as *The Exorcist, A Clockwork Orange* and *All the President's Men* – was not so encouraging to all young people. Director Juleen Compton, for example, was a self-made millionaire in property and a filmmaker with two independent films under her belt (both screened at Cannes). She went to Calley, a friend, looking for work in the early 1970s.

'Look, I'll just level with you,' Compton recalled him saying. 'I've got guys working here that have been directing shit for ten years waiting until they got a chance to direct. A small film comes up, I can't suddenly bring in a total stranger, somebody who has never stood in line.'[11]

Yet many young men never stood in line; they just got their chance. Warner Bros under Calley co-produced George Lucas's debut, *THX-1138*, and made Alan J. Pakula's second film, *Klute*. That's not to single Calley out: he was by all accounts one of the friendliest men in Hollywood, and women like Amy Pascal would hail him as a mentor. But his comment shows that the openness to new voices only went so far.

The roadblocks were even more considerable for would-be directors who did not have the advantage of being white. When Maya Angelou started seriously looking at filmmaking, she was already a Pulitzer Prize nominee and would soon be a Tony Award-nominated actress. She wrote a feature film, *Georgia, Georgia*, in 1972, and went to Sweden to study cinematography to enhance her campaign to direct it. But she was not given the chance, later saying that, 'in film, racism and sexism stand at the door', blocking her path.[12] Director and critic Stig Björkman was given the job instead, only his second feature. Angelou realised that, 'In every case I know I have to be ten times more prepared than my white counterpart' (another Black director, Gina Prince-Bythewood, would say *exactly* the same thing in 2020[13]). Angelou belatedly made her feature directing debut in 1998 with *Down in the Delta*, at the age of seventy. Roger Ebert called it a 'strong story, deeply felt'. Imagine what she might have accomplished with twenty-six more years' experience under her belt.

'If I were a man, I might have tried to be Orson Welles,' said Shirley Clarke, another female filmmaker who had independent films screened at Cannes and Venice but found Hollywood closed. 'But as a woman and an artist, it's impossible. Producers think of us in childlike terms ... they don't take us seriously.'[14]

The independent sector was slightly more open to women – or at least couldn't bar them from self-financed work. Gradually, through the 1970s, a few managed to make studio efforts as well.

Director Elaine May was already established thanks to *A New Leaf* in 1971. Her stellar career as a radio star and screenwriter extraordinaire had enabled her to make the leap to directing; her comedy collaboration with Mike Nichols had made legends of both. But May approached directing much as if she were still in improv, relying on endless takes and long spells in the edit room to shape her story. While she was endlessly sharp and incisive in her scripts (and with those of others) she dithered when bringing her own work to the screen.

Studios mistrusted her despite the success of *A New Leaf* and *The Honeymooners*, and she had endless battles over her final edits. Film critic Todd McCarthy (not to be confused with *Spotlight* director, Tom McCarthy) suggested[15] that May 'set back the cause' of women in Hollywood (harsh) but her 'bad' behaviour was no worse than many of her male contemporaries. It is possible that she became a handy scapegoat for the refusal to hire other women.

It's worth contrasting May's battles on 1975's *Mikey and Nicky* with, say, Warren Beatty on *Reds*, another project that went hugely over-budget and spent over a year in the editing room, from spring 1980 to November 1981. Both filmmakers were prone to huge numbers of takes, budget overruns and long edits; both were capable of great filmmaking and huge success. Neither was obviously commercial material. *Mikey and Nicky* went over budget by a higher percentage – from $1.8 million to $4.5 million – though *Reds* overspent by far more, going from $25 million to $35 million. But on *Reds*, the meticulous star director was ultimately cheered on by the studio, while Paramount actually sued May for control of *Mikey and Nicky*. May would not direct again for twelve years, and when she did the knives came out for *Ishtar* (which incidentally starred Beatty) long before anyone saw it. Beatty's film won Oscars; perhaps that made the difference – but then awards also skew male, as we'll see later.

While filmmakers like Joan Micklin Silver and Joan Tewkesbury managed to direct in the '70s, and actresses-turned-directors like Barbara Loden and Anne Bancroft, they didn't manage to build a sustained career the way that the men did. Stung by very public accusations of sexism, the industry opened the door to female directors – but only a crack. The American Film Institute (AFI) established a Directing Workshop for Women in 1974, in the hope of supporting more women into the profession. In its early years this programme accepted established, high-profile women – actresses like Nancy Walker, Bancroft and Lee Grant – in the hope that this would draw attention to the cause, rather than funding newcomers. Even with that support and with their own fame, it would take them until at least 1980 to make their first films. Bancroft and Walker would never make another after their efforts, *Fatso* and *Can't Stop the Music* respectively, were savaged by critics.

Women didn't get the same chances to find their feet, or to fly high and then screw up – which most of the early '70s greats eventually did, at least commercially. Coppola blotted his copybook with the vast budget overruns of *Apocalypse Now*, despite the film's subsequent success, and had a flop with musical *One from the Heart* in 1982. Michael Cimino hit big with *Thunderbolt and Lightfoot* and *The Deer Hunter* only to catastrophically crash and burn with 1980's *Heaven's Gate*, bringing down United Artists with him. Then, that studio was already teetering: audiences never flocked to Martin Scorsese's ambitious musical drama *New York, New York* as the execs had hoped. Peter Bogdanovich's first few films were made with his wife Polly Platt, a production designer who would go on to become an important producer and screenwriter. After Bogdanovich left her and Platt finally stopped working with him, his films experienced a sharp drop in success: *Daisy Miller*, *At Long Last Love* and *Nickelodeon* all under-performed, especially the latter two.

Some of those commercial misfires now look pretty great: *New York, New York* has been reassessed and even the famously disastrous *Heaven's Gate* has found fans since Cimino's lengthier cut was restored. But they came good too late. The New Hollywood era didn't *only* end because directors squandered that unparalleled artistic freedom on extravagant projects – but it didn't help. Many film fans would say that those disasters were a price worth paying for the masterpieces also created, and they might be right. But what is undeniable is that the moment of freedom, of possibility, was thrown away too fast for any women to grab the same chance.

It wasn't the only opportunity that vanished. If Hollywood in the early 1970s was open to experimentation, by the middle of the decade its executives were reassured that they had once again placed their finger on the pulse of America. They knew now that mass audiences, and not just niche exploitation markets, would watch violence, horror and crime quite happily. They knew that sex could sell, if carefully packaged. They knew that an edge of cynicism and rebellion was in line with the mood of the nation. And they knew that the cinema audience was still there, whatever the challenges of TV. *The Godfather* had shown that, but two slightly younger movie brats were about to show just how big the audience could get.

Steven Spielberg and George Lucas are now considered reliable blockbuster filmmakers, but they too were daring in their day. After some TV success, no one had a clue what Steven Spielberg was hoping to accomplish when he adapted the pulp thriller *Jaws*, and he seemed out of his depth as the film went over schedule and over budget. The shark wouldn't work, and anyway, shooting on water pretty much guarantees problems (ask Kevin Costner). Then, suddenly, it turned out that he knew *exactly* what he was doing when the resulting masterpiece broke box-office records – thanks in part to an innovative TV advertising blitz.

George Lucas's first film was the wildly experimental *THX 1138*, which landed him just enough acclaim to make the safer, deeply nostalgic *American Graffiti*. That was a bigger hit, whereupon he showed how *not* sensible he really was by making some weird space opera with Alec Guinness and a bunch of unknowns. *Star Wars?* A kids' title. Nothing important. Nothing to fundamentally change cinema so that studios would be aiming for half a *billion* dollars every time they hit the green light on a new project.

Spielberg and Lucas's success was not written in the stars, however much it seems that way in retrospect. But the success of those two films – and then *Close Encounters of the Third Kind*, and *Raiders of the Lost Ark*, and follow-on blockbusters like *Superman* from other filmmakers – was so overwhelming that it changed the whole face of the business. The studios would continue to play with violence and indulge sex, but Spielberg and Lucas had hit upon a way to return to the universal appeal of the big musicals and Westerns of the past – 'four-quadrant' films that appeal to men and women, over and under twenty-five – without losing the hipper, more cine-literate audiences of their own generation. They'd birthed the modern blockbuster and made it clear how great the rewards of success could be. You could make a fortune in merchandising! You could make *sequels*, with the same potential box-office rewards and considerably less risk! Such discoveries led directly to the 'high-concept' movies of the 1980s, where a single, highly marketable idea could be turned into a franchise – many of which are still being recycled now. *The Terminator, Aliens, Star Trek, Top Gun, Die Hard, Rambo, Rocky, Predator, Batman, Ghostbusters, Blade Runner*: we're still living in the shade of that era.

It's with Spielberg and Lucas that the lingering dominance of the movie brats becomes *really* clear. *The Godfather, Jaws, Star Wars,*

E.T. the Extra-Terrestrial and *Jurassic Park* in turn held the title of highest-grossing film ever made, and they come from just three filmmakers: Coppola, Spielberg and Lucas. If you count the slightly later-emerging James Cameron among the movie-brat generation (it's at least arguable), you'd add *Titanic* and *Avatar* to their total and have a clean sweep of every highest-grossing film between *Gone with the Wind*'s 1971 reissue and *Avengers: Endgame* in 2019. When it comes to going big or going home, the movie brats didn't seem to have a home to go to.

Of course, not all of this generation became box-office behemoths. Scorsese always trod a thornier path, one that was more concerned with masculinity, Catholicism, guilt, Catholic guilt or all of the above. But Scorsese has been at least as influential as the rest, with an astonishing number of young men naming *Goodfellas* or *Raging Bull* or *Taxi Driver* as their favourite film ever. It is practically impossible to find a male film-lover born in or near the 1980s who does not worship the ground on which he walks. His films provide a benchmark against which serious and important films today are measured. So does *The Godfather*. So does *Apocalypse Now*.

Consider the extent to which this generation still dominates movie discussion. Spielberg's scepticism about the studios' tentpole strategies (see Chapter 7) stirred up one hornet's nest in 2013; his doubts about Netflix's Oscars eligibility another in 2018. Scorsese dwarfed both controversies when he described the Marvel Cinematic Universe in 2019 as 'not cinema', creating a schism in filmdom and heartbreak for many Marvel-loving, Scorsese-worshipping film fans (it's OK, guys, you can still love both. Or neither!).[16] Few other filmmakers generate headlines to the same extent: Tarantino, perhaps, but that's it.

The movie brats became the grand old men of cinema, the arbiters of what it does and does not include. Some are still making great films (*The Irishman*, *The Post* – yes, really – *Silence*, *Lincoln* or Paul

Schrader's *First Reformed*). Many have also fostered younger talent. These men's legacy will be largely positive; they're talented and care deeply about cinema. They have made great, great films. But they were so successful – financially and critically – that mainstream moviemaking reshaped itself in their image. Hollywood adopted the same male focus that dominated the films these men made when they were young, and assumed that guys like these were the *only* ones who could make big movies. The rise of this new generation didn't teach Hollywood that it needed to stay open and keep taking risks; it taught the studios that they just needed more of *these guys* for ever. White guys in beards and baseball caps replaced the white men in suits, and there were only a few voices on the fringes shouting that something different was needed.

Feminist film criticism was born out of the same confluence of influences as the movie brats. The women who developed it had also devoured the old studio movies at every repertory cinema they could find, and read about the auteur theory in *Cahiers du Cinema*; one of the key figures, Molly Haskell, was married to the theory's American proponent, Andrew Sarris. 'We were very much guided by [auteur theory], we came very much out of that movement,'[17] says one of these women, Laura Mulvey. Essentially, they were movie brats, as passionately engaged with cinema as the men but rather warier of its power.

As directing became more macho, these women began to identify, and question, the way that women were portrayed onscreen. It wasn't the first time that feminist thinkers had questioned Hollywood; that started when the movies did. Alice Guy and Lois Weber wrote and spoke extensively about the role and purpose of movies back in the 1910s, and their films often centred on women's stories. In 1942 poet and writer Joy Davidman (best known these days as half of the love story *Shadowlands*) argued that the emancipation of women was 'part and parcel of the democracy we are fighting for' on the battlefields of the Second World War.[18] For Davidman it was therefore a matter of patriotic duty for cinema to avoid the thoughtless misogyny she saw in films like *Tom, Dick, and Harry* (1941). She also noted that, 'Now and then a movie actually discusses the "women question", although there is a significant lack of films dealing with the historic fight of women for independence in any spirit but that of mockery.' That remained the case until recent movies like *Hidden Figures* (2016), *On the Basis of Sex* (2018) and *Misbehaviour* (2020) and TV shows like *Mrs America* (2020). That's only one tiny area of representation, but it's notable that women's campaigns for equality were relatively under-filmed, despite happening on Hollywood's doorstep and sometimes in its corridors.

For decades, women were told, essentially, that our struggles – political or personal – were not of real concern, and our place was secondary to men. War movies, crime and Westerns are the stuff of legitimate cinema; the areas where women were allowed to function, like family life, were not. Films that *did* focus on traditionally female questions were dismissed as frivolous melodrama and lumped together as 'women's pictures'. Entire realms of the female experi-ence, particularly around pregnancy and birth, were ignored, partly but not solely because they were subject to censorship for decades. Other areas, like motherhood, were made the focus of female charac-ters' lives at the cost of every other desire. 'The basest of a man's ambitions (crime, espionage),' wrote Haskell, 'are often viewed with more respect than the highest (executive power, literary ambition) of a woman's.'

These feminist critics argued that such persistent messages could not help but infect us. The art that we consume not only reflects real-ity but shapes it; it teaches us what we can expect of the world. Journalist and screenwriter Marjorie Rosen was the first to shout this message with her 1973 book *Popcorn Venus; Women, Movies & the American Dream*. Rosen argued not only that women's role in film had been overlooked for too long, but that the movies could shape society as well. 'Because of the magnetism of movies – because their glamour and intensity and "entertainment" are so distracting and seemingly innocuous – women accept their morality and values. Sometimes too often. Too blindly. And tragically.'[19]

The Hollywood screen Rosen found was reserved, almost exclusively, for white, straight, able-bodied, cis women – and even that tiny slice of womanhood that was permitted comprised a minority of characters and a smaller minority of leads. When there *were* women, they were there to react to men doing things. Our beauty or sexuality might inspire men, but we would be almost entirely superfluous to the plot.

Much of what Rosen wrote remains relevant today. 'Is it a dream to presume that women could be delivered from the lethargy of television back to movies? Perhaps. But the pictures must exist, and women must know about them – which means a comfortable advertising budget and a neighbourhood run lasting longer than two blinks of an eye.' The same point has been made in recent times: female-focused films are still shown on fewer screens and given smaller ad budgets than their male equivalents.

Rosen also bemoaned the tendency of the New Hollywood to ignore women. She said that William Friedkin and Don Siegel were 'too busy turning violence into money', and noted that Bogdanovich, asked about feminism, had yawned that 'the whole subject bores me'. Even in 1973 she could see that roles for women were no better than they had been a decade or two earlier, and in some cases worse.

Rosen's book was swiftly followed by Haskell's 1974 *From Reverence To Rape: The Treatment of Women in the Movies*. Haskell began by discussing 'the big lie' of Western society, the idea of women's inferiority, and argued that, 'Far more than men, women are the vessels of men's and women's fantasies and the barometers of changing fashion . . . women in movies reflected, perpetuated and in some respects offered innovations on the roles of women in society.' Haskell despaired of the contempt afforded to so-called 'women's films', and of the wider moment in which she was living. Like Rosen she dissected each decade of movie history, looking at how the flapper girls of the twenties gave way to self-sacrifice in the 1940s. These overviews showed clear trends to prioritise men's stories over women's, to make women perpetually supporting characters while men save the day – or ruin it.

Arguably a bigger step forward in feminist film theory came in 1975 when film scholar Laura Mulvey wrote her ground-breaking article *Visual Pleasure and Narrative Cinema*. This introduced the concept of the 'male gaze' and the idea that, basically, women in film were generally reduced to objects to be looked at by men.

'I wasn't working in academia,' says Mulvey, who is now a professor of media studies and film at Birkbeck University. 'I wrote it really as a feminist polemic. It took a couple of years, perhaps even to the early '80s, before [the essay] built up a bit of steam. But it's extraordinary the way that it's persisted. I often say as a joke, or it's supposed to be a joke, that it's rather like the monster at the end of the movie. Every time you think it's gone . . .'[20]

That zombie-like longevity is due to the fact that her essay, with its potent mix of feminism and psychoanalytical theory, opened up a new way of talking about film. Mulvey stood at a unique crossroads. She was a cinema addict, reading *Cahiers du Cinema* at its height and spending the '60s 'absorbed' in classic Hollywood.

'I did know that cinema very well, and I truly loved it. I really learned how to think about cinema from that cinema, which I still think has extraordinary greatness to it. [But] the old Hollywood was dead. I had become really interested in a feminist theory of films.'

Mulvey started to notice the ways in which men and women's experiences were treated differently onscreen. She found that instead of being absorbed in the story of these films, she was watching from a distance, more critically than before.

Mulvey theorised that patriarchal society had shaped the stories that are told and how films tell them. Because patriarchal society believes that men are superior to women (Haskell's 'big lie'), films are designed so that men can narcissistically identify with the (male) characters who lead the action, men who are perhaps more heroic, more handsome or more daring than their real-life counterparts. These same attitudes ensure that women are reduced to objects, to be desired or pursued but rarely to act of their own volition.

For women to really lose themselves in a film, therefore, means adopting what Mulvey called 'metaphorical transvestism', requiring us to adopt the mentality of the male characters who drive the plot one moment and the women who seem closer to our own experience the next (Mulvey suggested that LGBTQ+ people would also have to take a similar shifting approach). It's something that will feel familiar to lots of women who grew up as film fans; we *had* to learn to identify with male heroes because who the heck else was there?

Mulvey's male gaze therefore describes a very specific type of viewer: it's not just male but heterosexual and masculine (the gay gaze is a separate thing). It's that lingering shot of Megan Fox at the open car bonnet in *Transformers*. It's the topless scenes in every *Police Academy* movie, and the hilariously gratuitous under-bum shots in every *Fast & Furious* film (they're so over the top it's almost sweet). But it's also the insidious assumption that the viewer who really matters is male – and a straight, cis, probably white, male viewer at that. It's an endless slew of films that tell men they can do anything, that they deserve the best, that they could quite literally be supermen.

In Mulvey's view, the female gaze is not a direct opposite: it's not as simple as all those topless shots of Chris Hemsworth in the *Thor* movies. After all, most films involving male objectification tend to play such behaviour for comedy rather than lust. Her female gaze is one driven by curiosity with the world: the detective stories that many women love, but also coming-of-age tales about women exploring life's possibilities for their own delight.

Later, Black intellectual, bell hooks, pointed out that the films that informed Mulvey's work were the white Hollywood work of the 1960s and earlier, where Black people were excluded almost entirely. hooks suggested that a Black female gaze would be an 'oppositional gaze', an awareness that you were not even considered worthy of notice. The gaze of Black women must therefore challenge not just the male objectification of women but also white supremacy. For Black people, staring at the screen is a political act, an act of daring. 'There is power in looking . . .' wrote hooks.[21] 'By courageously looking, we defiantly declared: "Not only will I stare. I want my look to change reality."' The oppositional gaze is aware that the viewer is not represented and challenges that lack; it comes naturally to Black women because they have been so under-represented for so long (there must, one imagines, be something similar for trans viewers and disabled viewers). Hopefully the need for such a gaze will decline as representation improves – but it is an important concept because it puts into words what we do *not* see onscreen, and reminds us of the pain caused by that absence of representation.

Queer cinemagoers, meanwhile, have to reckon with the way the male gaze means that lesbian love stories are often filmed with a straight male audience in mind, and therefore an emphasis on nudity and sex (*Blue Is the Warmest Colour*, for instance), whereas gay love stories – again, made with the consideration of straight men's preferences – tend to be non-explicit (*Call Me by Your Name, Moonlight*). That's beginning to change (*Carol, Portrait of a Lady on Fire*) – but it's still striking how often critics assume that the viewer is male. Zack Snyder's *300* is called homoerotic because it's full of near-naked men,[22] but no one assumes that Halle Berry's topless scene in *Swordfish* is there to titillate lesbians (though, you know, it probably does).

*   *   *

For an initially obscure area of film theory, these ideas exploded in the internet era, so that viewers became more savvy and began to challenge the pre-eminence of the male gaze. Films like *Hustlers* or the aforementioned *Portrait of a Lady on Fire* dispense with it entirely and just tell women's stories. Viewers have started to notice and object to blatant objectification – look at the outrage over the more sexualised portrayal of Wonder Woman and the Amazons in *Justice League* compared to their appearance in her own film.

But in recent decades and especially with the explosion of social media, film fans have begun to consider other ways to analyse how well films serve their female characters – and other under-represented groups. The feminist film critics of the 1970s laid the groundwork to consider how films portray women. Now there's an unruly but useful gamut of tests to analyse film.

The Bechdel-Wallace Test

The most famous test is the Bechdel Test, named after cartoonist Alison Bechdel (who prefers 'Bechdel-Wallace Test' after her friend Liz Wallace, to whom she credits the idea). It stems from her 1985 comic strip *Dykes to Watch Out For*, where one character says that she only sees films that feature at least two women, talking to each other, about something other than a man (a variation requires that the women have names). They're three criteria that sound remarkably simple, and yet over 60 per cent of Hollywood films fail the test. That's particularly foolish given that studies suggest that films that pass the test often perform better at the box office.[23] The entire *Lord of the Rings* series fails, as does 2012's *Avengers*. *Avatar* fails, as do the first two *Toy Story* films.

Obviously the test has limitations. *Gravity* fails because there are only two onscreen characters and one is male (there is a third speaking role, for an uncredited Ed Harris), and yet it is

---

female-centric. So we need other tests, as we'll see below. But what's striking about the Bechdel-Wallace Test is how difficult its low bar seems to be to pass and – this is key – how *few* films would fail a reverse Bechdel. If the criteria are that there must be at least two men, talking to each other, about something other than a woman, almost every film ever made will pass. If Bechdel-Wallace were entirely worthless as a means of assessing sexism in cinema, that disparity simply wouldn't exist.

Swedish art-house cinemas started rating films on whether they passed Bechdel in 2013, putting an 'A' rating on those that did.[24] In 2015 film critic Corrina Antrobus set up the Bechdel Test Fest in London, showcasing feminist films that pass the test. 'The response was incredible, and it showed that people wanted these stories, that there was a starvation for them.' Antrobus acknowledges the test's limits.[25] 'It's ridiculous, but those three rules make it an easy entry point to those that are intimidated by feminism. Feminism is open to everyone and [so is], you know, our double bill of *Magic Mike*. The point is, this is the absolute lowest demographic test, it needs to be progressed upon, which is why the other tests are so important.' Bechdel isn't the end of the discussion; it's the beginning.

The Mako Mori Test
Two Tumblr users, Chaila and Spider-Xan, proposed this test, inspired by Rinko Kikuchi's character in Guillermo del Toro's *Pacific Rim*. To pass, a movie must contain at least one female character who has her own character arc, independent of any man's story. Mako, in that film, fights for the right to pilot giant robot Jaegers, and overcomes her own childhood trauma while helping save the world. This test puts *Gravity*, for example, right back in play.

The Furiosa Test

The Furiosa Test was proposed by a Twitter user, Sean M Puckett, in 2015.[26] 'Your movie/game/book/play passes if it incites men's rights dipshits to boycott.' Yes, protests by misogynists gets you an instant pass (because there has to be some upside!). As the name suggests, it was inspired by *Mad Max: Fury Road*, where Tom Hardy's title character Max turned out to be markedly less important than Charlize Theron's Imperator Furiosa, much to the disappointment of a small contingent of online trolls. See also: *Captain Marvel*, *Ghostbusters* (2016) and every *Star Wars* film of the 2010s with the possible exception of *Solo*.

The Sexy Lamp Test

This test, proposed by comics author Kelly Sue DeConnick, is even simpler: could a female character be replaced by a sexy lamp (like the famous leg lamp in *A Christmas Story*) without significant impact to the plot? If so, the film fails the Sexy Lamp Test. Many Bond girls fall into the Sexy Lamp category, but some *do* offer exposition to the lead character, which means they technically pass the Sexy Lamp Test but fail the follow-up 'Sexy Lamp with a Post-it Note' Test: could the character be replaced by a sexy lamp with an explanatory Post-it stuck on?

The Smurfette Principle

This goes all the way back to 1991 and a *New York Times* article by Katha Pollitt,[27] and trips up some otherwise extremely entertaining efforts. If your heroes are a team of men featuring only one woman, she's your Smurfette. It's something that looks like a step towards equality while actually being closer to tokenism, because it means women can expect roughly one-fifth the attention given to men. It is rife in the *The Avengers* (Black Widow), *Justice League* (Wonder Woman), *Teenage Mutant Ninja Turtles*

(April), *The Hobbit* ('Tauriel), *Galaxy Quest* and *Star Trek* (Gwen DeMarco / Uhura), *Guardians of the Galaxy* (Gamora), *Predator* (Anna) and many more.

This problem has been a real focus for the Geena Davis Institute on Gender in Media, particularly as it pertains to children's TV. There, too, you often have teams of guys and a single girl, in everything from *Power Rangers* to *Paw Patrol* – or you did, until the Institute started highlighting the issue, and succeeded in achieving gender parity in children's programming in 2019. Madeline Di Nonno, CEO of the Institute, says, 'If we were able to have [our children] consume media that is not chockful of biases towards gender, race, LGBTQ, disabilities, could that be a positive factor in shaping their cultural view? That was the theory. Let's focus on what our youngest kids do, so we can stop another generation being laden with all this unconscious bias.'[28]

The Racial Bechdel Tests
There are several racial versions of the Bechdel-Wallace Test. Deggan's rule, from TV critic Eric Deggans of the *St Petersburg Times*, requires a show *not* about race to have at least two people of colour among its principal cast.

Journalist Nikesh Shukla proposed the Shukla Test in 2013 ('if you think that's arrogant, we could call it the Apu Test,' he added), which requires that 'two ethnic minorities talk to each other for more than five minutes about something other than race'.[29]

Bloggers Nadia and Leila Latif elaborated and set out five specific questions in 2016. 'Are there two named characters of colour? Do they have dialogue? Are they not romantically involved with one another? Do they have any dialogue that isn't comforting or supporting a white character? Is one of them definitely not magic?'[30] (That rules out the awful 'magical Negro' trope of films like *The Legend of Bagger Vance*.)

Finally the DuVernay Test, proposed by critic Manhola Dargis in 2016 and named for director Ava DuVernay, simply requires that people of colour 'have fully realised lives rather than serve as scenery in white stories'.[31] While it is the most recent of the lot, it's widely cited – but it's worth considering the specific questions of the other tests too.

A more specific racial test is the Morales Test, named for actress Natalie Morales (*Parks and Recreation, Abby's*) and related to Latinx representation. She asked that, '1. Nobody calls anybody Papi. 2. No dancing to salsa music. 3. No gratuitous Spanish.'[32] Producer Ligiah Villalobos proposed her own Latinx Test. You pass if: 'The film has a Latina lead and the lead or another Latina character is shown as professional or college educated, speaks in unaccented English, and is not sexualised.'

The Vito Russo Test
LGBTQ+ advocacy group GLAAD proposed the Vito Russo Test, named for the film historian (author of *The Celluloid Closet*) and GLAAD co-founder. It asks whether a film has an identifiably LGBTQ+ character, that they are not solely or predominantly defined by that identity and that their removal would have a significant effect on the film's plot (no gay 'sexy lamps', in other words). In GLAAD's Studio Responsibility Index, they found[33] that only 18.6% of 2019 studio releases featured an LGBTQ+ character, but only 73% of those passed this Test; a steady improvement on previous years.

The Topside Test
This test for trans characters, a woefully under-represented group, was proposed by Tom Leger and Riley MacLeod in their

zine *Is There a Transgender Text in this Class?*[34] While it's formulated for books, it works perfectly well for filmed media too. 'Does the book include more than one trans character? Do they know each other? Do they talk to each other about something besides a transition-related medical procedure?' If all three are a yes, you pass.

The Jenni Gold Test

Gold, a director who uses a wheelchair, asks two simple questions about disability inclusion.[35] 'Is there anyone in the world at all in the film or TV show that has a disability – in the background, under five lines, anything?' and then 'Is that character shown in a positive, non-stereotypical, three-dimensional way?' In other words, make sure that people with disabilities, both physical and mental, are present – people with physical or mental disability make up about 20 per cent of the population but less than 1 per cent of onscreen characters[36] – and that they are not entirely defined by their disability.

The Clit Test

This one is a *little* specific. This test asks that sex scenes show that clitoral stimulation is a 'central part' of sexual pleasure for many women (obviously not all women have clitori, nor are all people with clitorises women).[37] A film passes by 'showing, mentioning or even heavily implying clit touching, cunnilingus (oral sex for women) and women masturbating. Think a disappearing head or hand under the covers.' Failure to acknowledge the clitoris promotes bad and unsatisfying sex for women, so endless scenes of the missionary position with nary so much as a wandering hand do everyone a disservice.

Almost no film or TV show right now passes all of these tests. The dominance of films by white, straight, cis, able-bodied men is a real thing. That's always been the way – but it doesn't have to be.

If the New Hollywood failed to rewrite the rules the way we might have hoped, there could be a *new* New Hollywood: one that actually opens its doors to diverse voices. The feminist film theorists gave us the language to explain film's shortcomings so now we can challenge the system. First of all, we need to examine the stories we seem addicted to telling.

8

The Boring Legacy
Or, how franchises took over Tinseltown

IN 1956, actress Jane Wyman decided to move from film into TV. 'I could see that the era of simple movies that say something was over,' she explained. 'Blockbusters were the new rage. So I got out of movies while the going was good.'[1]

Actors and directors have been making the same dire predictions ever since, and they're not entirely wrong. Studios have moved towards a 'tentpole' strategy to make their money, concentrating their funds on fewer, bigger films. This means that a roster of five or six huge films per year consume the majority of a studio's production budget and advertising – but also bring in the majority of their profits. It's a return to the old 'A-picture' and 'B-picture' strategy of the early studio era, but on an even bigger scale, where a *Harry Potter* or *Pirates of the Caribbean* towers above perhaps ten smaller efforts. And if you're gambling $150 million or $200 million on each one, you need some reason to believe that it will pay off.

Increasingly, therefore, studios rely on 'intellectual properties' – or IPs – familiar brand names that they can adapt endlessly, sometimes to glorious effect. It could be a case of bringing a book to the screen: *The Lord of the Rings*, say. It might mean remaking a popular old film: a *Planet of the Apes*, maybe. It might be a belated sequel to something that retains cult appeal, like *Star Wars: The Force Awakens*. Often it's a reboot of a still-beloved franchise, like the last three

Terminator films or *Prometheus*. Or it could be a comic-book hero or literary favourite who can be updated, recycled or otherwise made fit for the modern day while bringing the fandom of fifty or a hundred years along with them. Everyone knows what to expect from a Sherlock Holmes, a Tarzan, a Superman.

'I totally understand if you're going to spend $200 million on something, people are worried for their assets,' one Hollywood producer told me. 'In some ways I will give Hollywood a pass. Show them the piece of IP with billions of followers [and] they will make it. All Hollywood is doing is consuming, building on, things that are monetised by the culture already. You gotta show the powers that be that the audience is there.'[2]

No executive ever got fired for greenlighting a *Batman* film (though some maybe should have been). There's safety for executives in following an established formula: even if the resulting film fails, it looked like a winner on paper. But this era of branded, sequelised and rebooted films is bad news for women, because almost all of the proven IPs were written decades ago, and are therefore stories about – sing along now – straight cis white men.

The level of dominance that franchises, sequels and remakes have in the modern era is unprecedented. An average of 2.5 original films per year have made the worldwide box-office top twenty this decade.[3] The least sequel/reboot/adaptation heavy year of the 2010s was 2016, where a whopping six original films worldwide made it to the top twenty. Those were *Zootopia*, *The Secret Life of Pets*, *Moana*,* *Sing*, Chinese film *The Mermaid* and *La La Land*. It was a victory for original programming, and indeed for female leads in three out of six cases, undermined only by the fact that sequels to four of those six have since gone into production. Otherwise the box-office charts are heavy

---

* Arguably 'Disney princess' is a franchise and this doesn't count, but I am erring on the side of generosity.

in old standards: *Mission: Impossible, Fast & Furious, Jurassic World, Transformers*. So how did Hollywood become *so* dependent on old favourites, and how can they work better for women?

Not all of this is new, of course. Since film first became an industry, there have been adaptations of popular stories, all the way back to *Trilby and Little Billee* in 1896.[4] Adaptations quickly grew longer and more ambitious. Georges Méliès' magical 1902 science-fiction film, *A Trip to the Moon*, was (loosely) based on the Jules Verne story of the same name; Alice Guy-Blaché of course appealed to an even bigger fanbase when she made *The Life of Christ* in 1906.

There have also been franchises for as long as Hollywood could crank them out, from Mickey Rooney musicals to Rin-Tin-Tin adventures to the early Batman serials. Even reboots and remakes are not a modern phenomenon. The famously fast-talking and practically perfect newspaper comedy *His Girl Friday* was a remake of *The Front Page*, gender-swapping reporter Hildy Johnson to add a romantic element to the editor/star writer relationship. *The Wizard of Oz* was adapted in 1910, 1925 (with a young Oliver Hardy) and 1933 before the 1939 version became definitive. *A Star Is Born* has been re-born roughly once a generation since 1932's original version, *What Price Hollywood?*.

Yet it also used to be that movie stars were their own selling points, that you could just put Julia Roberts or Tom Cruise or Denzel Washington on the poster and usually cover your costs. That changed in the mid-2000s.

Not only were the business conditions changing as studios tried to market their films simultaneously around the world to beat internet piracy, but internet gossip sites were going to town on previously reliable stars: even Tom Cruise was memed out of all recognition after his bounce on Oprah's couch (that was taken out of context and twisted into something demented). Gossip was suddenly a free-for-all and studios, risk-averse as always, were terrified. Humans are fallible. They do human things like shave their heads, say offensive things, or wear dresses shaped like swans to the Oscars. The star system was always a delicate balance, with the desires of those all too human stars in tension with the studios' desire to control them as products. As the internet era exposed stars to an unforgiving spotlight, the studios shifted further towards these IPs, which relied less on people and more on transferable, pure ideas that could be endlessly recast and recycled.

Admittedly, the trend was happening anyway: the business models demanded it. Counter-intuitively, it is *less* risky to spend vast amounts on an all-star product than to spread your risk across a modest spread. It takes an impossible number of indie breakthroughs to match the potential gains from a handful of blockbusters, made and marketed right. Alan Horn invested heavily in the tentpole model and enjoyed eleven record-breaking years at Warner Bros; he then moved to Disney and helped to make that the biggest studio in the world. 'Betting heavily on likely blockbusters and spending considerably less on the "also-rans" is the surest way to lasting success in show business,' says business professor Anita Elberse of Horn's strategy.[5] There's just one catch. Those big films *have* to work or risk the studio implosions, mentioned above, that Spielberg warned of back in 2013[6] – and working with a familiar brand increases the chances that they will succeed with audiences.

Certain sections of the media love to claim that Hollywood has run out of ideas, but it's not nearly that simple. Hollywood is just as full of gifted, daring filmmakers as it ever was – maybe more so as they (slowly) become a more representative bunch. Within the confines of franchises, directors like Ryan Coogler, Patty Jenkins, Taika Waititi and the Russo brothers have all made a significant mark and pushed the boundaries of personal expression possible on a nine-figure budget. Producer Jason Blum has overseen a hugely successful slate of low-budget talent at the other end of the financial scale, and a number of his Blumhouse alums have achieved great things: look at Jordan Peele's extraordinary race horror *Get Out* or the career of James Wan. Nor are those efforts alone. Films like *Moonlight, If Beale Street Could Talk, Hereditary, Leave No Trace, You Were Never Really Here, Coco* or *Widows* show real storytelling daring.

It's not that Hollywood has no new ideas. It's that the major studios – all part of huge, publicly traded companies – don't like to risk the sort of money it now takes to make a film on an unknown quantity. That's because the costs of making a film have risen and the film market has widened. The biggest films now sell on a worldwide scale; the days of aiming principally at American consumers are over. Where the US might once have provided 60 per cent of a film's worldwide gross, it is now perhaps half that. The more familiar the concept of your film, the better chance you have of selling in China and Brazil as well as the US and UK, and adding half a billion dollars to the gross. And ideas travel better than most stars.

'Back in the 1990s, you had plenty of macho blockbusters and "manly" action flicks, but you also had romantic comedies, legal dramas, and character studies that offered star vehicle possibilities to the actresses of the day,' explains Scott Mendelsohn, a Senior Contributor on Hollywood and entertainment at *Forbes*. He goes on:

> Sure, Julia Roberts wasn't going to headline *Air Force One*, but she would headline *My Best Friend's Wedding*. The drive towards four-quadrant tentpoles did a number on Hollywood, making and releasing the kind of mid- to low-budget studio program-mers that offered leading-role opportunities to women. It was less of an issue that Matt Damon got to headline *The Bourne Identity* when Ashley Judd headlined *Divine Secrets of the Ya-Ya Sisterhood* while Diane Lane headlined *Unfaithful*. But we know which kinds of movies still get made. Most of these films,

really most 'dude-centric' movies, tend to have a half a dozen major male roles and one pretty girl amid the crowd, and that single 'Smurfette' is usually cast as young and as conventionally attractive as possible. The kind of roles that male characters use to build a career, the kind of roles that actors like Jonah Hill can use to snag two Oscar nominations, just don't exist for women in most conventional studio fare.[7]

As that implies, the problem is and always has been money, and the fast-rising cost of launching a major studio film in the cinema. Some back-of-the-envelope economics might help make the situation clearer.

Studios don't get to keep all the money that a film makes at the box office; as a *very* rough rule of thumb, they keep about 50 per cent, so a film needs to earn back twice its production budget to break even. *Then,* there are marketing costs as well: launching even an average, non-blockbuster film across the US with a traditional marketing campaign costs about $30 million,[8] and can run into nine figures for a huge blockbuster. The sort of mid-level, star-led thriller popular in the '90s, a *Pelican Brief,* maybe, or *A Few Good Men,* would need to make at least $150 million to break even, and that's a high bar in today's market, with much of the same sort of entertainment on TV. 2018's *Vice* cost $60 million and made only $76 million worldwide.[9] *State Of Play* in 2009 (based on one of those great TV dramas, ironically) cost $60 million and made $88 million, despite an impressive cast.[10] These aren't even the truly catastrophic results, like 2010's *How Do You Know,* a star-led romance with Reese Witherspoon, Jack Nicholson and Owen Wilson that is estimated to have lost over $100 million (ironically, it recently found a new lease of life on Netflix).[11]

For nine months each year, this mid-budget market only really exists on streaming and TV. Why go to the cinema to see adults talk to one another? All the big stars are doing that already in the comfort of your own home, with longer running times that allow greater character development. Even in the other three months, awards season, any talky drama had better be a contender. Each January, the release calendars are littered with also-rans that didn't get the nominations, and they die a quiet death (think of *The Current War, Snowden, The Fifth Estate*).

So the chances of getting a Hollywood studio to sign off on that $40 million budget today are slim. Twenty-first century maths suggests that it's better to spend more on huge, familiar brands that can be trusted to reach a base level of appeal. Spend $130 million on your mid-level Marvel movie and another $100 million marketing it, and, barring Covid-19 or another worldwide disaster, it *will* take over $600 million worldwide.

That one-two combo of a familiar brand name and a marketing blitz works. If people liked your previous film, they will come out again. The stellar results of something like *Avengers: Endgame*'s $2.797 billion gross are testament to a ten-year charm campaign by Kevin Feige's Marvel Studios, directed with uncanny precision at winning the hearts of audiences across twenty-one at-least-solid films. Yet audiences are forgiving, to a degree: they'll give you multiple chances if you made them happy once. People kept watching *Pirates of the Caribbean* movies and *Transformers* movies for years after they ceased to be good, trying to recapture that initial high. It can take years of diminishing returns before the box office reflects that (there was a $500 million fall in takings from the second to the fifth *Transformers* film, and even it made a profit).

While the dominance of franchise filmmaking and the cost of these blockbusters is new, much of this is really the same old story. Substitute Abbott & Costello or Laurel & Hardy or Deanna Durbin musicals or Universal's monsters for the Avengers and you get the same effect. There have always been reliable sellers that anchor a studio slate. Give the people what they want, right? It's show business, and if audiences turn out maybe it doesn't matter how much it costs. Except that those soaring costs come with strings attached, and those strings are where things get problematic for anyone who isn't a straight, cis, white male.

That's because of what's 'proven' to attract audiences. That's because of the comics that are most established and book series that have most instalments. It's a new *Die Hard*, a new *Top Gun*, a new *Batman*. It's the same old names, over and over. Bond and Bourne and Batman and Boba Fett. You might get a new *Alien* or a *Terminator*, too – but note that the original female leads in those films appear to be negotiable presences in a way that Bruce Willis or Tom Cruise or Arnold Schwarzenegger are not.

That need for a thirty-year-plus track record is a problem that female leads, and female filmmakers, are going to have to negotiate, because they have only held a tiny minority of lead roles for the past century in Hollywood. If we're only re-adapting the hit films and comics that boys bought in the 1980s, then the lack of female leads in the 1980s will continue to shape the future. Yes, there are now LGBTQ+ comic-book characters, but most are recent additions and are not the characters with their own long-running titles and hordes of dedicated fanboys.

Consider a few examples. Sir Arthur Conan Doyle invented his consulting detective in 1887. Since then, Sherlock Holmes has become the most filmed character in cinema history. Holmes has been played by over seventy actors in more than two hundred titles, including an explosion of high-profile takes in the last fifteen years. Success breeds success, mostly for tall, restless men. Attempts by women to join the party have been limited: there was a Japanese, gender-swapped *Miss Sherlock* in 2018, and in 2020 *Enola Holmes* joined the pack, centring on Sherlock's much younger sister (based on Nancy Springer's novel).

Other properties over a century old include *John Carter* and *Tarzan*, both first published in the early 1900s and filmed in recent years,

166

though to disappointing box-office results. We have not only had *ten* live-action films about Batman (not counting serials or animation), who was created in 1939, but a series of hit animated films, LEGO spin-offs and, recently, TV shows about the young Commissioner Gordon and future butler Alfred Pennyworth. The joke in 2018's animated spoof *Teen Titans Go to the Movies* that we will soon see a spin-off film about the Batbelt seems increasingly plausible.

The problem with remaking the same old characters over and over is that they are mostly white, straight men. That's particularly noticeable in the biggest films of all right now, superhero movies. While they have only come to dominate cinema in the last twenty years or so, the stories being adapted date back as far as the 1930s, and that's shaping what we see in some significant ways. It's worth looking at superheroes as a synecdoche of this whole franchise-heavy, adaptation-centric business model. They are the biggest budget, biggest box-office behemoths right now, and they neatly epitomise one barrier women face in evening up the Hollywood picture.

Superhero movies offer a perfect demonstration of whose fantasies get to take precedence. They're made by (mostly) men who grew up reading comics that had been written for boys like them. These directors want to transmit the giddy feeling they had, reading these stories of daring and heroism, to a new generation. This is not a bad thing – but it has created an imbalance.

Superheroes are a peculiarly American mythology: put it down to rugged individualism, perhaps, but there's something about the model that fits naturally with the country's self-image. That's even before you put characters like Superman and Wonder Woman in red and blue, or create a guy who's outright *called* Captain America.

Like the Western before it, this mythology was then exported around the world. It became a framework for our conception of good and evil. The comics tell us that with great power comes great responsibility, and that it's worth fighting for truth, justice and the American way. For generations now, these have been the fantasy figures to which a certain type of person turns for inspiration and hope. But if almost all the figures we are thus turning to are straight white men, that says something not entirely comfortable about us as a society. There's at least a danger that we read the real world the same way as our comics, that we look to straight cis white men to save the day. Or, even worse, that we assume they already do.

Superheroes began in the late 1930s and 1940s, the so-called Golden Age of comics. There were some inklings of extraordinarily powered beings twenty years before, with Tarzan, Zorro or John Carter of Mars. The Phantom was out there fighting crime in 1936. But it wasn't until 18 April 1938, when a new title called *Action Comics* hit the shelves that the genre really took off (no pun intended. OK, kinda intended). *Action Comics* #1 had a new character called Superman on the front cover. He was the creation of Jerry Siegel and Joe Shuster, and he changed the picture.

Superman proved enormously popular, and in the search for imitators *Detective Comics* #27 launched a new character, Batman, in 1939. Not *technically* a superhero, given that he doesn't have extra-human powers, Batman fights crime with nothing but his wits, his fists and an enormous personal fortune. In 1940, the character now known as Shazam* followed, and in March 1941 Captain America was introduced, punching Hitler in the face, and the still undreamt-of Marvel Cinematic Universe gained its single best character.

It's not an accident that this Golden Age coincided with the build-up to, and battles of, the Second World War. Most of these heroes were created by young Jewish men, the sons of immigrants who believed

---

* Confusingly, he was called Captain Marvel for a *long* time. I'm using Shazam here for ease and because the *Shazam* and *Captain Marvel* movies came out in the same year and things could get complicated otherwise.

deeply in America and were appalled by the rise of fascism. Their ideal hero would fight for democracy and decency and protect those less able to go to war. While they might resemble the Nazi *Übermensch*, while one of them might even be *called* 'Superman', they were designed as a rebuke to Nazi thinking. Superman was an immigrant; Captain America a sickly, poor kid; Shazam a penniless orphan.

That's not to say that the comics always lived up to such ideals. Those early strips are full of racism, particularly in their characterisation of 'exotic' villains, and the casually sexist exclusion of women to minor roles and screaming hostages.

Except one.

In October 1941 Wonder Woman debuted, courtesy of a failed academic, Professor William Moulton Marston, and artist Harry G. Peter. Wonder Woman, aka Diana Prince, was an explicitly feminist hero, a woman sculpted from clay into perfection like Galatea. She was designed to be an intersectional feminist, though she too faced racist caricatures of villains in those early years. But at her best, she fought for workers' rights and against polluted milk, for example, and Marston flirted right on the edge of portraying lesbianism and bondage (it's worth noting that he lived in a polyamorous relationship with two and occasionally three women).[12]

Marston said, 'Not even girls want to be girls so long as our feminine archetype lacks force, strength, and power. Not wanting to be girls, they don't want to be tender, submissive, peace-loving as good women are. Women's strong qualities have become despised because of their weakness. The obvious remedy is to create a feminine character with all the strength of Superman plus all the allure of a good and beautiful woman.'[13]

His personal and rather breathless theories on submission aside, Marston was on to something that resonated with children around the country, and Wonder Woman was an immediate hit. She worked precisely because she gave women the role model they lacked.

Marston worked closely with his wife and lovers when he wrote, and their concerns shaped Wonder Woman's compassion and ferocity.

Yet Wonder Woman remained more or less a lone exception to the male-dominated mass of superheroes. After Marston's early death, DC turned down his wife's offer to continue writing her stories and sidelined Diana into giving fashion advice and – seriously – being secretary to DC's superhero team, the Justice League. This is a character with, canonically, roughly equivalent powers to Superman, reduced to being regularly kidnapped and rescued by her male colleagues. She was also subject to a crusade by the Catholic Legion of Decency, who saw her as a covert propagandist for lesbianism. Once again, the weight of censorship landed more heavily on a female character than on her male counterparts: Batman, chastised for his suspect relationship with Robin, kept going more or less unhindered, but Wonder Woman was dialled back almost to nothing.

That two-pronged crusade against Wonder Woman, by moral crusaders and her own editors, essentially ensured that she would have no serious competitors for a long time. Female comic readers (who always existed) were more or less ignored by the superhero genre for years. It was the '60s before the situation changed. That brought the Silver Age of comics, an era that came about when Marvel editor-in-chief Stan Lee, on the verge of quitting, decided to give some wacky ideas a try. In a four-year creative streak, Lee and artists like Jack Kirby and Steve Ditko created the X-Men, Spider-Man, Thor, the Fantastic Four, the Hulk and Iron Man. These new heroes were more relatable and more troubled than their DC counterparts, with less godlike powers. They were revolutionary in their shortcomings – and if they were almost all men, at least a few iconic women joined the ranks. Teams like the Fantastic Four and X-Men boasted the traditional ratio of one woman each: Sue Storm's Invisible Woman and Jean Grey's telepath respectively. It would be 1980 before a woman, the weather-manipulator Storm, led the X-Men, while Sue Storm languished for years as the bland, caring support for her team and didn't get a standalone comic spin-off until – and this is genuinely shocking – July 2019.

In turn, when filmmakers started trying to adapt these books for the screen, they catered to the same readers and their expectations. There were seven live-action Superman films and nine Batman films before Wonder Woman had a solo outing. The books have big fans (though not nearly as many as the films), and they want to see their core stories translated faithfully. Hollywood decided that meant sticking the guys front and centre – and sticking to the oldest, most established conceptions of the characters.

In these male-led films you inevitably have majority female love interests (because these films are also scared to make their leads gay; the X-Men's Iceman, for example, is still waiting to come out onscreen). And these women almost always end up being rescued by the hero because why else would the pair bump into each other so often? It's the easiest, laziest motivation in action films: put your hero's girlfriend in jeopardy. And it is fatally limiting for women. They can be smart, powerful and capable, but most still end up screaming for help. *Superman*'s Lois Lane (Margot Kidder), *Iron Man*'s Pepper Potts (Gwyneth Paltrow) and *Thor*'s Jane Foster (Natalie Portman) are world leaders in their fields – and yet.

The nastiest result of this tendency is that these women sometimes get 'fridged'. Fridging, as a verb, comes from comic-books writer Gail Simone.[14] It refers to an issue of *Green Lantern* in which he comes home to find his girlfriend murdered and her body stuffed in a fridge. Simone noticed that women in comics were killed, raped, maimed or de-powered far more often than their male counterparts. Those killed tend either to stay dead (which is otherwise vanishingly unusual in comics) or to come back physically weaker. Batgirl was left using a wheelchair after an attack by the Joker, but Captain

America's buddy Bucky came back with enhanced strength and endurance and a cybernetic arm. Gwen Stacy stays dead; Nick Fury comes back to life.

It's important to note that Simone did not – and does not – entirely condemn the practice. There are times when drama requires that one kill a supporting character to effect change in one's protagonist. But what rankles is this marked disparity between male and female victims. Simone said, 'My simple point has always been: if you demolish most of the characters girls like, then girls won't read comics.'[15] It's not just building a power fantasy for men; it's a way to communicate to female readers that this is *not for you*. And even so, women are so used to identifying with male characters (because that's all there is) that they still comprise a substantial minority of comic readers: some estimates are above 40 per cent.[16]

The practice of fridging has carried over into film. There are a *lot* of female deaths in these superhero films, from *The Dark Knight*'s Rachel Dawes to *The Amazing Spider-Man 2*'s Gwen Stacey to the *X-Men*'s Jean Grey. Twice. While Simone's term long ago entered the vocabulary of geeks, 2019's *Deadpool 2* killed off the (anti)hero's girlfriend Vanessa (Morena Baccarin), apparently without the screenwriters even being aware of the term.[17]

The imperilled woman is a phenomenon that goes far beyond the confines of comic-book movies, of course. It afflicts all those '80s action movies too: Riggs' wife and Murtaugh's daughter in *Lethal Weapon*, Arnie's daughter in *Commando* or John McClane's estranged wife in *Die Hard*. However competent, tough or smart a woman is (and Holly Gennaro is all three), there's a very high chance she's going to be held hostage or otherwise threatened. It's not as simple as some deep misogyny or a desire to endlessly portray the death of women (although there might be an element of that, sometimes, deep down). It's because the hero is almost always a man, and the person he cares most about is almost always a woman. So you're mostly going to hurt women to get at him – because he's far too stoic and manly to be rocked by anything else.

There simply aren't many other options for female roles in male-led action films. Where women aren't the love interest, they're sometimes a mentee: Rogue in *X-Men* or Batgirl in the dreadful *Batman & Robin*. If so, they will probably be rescued at some point. But they're rarely the mentor: that's Liam Neeson, Patrick Stewart, Stanley Tucci or, occasionally, Morgan Freeman. *Captain America*'s Peggy Carter – also a love interest not subject to being kidnapped – and the Ancient One in the Marvel Cinematic Universe (MCU) are rare exceptions.

These comics, and their films, are designed to give men the heroic model that meets their storytelling needs: characters who are strong and upstanding, morally certain, stalwart, beloved by women. When they tried to apply that model to super-heroines – *without* fundamentally changing it – it didn't work. *Supergirl, Elektra, Catwoman*: these were heroines made for men, in skimpy costumes (though still more modest than their physically improbable comic-book counterparts) and designed to appeal to a male audience. Look at 1984's *Supergirl*, throwing Kara Zor-El into a girls' school and giving her a giggling crush on the first handsome man she meets. Look at 2004's *Catwoman*, trying to convince us that Halle Berry is a homely weirdo who can't get a date. These women present no real challenge to the men they meet; they weren't intended to inspire girls to feel strong or free. They have only the superpowers that men are comfortable with.

These films, made with smaller budgets than their male counterparts and with little of their visual dazzle, underperformed at the box office – and a huge myth was born in Hollywood's executive suites. Women don't watch superhero movies, they said, and men don't watch superheroines, so we should stick to male-led blockbusters. Never mind any evidence (like the popular *Wonder Woman* TV show of the '70s) that suggested otherwise. Never mind successful action films with female leads like *Alien* or *Tomb Raider*. The myth took hold, and was stated in about as many words, by then Marvel Entertainment CEO Ike Perlmutter in a 2014 email that emerged during the Sony Pictures email hack.[18] Perlmutter is said to have nixed the inclusion of Black Widow merchandise in *Avengers* toy lines for the same reason,[19] and there were reports that he discouraged solo films for *Black Panther* and *Captain Marvel* (maybe that's why the studio made a film led by a raccoon before they got around to a solo woman) and objected to female villains.[20] It's fun to imagine the casting we might have had without him in the way: Meryl Streep as S.H.I.E.L.D. boss Alexandra Pierce instead of Robert Redford, maybe, or Rebecca Hall playing the major role she signed up for in *Iron Man 3* instead of a supporting villain.[21]

No one seemed to consider what women actually wanted to see until Patty Jenkins' *Wonder Woman* in 2017. That succeeded because it had a real sense of what inspires women. Jenkins knew that Themyscira, the home of the Amazons, needed to be a world where no woman holds back for fear of intimidating men, because they're just not a factor. She knew that Wonder Woman had to be matter-of-factly powerful but also compassionate. It never occurred to this Diana Prince *not* to be confident, and that is a powerful thing for little girls to see, and to model themselves upon. That's a female fantasy, even if it's one that we didn't know we needed.

The movie connected to the tune of over $800 million worldwide. Bang went the notion that women didn't like superhero movies and wouldn't go to see them. It was the tipping point. *Wonder Woman* also showed that the creative team matters, because Jenkins demonstrated quite powerfully that the female gaze can shape a better female hero, one that appeals to male *and* female audiences. The ongoing conversation about the lack of female directors in Hollywood didn't start or end with *Wonder Woman*, but Jenkins gave that issue an enormous boost.

It was a step forward. The film still places our heroine among men

174

for most of the running time, as if to soothe male viewers after the trauma of seeing a man-free world in the Themyscira scenes. Soon, our heroine was on a *Justice League* team as – yet again – the Smurfette, that one woman with five men. But this time she was the most popular of the lot.

Then *Captain Marvel*, the MCU's first solo female lead, appeared in 2019 and broke the $1 billion barrier despite a hate campaign by internet trolls. Its final act, where a villain tells our heroine that she needs to face him on his terms to *really* win his respect only for her to ignore him completely, is a feminist statement for the ages. It's a rewrite of those earlier movies, all those years of female characters being told they had to master themselves in order to be worthy. Once again, it was at least partly due to female co-director Anna Boden, who made the film with her partner Ryan Fleck.

This is still a cis, able-bodied and conventionally attractive form of representation, just like the super-men. There are hints that Wonder Woman might be bisexual or queer, but so far there are so few female super-characters that perhaps it should be no surprise that they are not, as a group, representative of a wider spectrum of womanhood. The next challenge will be to tap into the diversity on offer in the comics. Oracle, formerly Batgirl, became more powerful and more popular than ever in her wheelchair as a tech and information specialist. Batwoman is canonically a lesbian, and was played as such in her 2020 TV show, so how far behind can the big screen be? The Unbeatable Squirrel Girl has a curvier body type, and one of her allies is Koi Boy, aka Ken Shiga, who's a trans man. So there *are* characters out there who can open the doors wider if only movie studios would give them a chance.

It's also still a very white world, because the same executive myths that women don't sell these films were also applied to people of colour. Sometimes that was made explicit. Actor Peter Shinkoda, who played gangster Nobu on Netflix and Marvel's *Daredevil* TV show, claimed that a story delving deeper into his character's relationship with Wai Ching Ho's Madame Gao was scotched because the writers were told that, 'Nobody cares about Asian people.'[22] That's in a show steeped in Asian culture.

The tragedy here is that, again, there *are* characters of colour to adapt, or to use better. If the *X-Men* franchise broadly did right by Famke Janssen's Jean Grey and Anna Paquin's Rogue in its first two films, it consistently ignored Halle Berry's Storm and could never find a proper role for a fan favourite, the Asian-American Jubilee Lee. It wasn't until Marvel's *Black Panther* that we saw a story where Black women make up over half the principal cast, mentors and confidants and tech gurus and generals.

So far only a small number of superhero – or blockbuster – films feature diverse leads, but it is a growing number: *Black Widow*, *Wonder Woman 1984*, *Birds of Prey* and *The Eternals* followed in 2020 and 2021, with a sequel to *Captain Marvel* lined up. It matters that these huge films open their doors to women, and to non-white, non-straight people – and that they include people from those communities to tell the superhero stories that *they* need to hear. The last few years have shown that there is *no* reason to keep remaking the same white-straight-cis-able-bodied-male-led films to make money.

Now you might be thinking, 'Why not keep the brand names and change the casting? Why *can't* some of these roles be played by women – or anyone?' These are good questions. Changing aspects of the identity of a few characters or writing entirely new characters of a different sex, race, gender identity, physical or mental disability or sexual orientation could make your adaptation feel more representative of our times, or justify your remake beyond mere commerce. It can make stories that have been told a million times feel different because the mere fact of being a woman, or a gay man, or a blind man, will give that character a different perspective on both the action and the familiar elements that you might be leaving in place.

That's why, when shooting a new *Battlestar Galactica* TV series in 2004, showrunner Ronald D. Moore made the hard-drinking, risk-taking Starbuck into a girl.[23] He told an audience of TV critics that the move allowed him to avoid Han Solo comparisons. 'Making Starbuck a woman was a way of avoiding what I felt would be "rogue pilot with a heart of gold" cliché.' It's essentially the same character, but she *felt* entirely new because we haven't seen a million women smoking cigars with the lads and knocking back shots of whiskey. Also, Katee Sackhoff's performance was absolutely riveting.

The Ancient One in Marvel's 2016 *Doctor Strange* posed a thornier problem. In the comics he's a paper-thin stereotype of the wise old Chinese man, so director Scott Derrickson tried to sidestep that trope by casting Tilda Swinton instead. 'The first decision that I made was to make it a woman, before we ever went to draft, before we ever had a script,' Derrickson told Jen Yamato at the *Daily Beast*.[24] Unfortunately, he worried that casting an Asian actress as the remote, authoritarian figure would play into other 'Dragon Lady' stereotypes, leading to the character's whitewashing. In terms of representation, this one clearly is not a straight win, but at least there was some sort of thought process before they hired yet another wise old male mentor.

Gender swapping works fine where there's no real reason for the role to be played by a man. The concerned parent in *Flightplan* was switched from a father in the original script so that Jodie Foster could take the role. Superspy Edwin became Evelyn, and Angelina Jolie stepped up instead of Tom Cruise in *Salt*. Some of the biggest female names in Hollywood have started asking their agents to look for roles written as male; that's how Sandra Bullock came to star in 2015's *Our Brand Is Crisis*, playing a role that George Clooney – her onscreen brother and predecessor in the *Ocean's* franchise – had once considered. Bullock also starred in *Gravity*, after director Alfonso Cuarón faced down studio pressure to rewrite the story with a male lead.[25]

Yet this tactic of simply adding women can meet stiff opposition in geekier brands. Introducing new, female characters into an existing universe – Rey and Jyn Erso in the *Star Wars* universe, say, or two young women of colour as love interests in *Spider-Man: Homecoming* – draws opposition from certain internet denizens, who have been known to campaign rabidly against such tiny twitches towards equality through endless 'downvoting' in YouTube's thumbs-up and -down system and on review aggregator site Rotten Tomatoes' 'Want to see / Do not want to see' polls. They engaged in outright, ceaseless hostility to filmmakers and their stars on social media in some cases.

Even as a handful of successes have begun to dismantle the myth that only men want to see these films, a small handful of men are determined to bolster it. This startlingly vocal group are notably hostile to attempts to make superhero films about anyone other than white straight men. They're not only hostile to the possibility of a Black Batman, or Bond, or a female Captain America, but also to characters originally written as female, or Black, or LGBTQ+, getting a chance on the big screen.

The more women you cast in these stories, the more hostility you face, as one remake discovered. In 2015, Paul Feig started work on a new *Ghostbusters* film. As with the original, he looked to *Saturday Night Live*'s comic talents for his cast. Like the original film, he hired the best and brightest break-out stars, people with a track record of comedy filmmaking who he knew could open a movie. He persuaded the surviving Ghostbusters to make cameo appearances (the late, great Harold Ramis is represented by a bronze bust). And he brought in a bonus A-lister as comic relief, in the muscular and surprisingly hilarious form of Chris Hemsworth.

There was just one problem, as far as the internet was concerned. His four comic leads were women: Kristen Wiig, Melissa McCarthy, Kate McKinnon and Leslie Jones.

'All you hear from these guys is that you're a social justice warrior and you're politically correct and all these things,' says Feig, looking back.[26] 'So, first of all, could you please look at my career? All I do is work with funny women [Feig also made *Bridesmaids* and *The Heat*]. So why is it such a stretch that if I'm going to redo *Ghostbusters*, I know all these funny women and I'll put them in this movie? They're the funniest people I know! I love gender-flipping these genres, because, hey, I get to work with these wonderful women [and] there's so many established tropes that you're going against. You're getting comedy and fun out of the fact that you're doing something that hasn't been done.'

A certain section of the internet didn't see it that way. The casting announcement sparked months of torrential abuse and a vicious campaign against the film, and all those involved. 'We were the canary in the coal mine,' says Feig. Jones suffered the worst of the abuse (as *The Last Jedi*'s Kelly Marie Tran also learned, women of colour often suffer worse in these campaigns because many of these sexist trolls are also racists) and was driven off Twitter, where she was a delightful presence. That may sound minor, but it is not in the twenty-first century. For people in the public eye, a social media presence is important, not just a way to connect but a significant tool in the promotional arsenal and often a creative outlet. Ignoring abuse is not an option – and in any case, a chorus of death threats is not something that anyone should have to 'ignore'.

The film itself was fine, neither as stunning as the 1984 original nor as terrible as the misogynists claimed. 'The greatest moment for me, after all that shit, was when we won the Kids' Choice Award for Best Feature,' says Feig. 'After being told for three years, "Thanks for ruining my childhood" by middle-aged dudes, you go, "Okay, but maybe we made some children's childhoods. Now they've got new heroes and they get to play Ghostbusters." That's the prize. Isn't that what we want to do? Give stuff to a new generation [and] let them have their own hero? So, I mean, the positives are so much higher.'

The film underperformed at the box office, taking $229 million[27] on a near-$150 million budget (one that Feig said was inflated by years of development costs on several scotched ideas), so the internet hordes felt they had claimed a scalp, and were further emboldened to attack any project similarly smacking of 'wokeness' or, more accurately, women. The next along, *Ocean's 8*, fared better, but still had almost half as many dislikes as likes on its trailer on YouTube, an unusual ratio (absent gender) for a film of that sort.

The CW's *Batwoman* – not even a gender-swapped property – picked up more than four times as many dislikes as likes for its trailer, a higher ratio even than *Ghostbusters*. The MCU's first solo female lead (after twenty films), *Captain Marvel*, was targeted across the media. The trailer was down-voted, sure, but the more eye-catching result was that Rotten Tomatoes had to change its policies to prevent users from leaving comments prior to a film's release following 'an uptick in non-constructive input, sometimes bordering on trolling'.[28] This was decried as 'censorship' by the self-described 'fans' responsible.[29] Meanwhile, sexist users on Twitter tried to drum up outrage about star Brie Larson's mild request that outlets make an effort to send journalists who were not white and male to interview her (this, in their view, made her the *real* sexist and racist). Before the film's release, reader comments puts its 'Tomato' score well into the 'rotten' category; a continuing campaign by its naysayers has seen its audience numbers remain well under the Marvel average (critic's reviews, when they came, were 'Fresh').

The same attacks – the same negative pre-release commentary and accusations of 'woke' bias – affected *Black Panther*, and its mainly Black and heavily female cast. That, too, was review bombed, and critics who liked it were accused of positive weighting to try to compensate for its rare status as an African-centred story.

The common thread between these titles is not their quality but their leads. *Star Wars: The Last Jedi* drew similar outrage for daring to focus on (the new trilogy's lead) Daisy Ridley's Rey – never mind that Rey is no more improbably gifted than the original trilogy's Luke Skywalker.

If the self-appointed online custodians of big brands continue to display soaring levels of misogyny and hostility, then Hollywood might still find reasons to cast male leads in their biggest films. Yet there is reason for hope. The trolls' pattern of targeting certain films is becoming transparent. As more and more films succeed despite them, they seem less relevant; *Wired* magazine went so far as to declare them 'boring'.[30] The audience hunger for these films – particularly *Black Panther*, which drew Black and white audiences to the cinema in enormous numbers – is far more powerful than the haters. Meanwhile, films targeted for criticism by progressive groups have failed far harder than those targeted by misogynists: the white-washed *Ghost in the Shell* and *The Great Wall* underperformed to a greater degree (both were, admittedly, also worse films than recent *Star Wars* or Marvel outings).

It all shows that the trolls are, fundamentally, wrong. Audiences *do* want to hear from different voices with new perspectives, and they are voting with their wallets rather than easily manipulated online metrics. As more diverse films are greenlit and made, everything will change. If there are lots of female-led films (or Black-led, or gay-led, or you name it), then one can fail without any executives falsely concluding that no one wants to watch women anyway.

As time goes on, the materials available for adaptation are changing too. Maybe no one cares about John Carter anymore, but there are new properties. Stephen McFeely, screenwriter of the *Captain America* movies and two *Avengers*, says that, 'IP – horrible word

– created in the 2000s, 2010s and '20s already looks different. It's inevitable that it's gonna change, unless we're very pessimistic about gatekeeping, and I'm optimistic. Hollywood is greedy enough that they don't actually care where the money comes from as long as it comes in.'[31] Give them a few years and maybe we'll see a gritty live-action *PowerPuff Girls* movie, or the extended *My Little Pony* universe. Maybe Greta Gerwig and Margot Robbie's *Barbie* movie will kickstart a whole new world where studios search desperately for the female-led projects they'd previously ignored.

Or here's an even better idea. In his *Alien* script, Dan O'Bannon specifically wrote that, 'The crew is unisex and all parts are inter-changeable for men or women' – and Sigourney Weaver got her start because that gave Ridley Scott room to make Ripley a woman.[32] Why not do that far more often? Why not assume that, in an action-movie setting, people aren't going to have too much time to think with their genitalia, and might want to do other things? At that point we might end up, naturally, with more balanced casts. There's no reason not to. Except, perhaps, that male directors don't always consider it – and that's another area that needs to change.

9

The Auteur Gap
Where are all the female directors?

'I DON'T think women can be directors,' said Joan Harrison in 1957,[1] who the *New York Times* described in 1943 as 'the only producer . . . with a 24" waistline'.[2] 'To be a director you have to be an S.O.B.'

Harrison worked closely with Hitchcock and presumably formed her opinions on that basis – but she could be speaking for most Hollywood studio heads, up to and including the present day. Even now, there is a perception that directing is a man's job; that a good director may bellow and rage but will never weep or cajole. It's true that there have been great male directors, and we know about them because they got the chance to make films. But it's also the case that we can't compare like with like, because vanishingly few of their female contemporaries ever had the careers that would allow a direct comparison.

The fact is that if you *do* compare like with like – in budgets, in advertising spend and in the number of screens on which a film is released – films directed by women perform just as well as films directed by men.[3] The difference is that women do not generally get big budgets, or big ad spends, or a wide release. The difference is a long-held belief among studio executives that female directors don't have anything in particular to offer, and are not suited to directing (especially not big films) somehow by virtue of their female-ness, and are just an odd little minority that should occasionally be humoured. Female directors, as a result, often find themselves confined to documentaries or the smallest sort of self-funded indie movies and, even there, face barriers the men do not. And yet it never had to be that way.

'I believe a woman, more or less intuitively, brings out many of the emotions that are rarely expressed on the screen,' said Lois Weber once. 'I may miss what some of the men get, but I will get other effects they never thought of.'[4] Her contemporary Ida May Park agreed that, 'A woman can bring to this work splendid enthusiasm and imagination, a natural love of detail and a knowledge of characters. All of these are supposedly feminine traits, and yet they are all necessary to the successful director.'[5] A century later, we're still wondering whether they might have been on to something.

Of course, things are better now than they used to be. Between 1949 and July 1979, the major distribution companies released 7,332 films. A total of *fourteen* of those were directed by women (only seven different women), or about 0.19 per cent. In the mid-1970s, the Directors Guild of America counted three female feature-film directors among its ranks: Elaine May, Ida Lupino (by then retired from features) and Shirley Clarke*, who was also teaching rather than shooting at the time. May would make one more film before her career also ended.

It's not as though the studios, or the profession's representatives in the DGA, are unaware of the problem. Starting in 1979, the DGA's Women's Steering Committee – composed of Victoria Hochberg, Susan Bay, Nell Cox, Joelle Dobrow, Dolores Ferraro and Lynne Littman – spent a year analysing DGA hiring records, and presented

---

* Clarke, incidentally, had had her first film, *The Connection*, screen at Cannes in 1961 and her second, *The Cool World*, at Venice in 1963. She never made a third.

their findings at a 1980 press conference. The statistics showed the appalling reality of under-representation for women in the profession, including the horrifying statistic above. The group presented these figures to studios, producers and TV executives in an attempt to politely encourage some sort of movement, whether by affirmative action – one suggestion was that TV shows aim to hire one woman for every twelve men – or by encouraging recognition of unconscious bias. In that meeting the DGA women (and the DGA's feminist national executive secretary Michael Franklin) reminded the studios of the equal opportunities legislation that existed and asked them to consider if they were really abiding by it.[6] Their response, apart from a few angry words from one showrunner and a more encouraging response from the (famously progressive) Norman Lear, was general apathy. The Steering Group set up follow-up meetings with studios but were generally fobbed off on employees with no hiring authority, until the infamous 'Danish debacle', when the DGA invited everyone back in for a breakfast summit. Not one guest showed up. Most did not send apologies. It was clear that there was no appetite to improve the situation.

With no path to an amiable solution, the women of the DGA launched a suit against the studios in 1983 on behalf of 'women and racial minorities . . . who have not succeeded in gaining employment because of defendants' discriminatory employment practices'.[7] It failed. Fatally, after a studio counter-suit, the DGA was judged to be part of the problem and therefore could not be a co-plaintiff on behalf of its female members. The DGA had agreed rules for a seniority-based hiring system used by the studios, so their own regime was part of the issue for women – who had less opportunity to work and were therefore less senior. It was a crushing blow to any formal efforts to improve the situation, and at a Guild-wide level it more or less killed the issue. There had already been resistance in the Guild to the Steering Committee's suit (Elia Kazan spoke against it; Mel Brooks argued strongly in favour), and after it failed there was no appetite to challenge the studios further.

The organisation that should have been going to bat for female directors has been restrained in its efforts ever since. It does collect diversity statistics, in an attempt to shame the studios into further action, and has beefed up the language requiring diversity in its operating agreement with the studios, but these are limited measures. In the history of the organisation it has had only one female president, Martha Coolidge, who was in office from 2002 to 2003. Coolidge fought for improvement; she commissioned a report on diversity in the top forty drama and comedy TV shows that improved numbers in the short term.

But the Guild can also be a roadblock to change. Recent efforts – like a vote on whether to *have* a vote on creating a dedicated page for female members on the Guild website – met with resistance from male members of the Guild. There are reports from DGA and Directors Guild of GB meetings of male directors arguing that any steps towards promoting women should be accompanied by financial compensation to men, since they would be losing out as a result.[8] Their attitude seems to be that (white) men have a right to the plum jobs and any move to hire other people is taking something away from them – rather than simply fair competition at work.

The backlash shows a fear of increased competition, and affects efforts to improve racial diversity as well, where the figures are even worse. While people of colour make up over 40 per cent of the US population, they comprised about 15 per cent of film directors in 2019, according to UCLA's Hollywood Diversity Report 2020.[9] That was a relatively good year. The statistics for women of colour are far worse: Black women comprise less than 1 per cent of feature directors.

The reality is that it is not white men who are losing out. The disparity in hiring rates is so marked that the ACLU filed grievances with agencies including the Equal Employment Opportunity Commission in 2015, a case that is still ongoing at the time of writing. Things are improving slightly: female directors now hover around 15 per cent of the total each year, and between 2002 and 2013 they made a mere 4.4 per cent of the highest grossing films (which correlates roughly to the highest budgeted).[10] The situation is changing only very, very slowly as producers realise, first, that there is a reputational damage in failing to hire a diverse group of people and, second, that women can do a good job, and viewers like their work.

How did we get here? Yes, men took over directing in the 1920s and the qualities heralded by the auteurists only seemed to bolster their status. But we've had several waves of feminism since then: why are female filmmakers still such a small minority? A few myths have proved pernicious in keeping them down.

First up is simple: maybe women don't want to direct. This is a position that seems to be fairly widely held – whether admitted or not – among white male directors, perhaps because their ego demands that they have won on a level playing field. They figure that if women *really* wanted it, and were good enough, and worked hard enough, then they'd be directing the big movies. It's merely some sort of biological quirk that men dominate the results. This view was voiced in 2015 by director Colin Trevorrow, who stepped directly from the $750,000 budgeted Sundance hit *Safety Not Guaranteed* in 2012 to the 2015 blockbuster *Jurassic World*, budgeted at an estimated $150 million.[11]

'I want to believe that a filmmaker with both the desire and ability to make a studio blockbuster will be given an opportunity to make their case,' tweeted Trevorrow.[12] 'I stress desire because I honestly think that's a part of the issue. Many of the top female directors in our industry are not interested in doing a piece of studio business for its own sake.'

Trevorrow framed his tweet as a compliment to female directors' artistic integrity rather than casting doubt on their ability. But if he were right how come, just a couple of years later, studios have been able to find Cate Shortland, Niki Caro, Cathy Yan and Chloé Zhao to helm blockbusters? Gina Prince-Bythewood and the eye for action that she brought to *The Old Guard* was right there. Ava DuVernay had met with Marvel a couple of months before Trevorrow's tweet; Patty Jenkins was attached to *Thor: The Dark World* back in 2012. Did they all lose their integrity in the meantime?

Or is this just a comforting lie that male directors who got lucky tell themselves? This is not to pick on Trevorrow: he did a good job with *Jurassic World* and it can't be easy to be held up as an example of male privilege when he's been writing and working in film and TV for a decade. Then again, he *is* also an example of male privilege. He had opportunities that comparable women have not been given. Acknowledging that doesn't take away from his good work; it just adds nuance to the lack of similar success that other people have had.

Some female directors even internalised this belief early in their careers. The lack of role models made them doubt their own ambition. 'I really thought women didn't want to be directors and I was a crazy one who wants to be,' says director Lexi Alexander, who made *Green Street* and *Punisher: War Zone*. 'But then I started realising no, they *are* going to film school and then they become producers or executives or development people, because they don't land anywhere.'[13] Similarly, Allison Anders, director of *Gas Food Lodging*, said of her childhood love of movies, 'Even if I had known what a director was, I would have assumed that I couldn't do it because I was a girl.'[14]

Amma Asante, the director of *Belle* and *A United Kingdom*, virtually had to be bullied into her first directing job by an agent who believed in her more than she did. Having written *A Way of Life*, she was called in by Paul Trijbits at the UK Film Council to ask if she'd consider directing it and reacted with something like horror.[15]

> All I thought was, 'Why on Earth would *I* try to direct this film and ruin it? It's the best piece of work I've ever written. I need to entrust it to the hands of somebody who knows what they're doing.' In my mind at the time, that certainly wasn't me. Subconsciously, what I had in my mind was probably male. I hadn't been exposed to many other options. You want it in solid hands? Put it in a man's hands! So Paul Trijbits coming out with this almost felt like a blow. I still said no, but then my agent rocked up at my house on Sunday – and she never did that – and said, 'You will direct this film. That's just the way it's going to work.'

This is an intelligent, ambitious woman who had acted and turned screenwriter – and who didn't consciously consider directing until someone pushed her. That first film would win her a BAFTA, and she has gone on to tell diverse and interesting stories that might otherwise be overlooked. Asante says now that she realises, from her childhood fascination with Barbra Streisand's work on *Yentl* and her love of Scorsese and Spielberg, that there was a director inside – but it still took prodding to bring it out.[16] Streisand herself started to consider directing *Yentl* when she saw her then boyfriend, former hairdresser Jon Peters, put himself forward as director of the *A Star Is Born* remake.

'He said, "Maybe I should direct it,"' Streisand remembered.[17] 'He said this about himself. I said, "Man, if this guy thinks *he* could direct it, then *I* can direct it." Why am I so reticent here? He had such chutzpah.'

Self-doubt or no, these women still went for it – and despite their lack of role models, or occasionally chutzpah, there's no evidence that women want to direct less than men do. Women go to film schools in roughly equal proportions to men and have done for at least twenty years. Florida State University College of Motion Picture Arts, alma mater of Barry 'Moonlight' Jenkins among others, has had a number of years with more female students than male in the recent past, and the example of Jenkins means that the numbers of Black applicants there has also risen recently (they've also had at least one transgender student for the three years up to 2019).

The difference is in opportunity, that women are almost immediately encouraged into producing, writing or documentary work. There is nothing inherently wrong with those roles – directing features isn't for everyone – but such siphoning off happens disproportionately to women and continues at every subsequent career stage.

The good news is that the women who are breaking through, and being talked about, are changing that situation for the next generation. As Greta Gerwig says, 'I live in New York by NYU, and there's a lot of young girls who want to be filmmakers around, and they stop me on the street. Honestly, it's the sweetest thing. They tend to be very earnest girls who really want to write or make things. I am very honoured that they've chosen me as their leader for this time.'[18]

If we accept that women do want to direct, maybe they're not doing the right things? Maybe they're not hustling as hard as the men? But again, there's no sign of it. Women develop their own projects, just like men; they hustle and collaborate and build a CV; they work in independent film or TV to establish themselves. And yet, the title of director eludes them – and if they do manage to make one film, there's no guarantee they will ever make another.

Often women take some other job, hoping to move in to directing, but find they cannot make the leap. That was particularly tough back in the '70s and '80s. Joan Tewkesbury was a protégée of Robert Altman, who told her: 'If you really want to direct, nobody will let you unless you write a script.'[19] She wrote *Thieves Like Us* and *Nashville* for him – but when she tried to move into directing she had no luck with her own stories. She finally made *Old Boyfriends* in 1979 from Paul Schrader's script because that was the only chance she saw to make her first movie. Realising how unlikely she was to get a second, she took TV work – and was branded a 'television director' for ever after.

Some women strategise around that. Alma Har'el's breakthrough film was a documentary, 2011's *Bombay Beach*, and while it's a film she's (rightly) proud of, she admits that she was driven rather than drawn to the format.[20] 'I reached this point where I wanted to have more control. Nobody can tell you what to do on a documentary because it's so low budget, and it's so under the radar, that you're your own boss. A lot of women can pick up the camera and go and make a documentary without anybody saying no to them. So it's a gateway that is less monitored by the film structures, and by this unconscious or conscious bias that women can't handle bigger jobs. But documentaries were also the way to find my voice.' In her case it worked: her feature debut *Honey Boy* followed in 2019 and won considerable awards attention.

The shift from small film to big isn't always so smooth. When Lexi Alexander moved into directing in the early 2000s after a career in stunts, she had a clear game plan. She saw short films as a first step, so after studying filmmaking at UCLA she analysed the precise kind of shorts that were Oscar nominated, and made one of those: set in the countryside, in the South, thirty-eight minutes long, the sweet spot her research indicated. Lo and behold, she landed her Oscar nomination, and was able to build on that to make her feature debut in 2005 with *Green Street*. And then her model fell apart.

Alexander remembers now:

I had it all planned out. 'I thought, 'Okay, there is a lot more action being done than romantic comedies or drama, [and]

I've come from this world, so this is what I'm going to do.' It's probably the only reason I had a little bit of a career. But I remember *Green Street* winning all these prizes, and then the film didn't get distributed in America and Hollywood wasn't knocking. There were things that should have happened, that I saw happen to guys. And believe me, I was completely naive about this. I honestly thought Hollywood is all about making money and they would give a sock puppet money if they thought that sock puppet would make a good movie. I had no experience with sexism and did not see it at all.[21]

It's not that women don't do the same things men do; it's that these things don't pay off in the same way. Even success and awards don't seem to help women in the way they do male directors. Patty Jenkins' *Monster* won her leading lady, Charlize Theron, an Oscar in 2003. She wouldn't make another feature until 2017's *Wonder Woman*. Debra Granik launched Jennifer Lawrence's career with another Oscar-nominated performance in *Winter's Bone* in 2010, but wouldn't make another non-documentary feature until 2018's (blisteringly great) *Leave No Trace*. Barbra Streisand, the only woman (to 2020) to win Best Director at the Golden Globes, for *Yentl*, still waited eight years to make her next film – and *Yentl* was a financial hit.

There were eight years between Gina Prince-Bythewood's cult debut, *Love & Basketball*, in 2000 and her second film, *The Secret Life of Bees*. Lynne Ramsay had nine years between 2002's well-received *Morvern Callar* and 2011's stunning *We Need to Talk about Kevin*. It would then be six more before she made the definitive Joaquin-Phoenix-makes-over-his-body-and-kills-bad-people movie* with *You Were Never Really Here* in 2017. Why are we allowing talent like this to languish for years at a time? Eighty per cent of white female directors

* *Joker* sucks.

192

make just one film per decade (for women of colour the figure was 83.3 per cent), compared to just over 54.8 per cent of white male directors (for Black men 62.5 per cent).[22]

Amma Asante remembers hearing Gurinder Chadha, director of *Bend It Like Beckham* and *Blinded by the Light,* warn of this ten-year gap before Asante made her first film.[23] The younger woman vowed that she would not fall prey to it – but sure enough, she too had a decade-long gap. 'I would definitely take some responsibility and say that, for a period of time, for personal reasons, I ducked out. [But for the rest] I simply couldn't get anything off the ground. It didn't matter how many awards I'd won, or how significant and prestigious those awards were. They gave me a crack in the door and nothing more than that. I couldn't get myself any further than the commissioning stage.'

Some people blame biology: just as directors should be establishing themselves in their late twenties and early thirties, women are off having babies. Except that, if they're not working during that time, it is usually not by choice. Mimi Leder was offered her first TV directing job in 1987. Taking that opportunity meant weaning her daughter Hannah (now a filmmaker herself thanks to 2019's *The Planters*) after only three months and rushing back to work. 'My husband is an extraordinary man, and the opportunity was there and I took it,' she says. 'But I couldn't have done it alone.'[24]

Leder was lucky to have spousal and family support, and worked steadily for more than a decade while raising Hannah. After making *Deep Impact* when her daughter was twelve, one of the top ten films of the year, Leder took a year off to 'give her some time' – and 'lost a lot of opportunities because I had just come off a major, major success. But I have no regrets.'

She was lucky. Directors report financiers going cold when they went to meetings visibly pregnant, even though they would have long given birth before the proposed project was off the ground. Even an established actress-turned-director like Gerwig didn't mention her pregnancy while making *Little Women*, wearing a lot of A-line dresses and large coats so that no one realised she was six months' pregnant by the time the shoot finished (cast members thought she just had a new style). 'I was always scared about being a mother,' she told *Vogue*, 'in terms of what it would mean for what I was able to do.'[25] She turned in the rough cut of the movie and gave birth the following day; her maternity leave was cut short by the need for additional dialogue recording with Meryl Streep. Both the baby and the movie turned out well.

This sort of parental responsibility *is* a problem for some female directors, but it simply doesn't explain the disparity in work. Leder took one year off, but went eighteen without a theatrical release. Jenkins had one child between *Monster* and *Wonder Woman*, but that can only account for a tiny fraction of her missing time. And women without kids also struggle. The pressure on women in film to find childcare is an acute problem but that's far more true of women at lower levels than director; they can (hopefully) afford the necessary help, at least on bigger, studio films. So biology doesn't account for the attainment gap either.

There's one more myth that continues to be discussed: maybe women just aren't as good at directing – at least not directing *big* films. Maybe Joan Harrison was right and you do have to be 'a real S.O.B.' for those jobs, and maybe women are just too sweet and shy (please stop laughing at the back) to take the tough decisions. This view is less rarely voiced, but it's underneath, lurking behind every executive who refuses to take a meeting with a female creator, under the skin of every A-list actor who isn't sure he wants to go with someone with so little experience.

'The perception is that women cannot make commercially viable material so that women shouldn't be trusted to make blockbusters,'

Cate Shortland says.[26] 'I spoke to these two men and they were really great, and we spoke about working together. But when my agent [followed up] – and this is after I've directed *Black Widow*, which is a big-budget film – they told her, "We're just not sure that she's really interested in making commercial films." Isn't that interesting? There's still this perception that our work is domestic in tone and it won't cross over.'

The mere fact that women have not helmed the majority of block-buster films means that each one who does seems to start from the position of being suspect, a potential disaster in the making.

'Even the conversation that I'd never helmed a movie like this before,' says Patty Jenkins of her work on the first *Wonder Woman*, 'I'd helmed ten times what so many male directors who get these shots have done, and I don't hear the conversation about them, so that I don't understand at all.'[27]

When women *do* get the chance to direct something bigger, the perception that they're not quite up to it can lead to unhelpful inter-ference. Julie Taymor, the acclaimed theatre director, had to fight for her edit on her first two films, *Titus* and *Frida*, but 2008's *Across the Universe* presented a particular challenge when Revolution Studios head Joe Roth balked at Taymor's cut. Roth tested a version of the movie that was half an hour shorter, losing much of the film's polit-ical content and leaving out a gay character's orientation. When their disagreement became public, Roth said on the one hand that 'She's a brilliant director. She's made a brilliant movie', but on the other that, 'Her orientation is stage. It's different if you're making a $12-million film, or a $45-million film. No one is uncomfortable in this process, other than Julie. If you work off her hysteria, that will do the film an injustice.'[28] Women, in this reading, are 'hysterical' to want final cut of their work. Someone tell David Fincher, or Clint Eastwood.

'She went ballistic to save her child,' is how *Variety* described Taymor's reaction, another patronising form of words. Taymor ended up cutting four minutes and told *Variety*, 'If you were going to suggest radical cuts, you were going to make another movie. I stuck to my vision of this film. I never went into the histrionic scenes I heard about. I think women get that more than men.'[29] Ten years later, Taymor's opinion had not changed: 'Being a successful director on Broadway brings out all kinds of knives and hatred. But the misogyny business [in film] is true . . . It is sexist dialogue.'[30]

Crew can also make life difficult for a director in small but subtle ways: asking for repeated confirmation of instructions as if they didn't make sense the first time; persistently arguing back with requests or commands; even sabotaging footage in extreme cases. That's not common, but a tiny minority of hostile crew can make life miserable for even the most determinedly cheery director. One claim by a *Grey's Anatomy* crew member alleged that a Director of Photography (DoP) on that show had 'misused his position of authority to subject these female directors to verbal abuse and inferior terms and conditions of employment', and had sabotaged their shooting schedules by withholding key equipment. ABC settled the suit without admission of wrongdoing; the DoP remained on the show.[31]

'A common thing when I speak to female directors,' says DoP Polly Morgan[32] (*A Quiet Place 2*, *Lucy In The Sky*), 'I would hear that [when] they [told] a male cameraman what they wanted or the idea that they had, they got shot down, they weren't taken seriously or whatever. So they wanted to work with a woman because they wanted to be heard, basically, and they didn't feel that they were being respected.'

This idea that women aren't as good as men leads to crazy outcomes. After Streisand made *Yentl* she showed it to Steven Spielberg who told her, 'Don't change a frame.' This was spun by media reports into Spielberg acting as her mentor, instead of her peer. Directors show one another their work all the time; Pixar built their entire creative model around it. But when a woman does it, it is read to mean that she's insecure, shaky and inexperienced.

The fear of living down to these low expectations can also be a burden that men don't face. For example, to win a crew's respect many female directors will turn up hyper-prepared and hyper-focused. That's been Amma Asante's approach throughout her career. 'I have to go in planned, knowing exactly what my intentions are, because that's how you build confidence and how you hold on to confidence. A guy doesn't really get questioned if he changes his camera position three or four times. When women experiment, it can translate to them not knowing exactly what they're doing. I love being prepared, actually, but that's my only option. Men have more freedom.'

That may not sound like a big deal, but that lack of freedom and confidence to experiment, the inability to take intuitive leaps without losing the confidence of those around you, can limit your possibilities. It's like DNA pioneer Rosalind Franklin holding back on publishing her evidence of its helix structure because she was all too aware that a single misstep could cost her her career in science. If the consequences of failure are too high, you can never be as daring as those who have a safety net.

That fear of failure is why Patty Jenkins made her superhero movie debut with *Wonder Woman* in 2017 instead of with *Thor: The Dark World* in 2013. When she realised that she 'did not believe' in the story that Marvel was set on, she backed out. 'It would have been a huge deal,' she said.[33] 'It would've looked like, "Oh my God, this woman directed it and she missed all these things." That was the one time in my career where I really felt like, "Do this with [another director] and it's not going to be a big deal" . . . I don't think that I would have gotten another chance.' While replacement director Alan Taylor got disappointing reviews, he went on to make *Terminator: Genisys* and is due to release *Sopranos* prequel *The Many*

Saints of Newark in 2021. History suggests that Jenkins would not have fared as well.

That's because women are more likely to spend time, and receive longer sentences, in 'movie jail': the netherworld where you can't get hired after delivering a flop. Kathryn Bigelow won her Best Director Oscar for *The Hurt Locker* in 2010, but that was made on a shoestring budget after she was sent to director's jail following the financial failure of *K-19: The Widowmaker* seven years before. Mimi Leder went to director's jail after 2000's *Pay It Forward*; she wouldn't make another feature until 2018's *On the Basis of Sex* (a film, funnily enough, about gender discrimination), though she was able to work steadily in TV. *Vanity Fair* spoke to a Warner Bros executive at the time who said that her exile was due to 'hype outpacing abilities', and quoted him as saying, 'Everybody wanted to know if she was a journeyman television director or a feature director. *Pay It Forward* came out and people said, "Oh, she's a TV director." '[34] Even though *Deep Impact* existed. It's just not the sort of judgement you tend to hear flying around about men.

Catherine Hardwicke somehow got sent to jail after the huge success of *Twilight*, during which time she was branded 'difficult'. Lexi Alexander hasn't made a feature since 2010's *Punisher: War Zone*, a box-office flop that has become a cult favourite. Rachel Talalay's big-screen career was stalled when *Tank Girl* underperformed in 1995, though she's done great work on the small screen since (particularly *Doctor Who*). Elaine May has served the longest term of all: she hasn't been back behind the camera since 1987's *Ishtar*, a film that is not nearly as bad as you've heard.

Penelope Spheeris, who directed *Wayne's World* and *The Beverly Hillbillies* before the underperforming *Senseless*, explained:

> As a woman, when you do a movie that doesn't do well, then you're done. You're in director jail. I just took whatever job I

could get ... Like *Senseless*, they kept rewriting it and rewriting it. And I'm like, 'Dude, you guys, this is not working. Don't keep rewriting it. Let me just do the movie I signed up to do.' But they kept rewriting it, and it's in my contract that I got to do what they say, you know? And at one point, I said to Bob Weinstein, 'I don't think this works,' and he goes, 'This is my fucking money and I'm going to spend it any fucking way I want to.' And how are you going to argue with that?[35]

White men have landed in director's jail as well, of course: Richard Kelly, Frank Darabont, Josh Trank briefly. But their sentences are usually lighter and there tends to be a greater availability of good character references to ease their passage back into freedom. Trank delivered the famous flop *Fantastic Four* in August 2015; he was hired for his next job just over a year later. Gore Verbinski slipped up with *The Mexican* but was also back within a year with *The Ring*, and two years later was given the reins (or rather tiller) of *Pirates of the Caribbean: The Curse of the Black Pearl*.

It is even worse for directors of colour. In the early 1990s there were breakthroughs for young Black filmmakers, who – for really the first time – saw their films getting wide releases from big studios. But when these filmmakers came to pitch their second films, they found no appetite for original Black storytelling. According to a *New York Times* article that interviewed six of them – including Black women Julie Dash, Darnell Martin and Leslie Harris – they met with a surfeit of interference and a cripplingly racist system.[36]

'You think, "It's okay – you're like every other filmmaker," but then you realise, "No,"' said Darnell Martin, director of *I Like It Like That*. 'It's like they set us up to fail – all they wanted was to be able to pat themselves on the back like they did something.'

'When I would indicate that I'm here as a director to make films about Black women,' said Julie Dash, director of *Daughters of the Dust*, 'executives would say to me, "Why are you limiting yourself?" I was like, "I'm not. I want to see our stories on the screen that haven't been shown before. I'm bringing forth something new."' (Imagine a white man being told he's 'limiting' himself by only telling stories about white men.)

If you're a white man, you get multiple chances to fail. If you're a Black woman, you get none. The sign that we have achieved parity in directing will not come when we see exceptional women, and especially women of colour, succeed: it will be when decent female directors get another chance after a flop, just like the white men do.

Perhaps the biggest and most fundamental problem is that there's a tension between how directors are supposed to behave and how women are allowed to act. Directors are supposed to be decisive and direct, even to a fault. They should have a vision and be leaders of men who bring an entire cast and crew with them in support of some lofty goal, whether that be huge box-office or universal acclaim or, ideally, both. They should stand up for their film, shout down the naysayers and stick to their guns (possibly literally in the case of a few Hollywood legends). They are allowed to bluster, rage and even cry on set; they can and often do push their cast and crew to the limit. They are, in other words, allowed to be difficult.

But a woman who is decisive is treated as difficult. Not only may she be questioned on every aspect of her decision and forced to justify it ad nauseam, but she'll be treated as needlessly confrontational if she sticks to her guns. If she is direct, she will be considered a bitch. If she commands or shouts, she will be unhinged. If she's a Black woman, then she risks being slapped with the 'angry Black woman' stereotype for even the mildest of complaints. Yet how else do you get things done? Go back to Ida Lupino's model of wheedling?

'It's in the job description,' said Lynne Ramsay. 'You're a director, which means you need to make some tough decisions, and guide things, and say yes or no. I don't know any director who doesn't stick to their guns and their ideas on a project. But there is that thing where "difficult" as a guy and "difficult" as a woman is seen as a different thing.'[37]

Barbra Streisand said something similar:

We're just measured by a different standard. He's 'committed'. She's 'obsessed'. It's been said that a man's reach should exceed his grasp. Why can't that be true of a woman? 'Vanity' is another word they use for women. I saw it in a review of [Angelina Jolie's] *By the Sea*; I haven't seen the movie, but they call it her 'vanity production', because she's doing the jobs I did. But [if a man does it,] it's 'how brilliant. He's multifaceted, he's multi-talented, a multihyphenate.'[38]

So maybe women just have to be nicer, more retiring, a little softer. Except that's no way to win either. Then she doesn't have a backbone, can't stick to her vision or is just too emotional to behave profession-ally. That word, 'emotional', was thrown at Catherine Hardwicke on 2008's *Twilight*. She was never late, never yelled, never fired anyone. But one day, she went behind a tree and cried for a few moments when the weather and fate seemed to turn against the film. And that was enough.

'Emotional is a code word, as we know,' she says.[39] 'The "emotional" term is used on women all the time. If a man does it, oh, he's so passionate. If a woman does it, she's too emotional. It's classic gender bias.'

Once again the contrast is marked. Bryan Singer had a reputation for erratic on-set behaviour dating back before the first *X-Men*,[40] but was offered one big-budget film after another. David O. Russell famously came to blows with George Clooney on *Three Kings*,[41] but has no problem generating work. Oliver Stone had such a testy relationship with some of his actors that Sean Penn – *Sean Penn* – said that communicating with him was like 'talking to a pig'.[42] Richard Dreyfus called him a fascist.[43] But cry behind a tree for a minute and you're trouble.

Hardwicke was branded 'difficult' and was not invited to direct the sequel to her film, which made nearly $400 million on a $37 million budget. Every subsequent major adaptation of a young-adult novel in that era was directed by a man, including all the other *Twilight* films. Once Hardwicke proved there was a large audience, something that had previously been seriously in doubt, men stepped in to reap the rewards. And Hardwicke's own phone barely rang, just as it had been silent after her Sundance hit *Thirteen*.

This is another barrier for female directors. Success does not guarantee future opportunities in the way that it does for men, because men are usually invited back to direct the sequel.

What we might term 'franchise theft' with only some exaggeration occurs when you, a female director, make a film that is a larger hit than anticipated. Perhaps you have just adapted a young-adult novel about a teenager and a vampire falling in love. Maybe you're a respected theatre director who brought an Abba musical to the big screen and made it a sensation (scientists remain baffled). Or an artist turned director who adapted a soft-core erotica blockbuster successfully, or a rock documentarian who made one of the comedy hits of the '90s. It doesn't matter. Come the sequel, you'll be replaced by a man – and your own career will somehow never quite see the benefit of your success.

That was the case for Hardwicke on *Twilight*, replaced by Chris Weitz; Phyllida Lloyd on *Mamma Mia*, replaced by Ol Parker; Sam Taylor-Johnson on *50 Shades of Grey*, replaced by James Foley; and Penelope Spheeris on *Wayne's World*, replaced by Stephen Surjik. It's even the case on smaller-scale work: Alma Har'el won awards for a Sigur Ros video made for just $10,000, but it was still male colleagues who seemed to land the $300,000 or $500,000 jobs.

Some of these women might not have chosen to return to the franchises they birthed: Hardwicke says she wasn't actually keen on *New Moon*. But the point remains that it is rare for a man in the same position not to be offered the chance to return, and for studios not to accommodate their schedule. When women *are* invited back, they are not necessarily offered the perks of success. There was a long delay before Patty Jenkins formally signed on for the *Wonder Woman* sequel, reportedly due to her (reasonable) request for a salary bump.[44] Even after a huge hit, a raise was not automatic and her hiring was put in doubt.

'You know what's interesting?' asks Jenkins:

> Every single thing I've done in my career so far, everybody thought was going to fail and didn't believe in. That's my modus operandi. When I was making *Monster* with Charlize [Theron], it was a laughing stock. When I was making *Wonder Woman*, everybody assumed it was going to fail. When I'm making [the sequel, *Wonder Woman 1984*] everybody assumes it's not going to be as good as the first one. There's nothing I can do. I only make things that *I* believe in. I've never basked in the benefit of what some cool male directors have, where everybody's so excited for their work. I don't know what it is about women.[45]

Hiring doesn't work the same way for women as for men. It can't have hurt Trevorrow's career that established director Brad Bird told producer Kathleen Kennedy to hire him because he reminded Bird of his younger self – thus burnishing the younger man with a sense of inevitable destiny. It didn't hurt J. J. Abrams that he forged ties to Spielberg as a teenager and, again, reminded the director of himself as a young man.

It's called a 'similar-to-me effect' and it's a recognised phenomenon in the psychology of work. People with healthy self-esteem, who think they're pretty good at their job, figure that by hiring similar people they will replicate that success. Almost by definition, every major director and producer in Hollywood thinks they're pretty good at their job, so they keep hiring people like themselves.

It helps if you're one of the guys. Brett Ratner got his start in music videos because he 'knew where all the models' apartments were',[46] and, once he moved to LA, became friends with many survivors of the New Hollywood of the '70s, at one point living in Robert Evans' poolhouse for two years. He cultivated a reputation for throwing the *best* parties, all swarming with gorgeous young women around these much older men. There can be few female directors who have even attempted a similar path to success, but if they tried there would almost certainly be an assumption that they were sleeping with their mentors. At least one female director was told as much by potential older mentors, who kept their distance for her sake.

Such factors go unspoken; the official studio line is that female directors have the same chances as their male colleagues. Women go for jobs and are told that they *just* missed out to a guy who perhaps had more credits. And multiplied over time the guy is always going to have more credits, because they keep getting hired more.

Too bad, you might think. Not everyone gets every job they interview for, right? But directors may spend quite a bit of time and money on a presentation if they believe they have a shot. They may pay to have storyboards professionally produced, maybe even animatics, certainly a lookbook. This all has to be flawlessly presented to the executives who make the decision; many directors will spend more days per year pitching than on set. So if you're continually 'down to the last two' for a job, brought in again and again to pitch, that's costing time, money and effort – and if the executives know they're not planning to hire you, it's all wasted. There's potential reputational damage in always being the bridesmaid and never the bride too.

What stopped those other people hiring her? What's wrong with her? It can begin to look like no one thinks you're good enough, and that bodes badly for your future.

Some female directors have begun to notice patterns to these interviews, especially since the industry's lack of diversity became a scandal after 2017. Now they're more likely to get the interview, but just as unlikely to get the job at the end of the day. It's been compared to the 'Rooney Rule' in American football, introduced by Dan 'great-uncle of Kate and Rooney Mara' Rooney. This rule requires NFL teams to interview ethnic-minority candidates for head coaching and other senior football jobs. But the rule has been criticised as window dressing, making minority coaches subject to sham consideration before teams hire the white guy they already planned to hire. Seventeen years after the rule was introduced, the NFL had the same number of Black head coaches it did in 2003: three out of thirty-two.

It's a similar story with Hollywood. With the eyes of the world on them, studios have stopped claiming that there's nothing they can do to find more women, and more big films have made a song and dance about interviewing female directors. But if those executives then keep hiring men for most of the big jobs, it could actively damage rather than enhance their reputation to come second for the big jobs, and reinforce the belief that women just aren't good enough. The problem with such tokenism is that there's a statistical, psychological tendency to focus the choice between similar candidates when making a decision, because that's where the 'tough' choice lies. You are conditioned to see the more numerous sort of candidate as the 'norm' against which others should be judged. So if you have several men in consideration and one woman, there is a chance that you will subconsciously reject her as an outlier, immediately, and focus on the men who form the central pool of candidates to see which of those stands out.

Linda Chang, a social psychology graduate at Harvard, says that ideally you'd have a blind audition process for directors: watching their work without knowing who made it, for example. Director Alma Har'el's Free The Bid initiative did something similar in advertising and effected a huge uplift in the number of women hired; her Free The Work scheme is now trying to do the same in film and demonstrate to executives that there *are* women out there ready to work by making minority, female and non-binary directors' portfolios easily accessible.

To get past this tendency to dismiss the outlier you need what's called the decoy effect: a number of similar options to reset the norm and establish a different baseline. If you interview equal numbers of men and women, you might set a different norm. But you can't mandate a certain number of interviews for women or minority candidates, because then you run into a bias where decision-makers assume that the women and minorities are only there to make up the quota and are not seriously in contention. So the situation only changes when studios interview a truly diverse group *without* setting a quota; when they use a diverse interviewing panel; when they examine each candidate's achievements separately from their personality. Chang suggests that companies should be encouraged to settle objective criteria in advance and even decide how those criteria will be weighed. It would be a seismic change. And in the chaos of decision-making that drives Hollywood, a town where myth always seems to come before maths, it seems unlikely.

There may be no will to change. 'When it comes to what's onscreen I believe that it's unconscious bias,' says Madeline Di Nonno, CEO of the Geena Davis Institute on Gender in Media. 'When it comes to looking behind the camera and hiring, I think that's conscious bias. The industry has known the numbers on hiring for decades and decades. And [change] is so glacial.'

Director Martha Coolidge links the lack of women to the same root as the #MeToo movement. She told Deadline Hollywood:

> There is a sexual element, which is deeper than just stereotypes. There is a sex fantasy that holds over Hollywood. There are even some men in this game for the sexual perks ... and if they're screwing around all the time, and they want to be on a set where they are the king and they can f*ck anything out there, they're not gonna want women around who are like their mother or their sister or their principal. So they are not going to hire women in any important positions. They are going to hire cute women that are their prey and conquests. Even if it's just for eye candy, they don't want someone watching who might say something to their wife or their boss. And that is the truth.[47]

There *is* cause for hope, however. The problem of consistent work has begun to ease up, as public attention has begun to focus on the gender gap and studios have come under pressure to justify their failure to hire women. Marielle Heller, for example, released her first film in 2015, the excellent *Diary of a Teenage Girl*. She quickly followed that with *Can You Ever Forgive Me?* in 2018 and then the heartbreaking and heart-warming *A Beautiful Day in the Neighbourhood* in 2019. She says:

> I realised when I made my first movie how much I love directing and how much it felt like a natural fit for me. It was a surprise to be thirty-five and finding the career that I felt like I was meant to do, but that's what happened. I knew I didn't want to fall into that trap that a lot of female filmmakers fall into where it takes eight years to make your second film. So I jumped in pretty quickly, even though I had a young child and I was kind of scared to get back to it.[48]

Heller was able to move as fast as any male director, which is encouraging, and saw steadily escalating budgets on those three films: $2 million to $10 million to $25 million. It helped that she is exceptionally good, winning her cast Oscar nominations on the latter two films. But she has also taken the initiative to work differently – particularly on that third film, a story about American children's TV icon Mr Rogers.

'I learned how I can make these movies work with my life,' says Heller. 'Part of that was finding ways to work more sustainable hours. I said to everybody, "We can't make a movie about Mr Rogers where we all abandon our kids in order to make it. He wouldn't like that." So we did a lot of things to make this a more sustainable lifestyle.' Those accommodations included working through lunch to cut down the stop-start nature of some film days, which in turn enabled everyone to finish earlier and get home for the kids' bed or bath time. It suited Heller and her young family, of course, but it also suited many others on the cast and crew – and opens doors for women and carers in all positions.

Heller's situation is encouraging, as is the fact that Claire Scanlon directed Netflix's *Set It Up* while she was between seven and nine months' pregnant, giving birth a week after the film wrapped.[49] Women who have a successful film – critically, commercially or both – *are* beginning to get the big meetings that should follow. And in fairness, we should note that Hollywood is not alone in refusing to invest the vast sums in women's visions that they do in those of men. Joana Vicente, now head of the Toronto International Film Festival, was previously a producer who worked with several female directors. She says, 'We know that even start-ups that are led by women have a much harder time getting money invested. When you have a woman pitch a film or a start-up, everyone thinks that they know better, which they wouldn't do if it was a man pitching. It's really hard to get financing.'[50]

But it is an investment worth making. Hollywood is rife with executives who seem to assume that they cannot go wrong in hiring white men but in fact female directors, directors of colour and female directors of colour, the most under-represented group of all, perform extremely well for studios when given the support they need. The conscious and unconscious bias against female creators is hurting the bottom line just as much as it's harming their careers. Hollywood is betting against over half of its own potential.

Not only that, but hiring female directors is a quick way to get better representation across the board. Studies show that films with female directors hire 59 per cent female writers, compared to 13 per cent female writers on male-directed films; 43 per cent female editors compared to 19 per cent; 21 per cent female cinematographers compared to 2 per cent.[51] Hire more female directors and you begin to change the picture for the whole cast and crew.

Women also create better roles for female stars. Gugu Mbatha-Raw, for example, said about working with female directors:

Initially female directors were the ones who gave me the most nuanced roles to play – I gravitated towards films like [Amma Asante's] *Belle* and [Gina Prince-Bythewood's] *Beyond the Lights* because they were meaty, layered characters who were also written by women. It's what I'm interested in . . . But also I'm selfish as an actor – I want the meatiest, most layered roles, and if those are being offered and directed by women, then that's the role I want to play. I want the most challenging part.[52]

This opening of the doors is, of course, not automatic when you hire a woman. A female director still has to ask for a more balanced crew, ideally early and on every different shoot. Female producers may also think of this, but a mostly male team is far less likely to notice any disparity.

'Women employ women,' says Cate Shortland of the phenomenon. 'The same way people of colour employ people of colour. That's what's gotta change. I always work with women as producers, and there's not even a conversation about [hiring women]. It just happens. So I've always taken it as a given, since [her first movie] *Somersault*, that there would be a lot of women on the crew.'[53] On *Black Widow*, having not asked for a gender-balanced crew up front, Shortland found herself with Scarlett Johansson and 'about 200' men around them.

'In the end that really got me down. One day I burst into tears on set, because I felt that the men communicated with each other. And that was a fifty-year-old woman. That was the first time that had ever happened to me, and I never want that to happen ever again. What I would say is *we* have to make sure it happens, because if we don't, I'm sorry, it's not gonna happen.'

Things are getting better, but not to the point where we can become complacent. Lexi Alexander points out that there has been no fundamental, structural change in response to all the noise over the way women are hired – or not hired – for directorial jobs. The same people, mostly men, control the work; the same attitudes exist, even if they are not so public; the same stereotypes apply. Women who spoke out, like Alexander, have not been welcomed back to work. And for all the noise over individual women, the statistics remain pretty dire.

'Women comprised just 17 per cent of all directors, writers, producers, executive producers, editors, and cinematographers working on the top 250 (domestic) grossing films of 1998,' says Dr Martha Lautzen, of the Center for the Study of Women in Television and Film. 'That number increased to just 21 per cent by 2019. With all of the dialogue on this issue over the last twenty years, wouldn't we expect an increase of more than a measly 4 percentage points?'[54]

Diversity pushes have offered female directors the chance to shadow more established names, but while that can be valuable for newcomers to the profession, it's ultimately an unpaid and unsustainable practice. Qualified women want the chance to, y'know, *direct*. Just like qualified men. Mentorships and starter schemes are no substitute.

There has to be an effort to judge people on merit and not on whisper networks that proclaim women 'bitches' and end their careers. In the same spirit, a bit of training in unconscious bias for those with the power to greenlight would not go amiss. A woman with an opinion is not trying to scare you, harass you or be an unreasoning bitch; she's trying to get her film made. She's trying to be an auteur.

Agencies could also do more, putting women up for the biggest jobs and making an effort to ensure that there's transparency on pay. There's a danger, too, that agents use the much ballyhooed push for diversity as a sop to male clients who don't get jobs, reassuring the guys that they *were* the better candidate but that those ol' affirmative-action efforts ensured that the job went to someone else. Such lines may seem like comforting white lies, but they breed resentment and an entirely false image. Women are still a tiny minority of hires, as are non-white people. If any one of these people gets a job, it is almost certainly because they were the best candidate and not because of any diversity push. Men who know they have talent should accept that someone else just won out this time. Men without talent, well, maybe their time *should* be up.

'In the beginning, I did really think maybe they don't know how good we are,' says Alexander. 'I was very naive about it. It seemed very simple to me; the solutions were all there.'

But the solutions *are* there, if the studios will just grasp them. This doesn't have to be a male-dominated field. It doesn't have to be a white field. It could be a profession that reflects the audience and can speak to them directly. That will bring in more money than the alternative; films with diverse casts perform better than those with majority white or male casts.[55] And female directors, and directors of colour, are more likely to deliver those films.

But as we'll see, the men of Hollywood find it hard to let go of their privileges, or even to limit them to the scope of the law.

10

#MeToo
Making Hollywood safe for everyone

THERE'S A popular mall at the junction of Hollywood and Highland Boulevards in Hollywood, an architectural monstrosity modelled after the towering Babylon sets of D. W. Griffith's *Intolerance*. It stands above the Dolby Theater, where the Academy Awards have taken place since 2002. One pleasant aspect of the site is an installation called *The Road To Hollywood* by artist Erika Rothenberg, a colourful concrete and marble path that leads up a grand staircase from the street and in a winding circuit around the mall, punctuated by forty-nine funny or inspiring stories of those who came to Hollywood to seek stardom. 'As a viewer you are standing in Hollywood as you read them – and you can ponder how and why you came to be here, too,' says Rothenberg of her work.[1]

The path finishes with a sculpture of 'a glamorous old movie-style chaise longue', designed for tourists to sit upon, dream movie dreams and pose for a nice picture with the Hollywood sign in the background. Somewhere along the way, this stop on the 'Road' became colloquially known as the 'casting couch' (the mall used the term in its own Instagram posts, as did some tourists). In the wake of the #MeToo revelations in 2017 there were therefore calls for its removal, as it seemed to become a symbol of grotesque exploitation, a winking nod to something that is no laughing matter.[2] The mall's management temporarily moved the sculpture and covered it up with a tarp,

213

leaving Rothenberg in a rather awkward position as an outspoken feminist and supporter of the #MeToo movement. She got the piece restored, but not without effort. 'It took two months, a great lawyer, and my idea to add a personal statement about the work on a panel placed next to it,' she explains. 'There have been no further complaints. But what I like about public art is that the viewer's experience is as important as the artist's.'

If only the artist's experience had always been as important as the viewer's, predator producer Harvey Weinstein might not have got away with his behaviour for so long. Rumours had circulated for years prior to the 2017 revelations of his sexual assaults, after all. When Seth McFarlane announced the Oscar nominations in 2013 he told the Best Supporting Actress nominees, 'Congratulations! You five ladies no longer have to pretend to be attracted to Harvey Weinstein.' In 2012, on Tina Fey's show *30 Rock*, ridiculous actress Jenna Maroney (played by Jane Krakowski) announces, 'Oh please, I'm not afraid of anyone in showbiz. I turned down intercourse with Harvey Weinstein on three occasions. Out of five.'[3] As early as 2005, Courtney Love was asked for her advice to young women in Hollywood and said, 'If Harvey Weinstein invites you to a private party at the Four Seasons, don't go.'[4] Love claimed later that she was blackballed by her talent agency CAA for that remark. And long-time Weinstein collaborator Quentin Tarantino said that he 'knew enough to do more than I did' about cases of abuse, but mentally marginalised the stories he had heard as isolated incidents.[5]

The whispers were there, and yet they were fuel for jokes rather than fury. To naive outsiders and many in the business, they indicated that Weinstein tried his luck, hit on beautiful women, and sometimes had success. But that wasn't the half of it. Harvey Weinstein was a flamboyant producer, a big noise in getting the world to pay attention to independent and foreign-language films and a major force in driving Oscar campaigns. He donated to all the right causes, had all the right friends. That's why, if you weren't online or paying attention that week in October 2017, Weinstein's downfall started slowly. There were whispers that some sort of exposé was coming. That seemed both shocking and not. Everyone knew he was not a nice man, a bully and a boor. There had been swiftly buried accusations of sexual misconduct in the past. But a credible report of not just groping but *rape*? That was more surprising, and yet. The worldly among us did not seriously expect much to come of it; it would probably be brushed aside as usual.

That is what always happened; the news cycle moves too fast for any such claim to make an impact. It felt like realism rather than cynicism to assume that Harvey would shrug it off as always. But this time something changed. A critical mass of pain, outrage, and defiance had been reached; some sort of dam of despair had given way. The reporting, first by Megan Twohey and Jodi Kantor and then by Ronan Farrow, then by a host of others, was strongly sourced and impossible to ignore. Women all over the world started to speak out in support of his accusers, and in solidarity with them, using activist Tarana Burke's hashtag campaign #MeToo. The movement rolled on, and rolled over some abusers, and kept going, and caught almost everyone by surprise. It was a shock to learn how deep the rot went, and how many predators thought they could get away with so much for so long. It was appalling to think how many people were made complicit in their schemes, how many counselled silence, how many listened because they saw no other choice. And it was a shock to gradually realise that one of Hollywood's most fundamental power imbalances, and its oldest, could be challenged and, perhaps, changed. #MeToo shifted Hollywood's self-image in a fundamental way – and if it has not yet entirely changed the balance of power, it has at least empowered victims to speak up.

*   *   *

Harvey Weinstein may have been spectacularly evil in his predations, but he was not alone, nor was he the first to demand sex for success. It's worth taking a moment to look at the history of actresses being sexualised, because there is a long tradition of abusing women involved in performing that carried over to the screen as soon as film began. That context helps to explain why Weinstein got away with it for so long.

For centuries in Europe, women were discouraged or banned from going on stage. In the 1600s a new and daring art form, opera, shook things up by allowing women to sing and act, and the traditional theatre followed. Almost immediately – and probably because of lingering discomfort from the innovation – rumours spread that female actors were loose, overly sexual and probably whores. Pretend to be one thing for the pleasure of a watching audience and, apparently, you are capable of pretending all manner of things for a different sort of paying customer.

Some actresses leaned into their racy reputations, of course, and built successful careers on the false promise that any viewer could be in with a chance. In the nineteenth century, ballerinas at the Paris Opera were habitually sponsored by wealthy male patrons called '*abonnés*', who had their own private entrance to the backstage area where they could meet (and grope) the ballerinas up close and personal. You can see these figures gazing at the dancers from the shadows in many Degas paintings. In the late nineteenth century, a few storied tragediennes like Sarah Bernhardt began to convince at least some people that it might be possible to be both respectable and an actress, though the majority of vaudevillians were still eyed with suspicion. Then came the movies, and the frenzy that drove generations of lovely young people to try to grab a piece of that magic. As they flocked to Hollywood, so did the predators.

It's hard to talk about #MeToo without talking about the 'casting couch', the trade of sexual favours for acting roles, rumours of which have haunted Hollywood since the very beginning. Some of those rumours were true. It was Joan Crawford who is generally credited with saying, when accused of sleeping with the boss, 'Better the couch than the cold, hard floor', but it could have been any number of similarly cold-blooded, pragmatic starlets.

For some of those penniless young women, accepting the exchange might have been worth it. Some people mean it when they say they would do anything for a role, and see a consensual sexual transaction as a legitimate choice. The purpose of this chapter is not to question their decision because the problem is not those who, given a choice between success at a sexual price and the potential ruin of their career by a jealous executive, choose success. The problem is those who toy with lives in that way. It's also worth noting that there was, of course, no enforceability in such an exchange.

To be clear, there is no scenario where an executive offers a job in exchange for sexual favours without in some way exploiting their position. There is no legitimate work, even in the porn industry (which actually has better safeguards for stars), where someone is entitled to demand sex as part of their job. Anyone asking – openly or in coded language – for sex in exchange for success is in the wrong. Every single casting-couch transaction therefore has someone in the wrong, and that person is the one asking for sexual favours from a position of higher institutional power. There is absolutely no grey area. Not 'boys being boys', not someone legitimately thinking the other party fancies them (in that case, hold your proposition until after their work is done), not the impression that they have a right to make the demand as a perk of their position. If it *were* a legitimate perk, it would not have operated under such conditions of secrecy. If it were legitimate, trade magazines like *Modern Screen* would not have claimed, in 1941, that: 'The day of the "Casting Couch" . . . is almost dead . . . today's Hollywood parties are pretty dull and business-like affairs.'[6] If it were legitimate, columnist Sid Skolsky would not have talked about 'the nightmares most of our Hollywood females go through' around the same time.[7]

The brutal truth is that not every woman was able to shrug off this kind of harassment. Marilyn Monroe, in her autobiography *My Story*, talked of being passed around from man to man, and described Hollywood through their eyes as, 'an overcrowded brothel, a merry-go-round with beds for horses'.[8] Monroe told stories of narrowly escaping harassment at the hands of a 'Mr A', who is thought to be Columbia Studios president Harry Cohn, a widely acknowledged creep who also spied on Rita Hayworth.

Fay Wray, star of *King Kong*, recounted how she was ordered into Darryl Zanuck's office in 1933 and told that she could become a big star at Fox. She said that Zanuck promised her a role opposite Clark Gable in an adaptation of Jack London's *Call of the Wild*. 'A contract at Twentieth Century would have saved me from slavery in B pictures,' she told James Bawden.[9] 'Then he tried to kiss me and I ran out sobbing. If I'd played along, who knows how far I would have gone?' Zanuck was notorious that way: when an assistant modestly stood in front of him once as he urinated in a studio flower bed, he laughed and said, 'If you know a young lady on the lot that hasn't already seen *this*, I want her in my office by five tonight.'[10]

Esther Ralston, star of *Tin Pan Alley*, turned down a proposition by Louis B. Mayer and was told, 'You'll never get another picture in any studio in town.' Her MGM career ended there, though she did manage to make one more film at Universal.

These are the rare stars who even alluded to the casting couch publicly, though many more talked about it in private. A code of silence – the same one we have seen around Weinstein – prevailed, though women tried to look out for one another. Anne Baxter, working on her first film, *20 Mule Team*, at the age of sixteen, was warned about co-star Wallace Beery's 'busy hands', and was shielded by the star next highest up the bill, Marjorie Rambeau, who at fifty was apparently not at risk.[11] On Baxter's next film, *The Great Profile*, she witnessed silent-era star John Barrymore harassing her co-star, Mary Beth Hughes. Welcome to Hollywood.

On early twentieth-century Broadway – where the 'casting couch' phrase originated – the demand for sexual favours from chorus girls was so common that it wasn't worth mentioning. That became the way in Hollywood, too: there were jokes about it, but the *victims* rarely spoke of it. Dorothy Dandridge was an exception, detailing her encounter with Harry Cohn at some length, though the account was published after her death.[12] Like some proto-Weinstein, he met her at the door in pyjamas and a purple robe and held out the possibility of work at Columbia in return for sex. Dandridge, well aware of society's views of young Black women, was wary. She called him on his pass before he even made it, but eventually made the bargain because she decided she liked Cohn and because she wanted her chance at stardom. 'I never worked at Columbia Pictures again, but when you gamble, you lose as often as you win.'

As well as the usual social stigma linked to any sex for women in the twentieth century, some who were invited to use the casting-couch route to success went on to wonder if they were really good enough, and came to doubt themselves. This result is insidious and cruel, but it's a feature and not a bug of sexual domination by one sex over another. Monroe, the most desired woman perhaps in human history and a genuinely gifted actress, never trusted her own talent. She maintained that she never used the casting couch, though she was widely assumed to have done so because of the way she looked and the roles she played. Her insecurity about her own abilities caused frequent panics before she was due to work, in turn leading to lateness, line-flubbing and a reputation for unreliability. Of course, not all of that neuroticism was down to her treatment by her movie studio bosses – she had an unhappy childhood and a history of abuse before she reached Hollywood – but it would be foolish to claim that none of it stemmed from persistently being treated like a sex object, even at the height of her success.

You might have thought that things would have improved once the repressive, hypocritical '50s came to an end and the free-love era of the 1960s dawned, but the same problems persisted. The groovy '60s just meant that powerful men saw their sexual appetites as something they no longer had to hide, sleeping around with abandon. In Peter Biskind's account of the cinematic rebirth of the 1970s, *Easy Riders, Raging Bulls*, men sleep with whoever they want – because how else to show that you have arrived, that you are powerful?

Some of those men were sleeping with startlingly young women and girls. Actor and director Dennis Hopper apparently tried to seduce a schoolfriend of his daughter's when he attended her high-school graduation.[13] Director Roman Polanski pleaded guilty in 1977 to having unlawful sexual intercourse with a minor, Samantha Jane Gailey, when he was forty-three and she was thirteen. That was a plea deal to a lesser charge after he was indicted on five counts, including rape by use of drugs, sodomy and perversion. Polanski fled the US upon learning that he might face jail time rather than probation, and has never returned.

Many excuses have been made for the director, and many big stars have worked with him since. Perhaps the plea deal succeeded in obscuring the fact that the complaint was not simply Polanski having intercourse with a too-young but otherwise willing person. Gailey's witness statement made it clear that this was very much 'rape-rape' (a term Whoopi Goldberg unfortunately used to try to distinguish 'mere' underage sex).[14] The excuses big stars and producers made (and continue to make) for working with Polanski rely on this idea that he was merely unfortunate in being mistaken as to the girl's age, showing that pleading to a much lesser offence than the one with which you are charged can distort the picture, and that there is a lot of wilful blindness when it comes to women's welfare.

While Polanski's conviction gets only a passing mention in the Biskind book, the author reports that Polanski carried around the panties of his murdered wife, Sharon Tate, for years after her death, and refers to parties where the director would run out to take pictures of topless 'teenyboppers' 'with braces' diving into the pool.[15] Polanski's autobiography[16] tells the same story, of girls visiting him 'all between 16 and 19 years old' and that they were there 'not necessarily to make love – although some of them did'. He also mentions having sex with fifteen-year-olds when he was an adult.

Nor was Gailey's the only accusation of sexual abuse ever made against him. *The Golden Child* actress Charlotte Lewis, who appeared in Polanski's *Pirates* as a teen, said,[17] 'He sexually abused me in the worst possible way when I was just sixteen years old.' He has also been accused of assault by multiple other women.[18] But according to Polanski, his legal trials are not his own fault but down to a prurient society that just wishes it had his nerve.[19] 'If I had killed somebody, it wouldn't have had so much appeal to the press, you see? But . . . fucking, you see, and the young girls. Judges want to fuck young girls. Juries want to fuck young girls. Everyone wants to fuck young girls!'

Well, some predators do. Actress Eliza Dushku appeared in *True Lies* when she was twelve and says she was sexually assaulted by a stunt coordinator on the film (he denied the allegations). She wrote, 'I remember vividly how he methodically drew the shades and turned down the lights; how he cranked up the air-conditioning to what felt like freezing levels, where exactly he placed me on one of the two hotel-room beds, what movie he put on the television (*Coneheads*); how he disappeared in the bathroom and emerged, naked, bearing nothing but a small hand towel held flimsy at his mid-section.'[20] Dushku told family members and her on-set chaperone, Sue Booth-Forbes, about the assault at the time, and Booth-Forbes claimed that she reported the matter to 'a person of authority' only for no action to be taken. Dushku believes that the same man retaliated following that report by allowing her to suffer an injury during a stunt while shooting the film's climax.[21] Tom Arnold, Jamie Lee Curtis and director James Cameron all expressed horror at the revelations in January 2018, and said they would have acted had they known. But whoever *did* know at the time did nothing to inform them. The same man was the target of further accusations by two other women, one of whom was only sixteen at the time.[22]

Back in Judy Garland's day she talked about uncomfortable moments being asked to sit on Louis B. Mayer's lap, and, according to biographer Gerald Clarke, she was subject to being fondled by Mayer as she grew older.[23] Garland finally stood up to that manhandling, and Mayer affected hurt: didn't she know he loved her?[24] In more recent years, director Victor Salva has somehow maintained a career in Hollywood even after a conviction for sexual misconduct against a twelve-year-old actor in 1988. Martin Weiss, a manager of child actors, was sentenced to a year in jail in 2012 after pleading no contest to two charges of oral sex with a child under fourteen.[25] A casting agent who worked on *Super 8* was also found to be a convicted sex offender.[26] Eighties child star Corey Feldman has spoken out about creepy behaviour he witnessed, and said that his peer Corey Haim was raped (Haim died tragically young).[27] 'Any industry that has that much power and is that competitive . . . after a while, it starts to become [about] who can take the most abuse,' Evan Rachel Wood, an abuse survivor, said in Alex Winter's *Showbiz Kids* documentary. 'Because somebody's waiting in line to take your place. So you just start to allow yourself to be abused in some form or another – every actor is guilty of that . . . There's always going to be somebody willing to take abuse and stay quiet.'[28]

Men of all ages have also been prey to assault. Several young actors, led by actor Anthony Rapp, spoke out against Kevin Spacey.[29] Rapp said Spacey made a pass at him when Rapp was just fourteen (Spacey was twenty-six at the time). Actor Terry Crews was groped by a high-level executive, and felt he could not speak out or be judged an 'angry black man'.[30] *The Mummy* star Brendan Fraser was left depressed by a similar assault, saying that it 'made me retreat. It made me reclusive.'[31] James Van Der Beek, star of *Dawson's Creek*, was 'cornered' when he was younger and made to feel powerless.[32] Man, woman or child: anyone can be a victim to predators, and while they exist everywhere the Hollywood environment is conducive to them. There are big enticements to stay quiet and not rock the boat, and low accountability. Until recently, at least.

This context to Weinstein's behaviour should make it more monstrous, not less. Here was a guy who saw himself as an innovator and disruptor, someone who challenged the bigger studios by distributing daring films and who launched great artists to major success. Harvey wanted to be remembered as a revolutionary and a visionary, but his vision reached no further than his own pleasure.

As if the sexual assault wasn't enough, there was also the career fallout. Harvey Weinstein cautioned directors against hiring victims who resisted him, calling them 'difficult', and so, for example, Peter Jackson hired Liv Tyler instead of Mira Sorvino or Ashley Judd because he trusted the guy.[33] 'For so many years this has happened to me,' said Rose McGowan of her trauma after being attacked by Weinstein. 'It's just a hijacked life. I was sexually assaulted after I was already famous. And then I got blacklisted right away. So what do you do then? . . . You take subpar work; you take scraps. You take what you can get.'[34]

Looking back, it certainly seems like the suddenly sputtering careers of Rosanna Arquette, Claire Forlani, Sophie Dix, Heather Graham, Heather Kerr, Annabella Sciorra, and so many more, might have been the result of similar whisper campaigns after they rejected Weinstein. 'There was a significant drop in careers,' said Arquette, who had BAFTA nominations, a Golden Globe nod and *Pulp Fiction* behind her when she was assaulted by Weinstein, and who disappeared into small films for years afterwards.[35] 'We've gone from the top of A-lists to bottom of the C-minus list within minutes. Gossip . . . A dinner party . . . "Be careful, she's a pain in the ass . . ." People listen to that. And it's not true!'

Sorvino definitely felt 'iced out', though she did work with Weinstein's company again in small roles.[36] Graham was offered her pick of films in an early 2000s meeting with Weinstein, but when she refused to go alone to meet him at his hotel, the offer suddenly vanished.[37]

Sciorra was coming off hit lead roles with *Jungle Fever* and *The Hand That Rocks the Cradle* when she was raped by Weinstein. 'From 1992, I didn't work again until 1995,' she said [some of the films she made in 1992 were released the following year]. 'I just kept getting this pushback of, "We heard you were difficult . . ." I think that that was the Harvey machine.'[38]

'I don't think he hated anything more than the word "no",' said Salma Hayek of Weinstein, speaking about his rages when she turned down his advances and his threats.[39]

If #MeToo taught us anything, it's that for every person who ever got ahead via the casting couch, there were one hundred who felt demeaned, abused, injured or made distraught by it. There were lives turned upside down, even destroyed by it. There have been mental health problems, substance abuse issues and even suicides linked to sexual abuse as part of a culture whereby (mostly) powerful men demand sexual favours of (mostly) less powerful young people.

The casting couch was a long-standing joke in Hollywood, the stuff of porn fantasy and wink-wink, nudge-nudge ribaldry, but for its victims it is deadly serious. It is sexual assault, sexual exploitation and even rape, and it is not an ordeal that anyone should face as the price of following their dreams. When asked, decades ago, about the women who refused to have sex with powerful men, Bette Davis said,

'Well, more careers were nipped in the bud *that* way than any other . . . It was terribly unfair – much more unfair on the actresses.'[40]

Weinstein's bullying was often public; employees lived in fear of his temper, and filmmakers learned to anticipate sometimes acrimonious battles for the final cut of their films.

The thing that not everyone knew was that Weinstein was also using his position to attack women. With the weight of his success behind him, with his reputation as a taste-maker, people were naturally desperate for his support. He could, and did, launch careers. He could, and did, win people Oscars. The most talented people in Hollywood took his calls and believed what he told them, so if he told them you were good, you might be hired. But for many, taking a meeting with him turned into a nightmare.

It seems strange to many outsiders, but a lot of Hollywood meetings take place in hotel rooms. Offices can seem too impersonal, and anyway executives like Weinstein spend a lot of time travelling, so they and their staff take over massive hotel suites during festivals and events. Some people are too famous to sit in a restaurant or coffee shop without being bothered by fans or professional admirers. During Cannes or Oscar season, there's a non-trivial chance that rivals might overhear your conversation in a crowded restaurant. Hotel rooms, or a suite, make a more practical base of operations. Hotel staff often remove the beds, add desks and keep a running supply of coffee and pastries, so that they become, essentially, luxury office space. Almost every celebrity interview a journalist ever does will be in a hotel room. It's not necessarily something that would ring alarm bells even for a wary young woman. Many of the women Weinstein preyed upon were assistants rather than stars; they are expected to deliver things to their bosses, even if those bosses are at home or at a hotel, and that too is normal.

What's not normal is for a producer to be wearing only a bathrobe in that room. What's not normal is him flashing the actresses who come to see him, or asking for a massage, or insisting on giving one. What's not normal is sexual assault, or being chased around the room as you try to escape sexual assault, or having a large man hammering on the door of your room because you're both at the same hotel for the same premiere. What's not normal is rape. But that's what Weinstein did, as described by scores of victims, and he got away with it for decades because his victims were too scared, too scarred or too wary of disbelief and reputational ruin to come forward.

British actress Sophie Dix suffered a typical Weinstein experience. Invited to the producer's room to watch the rushes of her film, she was assaulted instead. She said:

> As soon as I was in there, I realised it was a terrible mistake. I got to the hotel room, I remember talk of a massage and I thought that was pretty gross. I think he showed me his big back and I found that pretty horrid. Then before I knew it, he started trying to pull my clothes off and pin me down and I just kept saying, 'No, no, no.' But he was really forceful. I remember him pulling at my trousers and stuff and looming over me and I just sort of – I am a big, strong girl and I bolted . . . ran for the bathroom and locked the door.[41]

When she tried to emerge she found Weinstein masturbating, so locked the door again until she heard room service arrive, whereupon she took the opportunity to escape. The incident left her disillusioned ('I decided if this is what being an actress is like, I don't want it'), and she became a screenwriter instead.

Ashley Judd was also asked for a massage when she went for a business meeting in a hotel, a breakfast appointment after a night of shooting, and thought, 'How do I get out of the room as fast as possible without alienating Harvey Weinstein?'[42]

Weinstein's operating procedure was to use his female assistants and sometimes female casting agents as unwitting Judas goats. Their presence reassured his targets that this really *was* a professional meeting. But Weinstein would dismiss these employees almost straight away, and his targets would be left in the tricky position of either kicking up a fuss over what could be nothing or staying in the room alone with a man in his bathrobe. Weinstein employees like Lauren O'Connor, one of the first to speak out about his behaviour, raised the alarm about these patterns.[43] But they too were silenced with payouts and NDAs (non-disclosure agreements), two solutions that go hand in hand. Complainants agreed to settle in the knowledge that it is almost impossible to get a man convicted of sexual assault without witnesses or DNA evidence – especially a powerful and well-connected man – and frequently even if you have one or both. Any realistic lawyer would counsel a settlement, even at the price of silence. Arguably, they have a professional *duty* to counsel settlement because the odds of any other 'successful' outcome are so remote. RAINN, the Rape, Abuse and Incest National Network, estimates that for every 1,000 sexual assaults in the United States, 995 perpetrators will walk free.[44]

That advice to settle perpetuates the culture of secrecy and the impression in some misogynists' minds that accusations of harassment and assault are only a money grab – though from a purely practical viewpoint, in any individual case a settlement probably *is* the best possible and probable outcome. Going to court isn't even a coin toss, it's a trial by fire with little chance of success. Defendants therefore push for confidentiality agreements in settlements and are left free to continue their abusive behaviour, still in positions of power and responsibility. Complainants agree to it because what else is there?

Lawyers push especially hard to settle cases when the accused is someone rich and powerful, and not just because they want a share of the proceeds (as can be the case in the US; in the UK fees are separate from awards). The more powerful the accused, the more they will try to bend the odds in their favour. Weinstein used an elaborate network of lawyers, detectives and muscle to intimidate those who bothered him, as recounted in Farrow's *Catch and Kill*. It was easy to take a payout, and almost impossible to achieve any other meaningful result, so the accusations always died down. Until, in a trickle and then all in a rush, they blew up in October 2017.

The accusations this time were coming not from unknown secretaries or assistants but from big names, courageous stars like Judd and McGowan, and they were not silenced. The claims came so thick and fast, in fact, that Weinstein did not comment on each one individually – though he did specifically contradict Lupita Nyong'o and Salma Hayek: as Hayek pointed out, the two most prominent women of colour among his accusers.[45]

The meticulously reported work of Jodie Kantor and Megan Twohey in the *New York Times* established the case against Weinstein, and every interview with a Hollywood star in the next few weeks added fuel to the fire. Actress after actress was asked about sexual assault, and an astonishing number of them suddenly started to talk about it. Sharon Stone, asked about it in January '18, laughed for a long time before telling *CBS Sunday Morning* matter-of-factly, 'I've been in this business for forty years, Lee. Can you imagine the business I stepped into forty years ago? Looking like I look, from Nowhere, Pennsylvania? I didn't come here with any protection. I've seen it all.'[46] Her matter-of-factness gives you some idea how prevalent assault has always been. Of *course* you would be sexually harassed and sexually assaulted. How naive of an interviewer to think otherwise.

Lupita Nyong'o wrote a powerful piece on her experiences with Weinstein when she was a student at Yale Drama School. She said he attempted to force alcohol on her and later asked if he could give her a 'massage'.

> I was entering into a community that Harvey Weinstein had been in, and even shaped, long before I got there. He was one of the first people I met in the industry, and he told me, 'This is the way it is.' And wherever I looked, everyone seemed to be bracing themselves and dealing with him, unchallenged. I did not know that things could change. I did not know that anybody wanted things to change. So my survival plan was to avoid Harvey and men like him at all costs, and I did not know that I had allies in this.[47]

Every one of his victims thought she was alone. Every one was told that other women were more willing, more amenable, and that they would be more successful as a result.

What's striking is that Weinstein seemed to have no sense that anyone was beyond his reach. The regal Cate Blanchett said that she 'wouldn't do what he was asking me to do' so that Weinstein told her, 'We're not friends.'[48] He made a pass at Angelina Jolie as a young starlet, though her father was established star Jon Voight and she was already fierce and outspoken. Ashley Judd, of course, was the daughter of country music star Naomi. He pressured Gwyneth Paltrow for sex, knowing she was the daughter of well-known producer Bruce, goddaughter of Steven Spielberg and, at the time of the incident, girlfriend of Brad Pitt. Paltrow told Pitt about the incident, and he threatened to kill Weinstein if he didn't back off.[49] But Weinstein still tried. And if *Gwyneth Paltrow* wasn't safe, with her connections, then clearly no one was.

Weinstein later made Paltrow an unwitting accomplice. As Kantor and Twohey chronicle in their book about the scandal, *She Said*, the producer held up Paltrow as a model of the sort of fame and fortune that awaited women who went along with his requests. He took credit for launching her career, for getting her an Oscar, and implied to other targets that he did so only because she granted him sexual favours. Merely being associated with Weinstein meant that Paltrow was an unwitting patsy used to lure in new victims. Escaping assault at his hands was only half the battle. Each woman in his orbit was a name he could claim to have helped. Even after the accusations started to come out, he tried to defend himself by trumpeting the fact that Jennifer Lawrence and Meryl Streep had said they were not harassed by him, a use of her words that made Lawrence also want 'to kill him', she said.[50] Even Streep had to explain that not everyone knew,[51] or some at least would have spoken earlier (she too had been a victim of harassment in her younger years, though not at Weinstein's hands[52]).

It's important to be clear that the assaults on stars were not the worst assaults Weinstein carried out, nor the only ones, and that he is far from alone in preying on women in a work setting. Sexual assault is not only or mostly a problem of Tinseltown. If it were, we could just shut the place down, arrest all the men and sexual crimes would vanish for ever. But the public fascination with Hollywood wrongdoing paid off for once; it directed attention to the wrongdoing and not just the Hollywood part. The celebrity of those rich, prominent (mostly) white victims helped to do what years of campaigning alone could not. They made the mainstream media focus on sexual misconduct, over a long period and to a degree never really seen before.

A bunch of gorgeous women wearing all-black to the Golden Globes – as most attendees did in January 2018 – and escorting ground-level activists may not be the concrete change we wish to see in the world, but it kept people from turning away from reality. These celebrities should not get the credit for the grass-roots work that had been done for years before and since by people and organisations like Burke, RAINN and Sexual Assault Awareness, but their fame boosted the conversation. They forced the world to listen long enough to learn that sexual assault was not an occasional thing done in dark alleys by oily-haired men in trench coats but a lived, daily reality for much of the world. The Time's Up initiative launched in the wake of the scandal immediately acknowledged that the problem was not a Hollywood one by focusing on far more vulnerable women in far more financially precarious fields. Privileged Hollywood victims and their allies donated to Time's Up's legal fund to support farm labourers, McDonald's workers, nursing school students, FBI recruits and more.

Celebrity examples encouraged other women to speak out and hope that they would be believed, women in finance, politics, sport, media, tech and a hundred other industries. Legislation was introduced in the US Congress to toughen up the rules protecting staff from sexual harassment. Celebrities made sexual assault not a matter of whispers but of big splashy headlines.

This says uncomfortable things about the ways that we, as a society, value women or believe women, and says horrendous things about our willingness to trust women. Do we only care about assault victims if they also have an Oscar nomination? Has the structure of the world changed enough so that a non-glamorous victim will now be taken seriously in the media, in the courts and by her bosses?

And how many women will it take? If the Bill Cosby case – where the comedy legend was convicted of aggravated indecent assault following accusations by more than sixty women – showed anything, it was that it takes a huge number of accusers to bring down one powerful, famous man. More than eighty women accused Harvey Weinstein before he was permanently removed from his position of power. It took twenty years of cases against R. Kelly before he went to prison. Accusations from over twenty women have failed to make much impact on Donald Trump. What *is* the magic number? Is there some equation that explains how many women we need to accuse a powerful man, and does that number vary depending on how established he is and how famous they are?

That's important because it highlights how much resistance every woman *outside* film faces when making a claim of sexual discrimination, harassment or assault. Even with the most recognisable women in the world complaining of it, the movement still struggled to get past the 'he said, she said' barrier and convince people that there was a real problem. Even in Weinstein's case there was scepticism at first, only overturned as the complaints climbed into the tens, the twenties and higher. That means that the #MeToo campaign has a long way to go, because our society should not require scores of victims before we act, nor should star power determine whether your harasser or assailant ever faces justice. HR structures and the law have failed women for so long that women had learned not even to complain of assault in many cases – which was, of course, the point, further empowering the system to protect the men it felt could not be spared.

It's a situation born of patriarchy that could not have been better engineered to protect the accused, though it can sometimes fall short of total protection. It emerged in March 2020 that, prior to his firing from the Weinstein Company, Harvey Weinstein reached out to billionaires and backers, friends and peers, to plead for letters of support that might convince his own company to keep him on.[53] There is no evidence that he received replies from most. His own brother and long-term partner Bob wrote back, 'U deserve a lifetime achievement award for the sheer savagery and immorality and inhumanness, for the acts u have perpetrated [sic].'

On 24 February 2020 Weinstein was convicted on two charges of rape in the third degree and sexual assault in the first degree in New York City. Weinstein had hobbled into court every day on a Zimmer frame;

he left it behind after the verdict, like a prop that had outlived its usefulness.

In response to the verdict, #MeToo founder Tarana Burke issued a statement saying:

> Today, a jury confirmed what we all know: Harvey Weinstein committed sexual assault. This wouldn't have been possible without the voices of the silence breakers in and outside of the courtroom, the survivors who courageously testified, and the jurors who, despite an unrelenting and unethical defense strategy, voted to find an unremorseful Harvey Weinstein guilty . . .
>
> For some, this has been a Hollywood battle between famous actresses and a larger-than-life producer. Some have tired and begun to ask whether we should care about these Hollywood celebrities.
>
> We would do well to ask ourselves how many of these women's names we can actually remember, beyond the bold-face few? Certainly, Harvey's name will be seared in our collective memories, but many of the survivors will be quietly taking stock of the impact.
>
> How many careers were derailed? How many entry-level assistants were fired or silenced? How many jobs were lost? How many news stories, that could have exposed Harvey sooner, were censored? How many people could have spoken up, but didn't? All in the name of protecting a violent sexual predator.[54]

That's the other side to Weinstein's predation. The women on whom he preyed were fearful that he could ruin their careers – and in many cases, he *did*. That '90s actress you loved in that indie who seemed to disappear from film? There is a non-negligible chance that she fell victim to a Weinstein whisper campaign. Darryl Hannah has recounted how she turned Weinstein down and suddenly found herself left behind by the Weinstein jet that the rest of her cast mates were travelling on. 'I did tell people about it,' she said, 'but it didn't matter.'[55]

Despite relentless intimidation and dirty-tricks campaigns by Weinstein associates, eighty women came forward with accusations against Weinstein. These women are not famous, and had no wish to become so in many cases: no one wants to be a famous victim of rape by a monstrous man. Our society still looks down on rape victims – more, sometimes, than on rapists. 'I would never put myself in that situation,' said Weinstein's female defence attorney callously, when she was asked if she had ever been a victim of sexual assault. But she's lying. Everyone has been in the situation where you *could* be raped or assaulted, because it happens to women every day in spaces that should be safe. She was just lucky enough not to meet Harvey Weinstein in those moments.

And of course Harvey Weinstein – and others like him – had an entire ecosystem of support. The lawyers alone could see off many accusers. As former Weinstein lawyer Lisa Bloom put it when advising a public relations blitz on Weinstein's behalf, weaponised against his accuser Rose McGowan, 'You [Weinstein] should be the hero of the story, not the villain. This is very doable.'[56] Bloom suggested planting an article that would paint McGowan as 'increasingly unglued' so that she would be 'discredited'.[57]

There was also the unpaid help, the friends and associates who suspected something but did not speak out. There were the agents who sent actresses to meet with Weinstein despite, surely, suspicions that he might be at least sleazy. Predators like Weinstein are surrounded by networks of people covering up, laughing it off or not paying attention. Everyone seems to believe they have a vested interest in keeping these men where they are because they believe that the best they can hope for are crumbs from their table, rather than success in their own right. There is, essentially, a whole culture of men who envied Weinstein his access to these women, and did not particularly consider the possibility that the women might have feelings in the matter.

That's how Weinstein's case reverberates far beyond Hollywood, which as a petri dish offers a particularly strong mix of unchecked power, money and sex but is not otherwise unique. Harvey Weinstein may have been more violent and more prolific than many, but he is not alone. Lanny Davis, an attorney and frequent crisis counsellor who worked for Weinstein, spoke to Megan Twohey for the *New York Times* story about Weinstein and confirmed that he had made 'eight to twelve' settlements to women. Twohey asked Davis if he considered that normal. 'I do,' he replied matter-of-factly.[58] That's a mind-blowing detail: up to a dozen such payouts might be considered *normal*. How many undiscovered Weinsteins are there out there?

After that initial flurry of reports on Weinstein sexual harassment scandals were uncovered at CBS, Google, McDonald's and in the world of yoga. Some of the other cases that emerged from the rolling storm of #MeToo revelations were less obviously monstrous, unless you look at it from the point of view of the victim – which, of course, no one did for the longest time.

One revelation that came as a shock to most was the case against John Lasseter, the founder of Pixar Animation, head of Disney Animation since 2006 and chief Imagineer for the Disney parks for over a decade. He is a nailed-on genius, an apparently avuncular fellow determined to single-handedly bring back the Hawaiian shirt (still a laudable aim). Yet the guy who made the sublime *Toy Story* films was also a persistent harasser of female staff.

The story broke in the *Hollywood Reporter* that Lasseter had been 'grabbing, kissing [and] making comments about physical attributes' towards female colleagues.[59] In November 2017 he released a memo to staff that said, 'It's been brought to my attention that I have made some of you feel disrespected or uncomfortable . . . I especially want to apologize to anyone who has ever been on the receiving end of an unwanted hug or any other gesture they felt crossed the line in any way, shape, or form.'[60]

But female staffers said that his statement didn't go far enough, that his gestures went beyond 'unwanted hugs' – though, to be clear, nowhere near the levels that Weinstein reached. Worse, aside from the physical harassment, Lasseter's actions created an atmosphere that made sexism acceptable in the larger ranks of male employees. Bad apples were still a small minority, but they were allowed to remain in the barrel, rotting the trust of every woman they encoun-tered. The Pixar Sparks short film *Purl*, about a small, female ball of wool trying to fit in among her male, human colleagues, reads as a chilling representation of life at Pixar for women in light of these allegations: hostile, unwelcoming, and quick to dismiss the outsider.

As reported by former Pixar artist Cassandra Smolcic, the fact that Lasseter was likely to inappropriately hit on her meant that her exposure to him was limited. 'We've decided it's best if you don't attend art reviews on this production,' she remembers her female art department head telling her. 'John has a hard time controlling himself around young pretty girls, so it will be better for everyone if we just keep you out of sight.'[61]

That might seem wise, managers looking out for women's safety. Except that they're doing so by leaving women out of the conversa-tion, by limiting their opportunities to impress their bosses and move up the ranks. And they're doing so because they *know* that the working environment is unsafe and unfair. If your boss is only going to see you as a piece of meat, how do you convince him you're also a person with a huge amount of creative talent to offer? If you can't trust the people above you to behave appropriately in a meeting, how can you trust them to see your worth as an artist? There have been anecdotal reports from post-MeToo Hollywood that this sort of professional distancing has been a common response, that high-powered men are modelling themselves on the ridiculous example of American Vice President Mike Pence and refusing to see female employees socially or one-on-one to protect themselves, as if every woman were a lawsuit waiting to happen. Such a response can never lead to equality. Segregation never does.

For all the noise and thunder of #MeToo, some at the very heart of the complaint will never hear it. Men accused of harassment and worse have, for the most part, decided that they are the real victims here. Ahead of his trial, Harvey Weinstein gave an interview to the *New York Post* where he complained that his good works had been overshadowed by the accusations against him.[62]

This nonsense prompted a dignified reply signed by twenty-three of his accusers, who wrote, 'He says . . . he doesn't want to be forgotten. Well, he won't be. He will be remembered as a sexual predator and an unrepentant abuser who took everything and deserves nothing . . . We refuse to let this predator rewrite his legacy of abuse.'[63]

Other men caught up in the #MeToo storm saw life return to normal quite quickly. After Louis C.K. admitted the truth of the accusations that he masturbated in front of female colleagues without their consent in November 2017, he went back to stand-up, starting with unannounced appearances at the Comedy Cellar in New York in 2018 that, by definition, meant attendees who might not have chosen to see him found themselves confronted with his presence.[64] At least this time he was fully dressed. It's a far cry from his apologetic statement, which said that, 'I have spent my long and lucky career talking and saying anything I want. I will now step back and take a long time to listen.'[65] That 'long time' was about a year, as it turned out.

TV showrunner Matt Weiner was soon back on TV with *The Romanoffs*, despite accusations from a *Mad Men* writer that he told her she was obliged to let him see her naked (he said he does not remember saying that).[66] James Franco went on starring in *The Deuce* despite allegations of sexual misconduct and unprofessional behaviour (he denies both), and Bryan Singer, who had been accused in a lawsuit of sexually assaulting a seventeen-year-old boy (charges he too denies), was signed up to direct *Red Sonja* in September 2018. That job did not stick, however: he was subsequently replaced by Jill Soloway after problems finding a distributor for his take. Roman Polanski, who still awaits justice in the US, continues to make films. His 2019 *An Officer and A Spy* concerned a famous miscarriage of justice, and its press notes contained an interview with Polanski where he was portrayed as a victim of 'present-day neo-feminist McCarthyism'.[67]

John Lasseter[68] was snapped up by animation studio Skydance in January 2019 to consult on their projects,[69] only for Emma Thompson to resign from the studio's film *Luck* in protest.[70] 'Much has been said about giving John Lasseter a "second chance",' she wrote in an open letter. 'But he is presumably being paid millions of dollars to receive that second chance. How much money are the employees at Skydance being paid to GIVE him that second chance?'

And there's the rub. There is sometimes an impulse of sympathy to those accused of these misdeeds, largely but not only coming from men who can imagine behaving inappropriately themselves if given the chance. There is a (slightly more commendable) insistence in other quarters on the rule of law, that people accused of criminal acts but not convicted be given the benefit of the doubt. But given the shortcomings of virtually every criminal justice system in the world in respect of sexual assault and harassment cases, and given that many cases become a 'he said, she said' toss of the dice, that is always going to be a high bar that leaves many accusers free to continue their predations. It may be a too-high bar to allow a functioning film industry. The mere suggestion of being 'difficult' or 'emotional' can see a woman blackballed and essentially prevented from working for years, as we've seen in the case of Weinstein's victims and in regards female directors. So how come multiple allegations of sexual abuse don't seem to have much effect on men? Our hands cannot be tied by overwhelming sympathy towards the accused; that *must* be balanced by consideration for victims. Records must be kept of accusations and investigations so that a pattern of abuse can be spotted before it claims scores of victims, as Weinstein did. Settlements that muzzle accusers have to be addressed: ideally outlawed, certainly limited where there is a public interest in transparency. The industry that profited from those settlements has to find a new way to make money.

It's also important for people who have power to speak out. In October 2010 Mel Gibson was cast in a small role in *The Hangover Part II*, shortly after the revelation of his verbal abuse of ex-girlfriend Oksana Grigorieva that included sexist and racist language (she also claimed that he had punched her, which he denied), and a little longer after his sexist and anti-Semitic remarks when arrested for drunk driving in 2006. According to a 2011 article, many gay and female crew members were intensely uncomfortable with Gibson's casting in the film, but it was only when star Zach Galifianakis spoke out that Gibson was replaced by Liam Neeson.[71]

The same report suggested that many of the (straight, presumably) male crew members thought that Gibson deserved a 'second chance' (by any measure it would be a third or fourth) and saw the recasting as a 'blacklisting'. There was reportedly a sense that any of them could have been guilty of the same misdeeds. This is the *other* 'me too' attitude, the awareness on the part of some men (#NotAllMen, guys) that 'they too' might try their luck if they felt sufficiently powerful. This counterweight really gets to the root of why so many people advocate softly-softly approaches to sexual harassment, and also problems like racism. So few consciences are clean that a huge number of people would grant unlimited further chances to wrongdoers because they're aware that condemnation would be hypocritical.

Maybe too many of us are hypocrites to change anything. Maybe too many of us are aware of having thought of an unkind slur at some point, of having generalised, of having behaved in a way that now makes us ashamed. Yet there comes a point where being a little hypocritical is no longer the greater evil. It's better to be a little hypocritical and condemn behaviour that we now consider beyond the pale than to stay silent and condone it, to signal that it's not such a big deal and anyway there is no hope of real change. So let's be hypocritical and signal that we have all moved forward. Give people a second chance by all means, after they make true and significant efforts at restitution and responsibility. Don't just give them a second chance because they went away for a little while and are now back. For most of the world, outside of the most privileged classes, second chances must be earned and not just given out of guilt. Maybe it's time that rich men learned that too.

The big danger is believing that the hard work of #MeToo is done now that Harvey Weinstein is in prison, that the reckoning has been reckoned. This is no time for complacency; the structure that enabled and protected Weinstein remains in place. The legal system has shown no great movement in the statistics on convictions. Most powerful people in Hollywood are still men, as are their corporate bosses, and experience suggests that they will still care more about their male peers than they do about less powerful accusers.

More to the point, there's no undoing the damage. Studios have not obviously rushed to hire Mira Sorvino, Ashley Judd, Rose McGowan or the rest now that they know how their careers were unjustly stymied. The women who spoke out have not benefited, and most remain locked out of the professions they once pursued by corporate disinterest or their own disillusionment. Some may have a monetary settlement, but you don't go into film just to make money.

You go into film because you want to be part of creating something magical – and instead these women were assaulted, and told that the magic only existed for someone else.

So it takes a little searching to find a silver lining to this cloud. It's good that the publicity has drawn out some of the poison, and has shown companies the reputational and fiscal damage that can result from these rogue agents. Social media blitzes hurt; consumer boycotts and tumbling stock prices hurt even more. Unexciting and unsatisfying as it is, the economic picture has to change for the predators to really be weeded out of Hollywood. Way back in 1921, it was the plummeting number of viewers following the Fatty Arbuckle scandal that drove Hollywood to clean up its act, not any concern for Virginia Rappe. So it goes today.

One big positive of the #MeToo movement was establishing a sense of camaraderie between women where, often, there had been isolation. Many women spoke out about their experiences as opposed to covering them up in misplaced shame, and others will know in future that they are not alone. It forced Hollywood, and many other industries, to finally confront their sexist assumptions about women and has led, slowly, to concrete and practical changes in the way that some things are done. Like, for example, sex scenes.

Sex scenes aren't always a big deal – or even if they are, they may not be a cause for angst. Shirley MacLaine, remembering her nude scene in 1963's *Irma la Douce* in 2019, told me, 'It was a big deal for me to do that nude bath-tub scene. But I did it as a gift to Billy. And the crew! [laughs] I don't remember any special stuff that day. Being a dancer it didn't matter to me where I changed clothes, so, eh, I think I had a dancer's towel and I held it up, or something like that, and then I got in the tub.'[72] Similarly, Amy Schumer amped herself up listening to Beyoncé before her scenes in *Trainwreck* – and then just did it.

Many stars are blasé about disrobing, but it's not always so simple. There have long been complaints, particularly but not only from actresses, of sets suddenly becoming crowded before nude scenes, with gawking executives or non-essential crew. Sometimes actors are not made aware what, or how much, nudity and sexual content a role will involve when they sign on, and then feel pressured once they're on set. That *Last Tango in Paris* situation describes one such incident, but there have been thousands. Quite often, the sort of exploitation film and risqué, R-rated efforts that featured extensive nudity or sexual scenes are also the films that cast young, not-yet established actors, who often feel obliged to do whatever is asked of them or be branded 'difficult'.

That's not a far-fetched worry: established star and Golden Globe winner Ruth Wilson was apparently so described after objecting to the frequency and degree of nudity required of her in TV show *The Affair*.[73] It's been reported that those concerns are the reason she left the show. Where some directors want to leave room for spontaneity, the result might leave their cast open to discomfort. For example, director Jean-Marc Vallée said of a sex scene in *Wild*, 'It wasn't specifically planned for this guy to take Reese [Witherspoon], to turn her on her back, and take her from behind, but it just happened as we were shooting.'[74] Witherspoon does not appear to have objected – but another actress might not have been comfortable with suddenly being hauled around without warning.

Even after a scene is shot, an actor may not feel comfortable with the take chosen or the angles used if the result is unexpectedly revealing, and may want some control over images of their body. If you think such worries are a little prissy, consider the letter that film blogger Jeff Wells sent to director James Mangold in 2007 after seeing his remake of *3.10 To Yuma*, begging for stills of actress Vinessa Shaw's nude scene. 'Please tell me there's somebody on the *Yuma* team who can slip me some stills of shooting that day . . . please. I'm serious . . .

as one good hombre to another . . . I'm not a sleazebag either . . . At the very least it would be great to grab some frame captures from the film itself. Or some unused footage of Shaw and Crowe doing whatever.'

Mangold, appalled, released the letter rather than the photos. Wells was unrepentant, telling entertainment news site Deadline, 'I really don't see what the big effin' deal is, except for your having posted a private e-mail that had nothing to do with anything except a surge of hormonal intemperance on my part.'[75] How many other emails had people like him sent? This is not actresses being overly sensitive; it's women's bodies being bartered without their knowledge.

None of this is to say that anyone should be ashamed of their body or worried about who sees what. The point is that it should be their choice. And that's why the industry has responded to #MeToo with one major step forward, by finally bringing in intimacy coordinators as standard to oversee intimate, sexual or nude content, and ensure that everyone's happy with what's happening. Major content producers like Netflix and Amazon have announced protocols requiring intimacy coordinators for their productions, and the actors' union SAG-AFTRA added its own framework of standards for sex scenes.

Ita O'Brien is an intimacy coordinator and created the Intimacy on Set guidelines. Essentially these ask filmmakers to treat intimate scenes in the same way that they treat health and safety considerations or stunt work: to assess what's needed in advance, discuss it with those involved, get their consent and keep talking to ensure everyone's safety and happiness. The guidelines cover rehearsal as well as performance and require open lines of communication if there are changes, so that actors aren't suddenly ordered to do something they hadn't agreed to. More importantly, it gives the cast a means to negotiate, and puts a professional structure in place instead of an ad hoc and sometimes exploitative set of relationships.

'Historically it could be anything from feeling awkward to feeling harassed to feeling absolutely abused,' says O'Brien. 'Often people say, well, the best-case scenario is that you get on well with the other actor and then you just hope that the intimate content is going to be all right. And, of course, that's not good enough.'[76]

Different actors may have different points of vulnerability: someone might be happy to portray sex but absolutely uncomfortable with showing a particular body part, or vice versa. So the intimacy coordinator is an advocate for every performer, and a neutral party to play the go-between for, say, an uncertain young actor and an overbearing director. Some productions are more keen to have that in theory than in practice – producers have occasionally asked intimacy coordinators to rubber stamp their production without real involvement – but that should become rarer as the practice becomes increasingly normalised. Every film released comes with a seal of the American Humane Association promising that 'No animals were harmed in the making of this movie'; wouldn't it be nice if the same could be said of the people?

Sexual performances can be risky for the future health of those involved – men as well as women – because a bad experience could cause an actor to avoid all work involving intimacy for years afterwards, to the detriment of their career as well as their mental health. If an intimacy coordinator does their job, the result is safer sex.

'What I'm finding is that the structure of agreement and consensus actually gives a voice for the men who are uncomfortable with what they've been asked for,' says O'Brien. 'A lot of their concern is that they're going to make sure that what they're doing to their fellow actor is okay for them. So now we've got a professional structure, they don't have to overly compensate, and that's really important. It's giving a voice to everybody who is vulnerable.'

This might seem like a side issue to #MeToo and #TimesUp, and in some ways it is. But it's also linked to a fundamental change of mentality and a shift in power, creating a filmmaking system that builds in consent and respect as basic values. Ironically, a code governing sex scenes might finally overturn this idea that it's okay to compare actors to sex workers, because it makes everyone absolutely clear on what the boundaries are, with no room to plead ignorance. So it's part of the long-overdue attempt to professionalise Hollywood and remove its seedier underbelly. And that push towards safety and professional equality has another big barrier to overcome: money.

11

Pay It Isn't So
How to end the pay gap

ETWEEN JUNE 2018 and June 2019, the top ten highest paid actresses in Hollywood made a total of $315 million.[1] Unless you're Jeff Bezos, that probably sounds like a lot, and objectively it is: more than Larry Ellison paid for his private Hawaiian island in 2011, for example.[2] But during the same period the top ten highest paid men made almost $600 million; enough to buy two out of three of the world's most expensive yachts. So when women complain that they're not paid equally to men in Hollywood, there is good cause to believe them.

Much of 2019's disparity comes from one movie: the highest paid actress was Scarlett Johansson, and a majority of her estimated $56 million income came from *Avengers: Endgame. Five* of her male co-stars were among the male top ten earners, so if the Avengers had a completely equal gender split the overall story might have been less skewed. Still, the highest earning man of 2019, Dwayne Johnson, was not part of that film and he made $89.4 million. The lowest earning man of the top ten, Will Smith, made a reported $35 million, which would have put him joint third on the ladies' list.

These massive gaps in earnings have been consistent for decades. In 2014, the top ten male actors earned $419 million compared to $226 million for the top ten women.[3] In 2017, the picture was even worse: $488.5 million for the men, $172.5 million for the women.[4] The top-earning actress that year, Emma Stone, would have come fifteenth on the men's list. Men consistently earn more than women, at the highest as well as the lowest levels of the industry. A 2019 study found that female stars earn $1.1 million less per film than men of similar experience, *after* factoring in previous box-office success, awards won and even Twitter popularity. In action cinema the gap is even higher, at $1.8 million.[5] The gap gets bigger with age: over the age of fifty, men earned on average $4 million more than comparable women. Patricia Arquette was not making things up when she called for equal pay in her Oscar acceptance speech in 2015. She was addressing a real issue – and one that had not progressed *at all* since 1980.

Now no one should cry themselves to sleep at night because Scarlett Johansson 'only' made $56 million after she appeared in the highest-grossing film ever made (unadjusted), and no one is saying that The Rock is not a jewel of a human who deserves the riches of an Oceanic demi-god. Still, it's a neat illustration of a wider imbalance. Star salaries may seem obscene, but if you're a capitalist you don't get to complain about them: these people bring in punters, and deserve to be rewarded for that contribution to a film's success. If you want to rail against people who don't contribute much while making vast amounts in Hollywood, there is a *long* list of pay packets to cut before you get to the bold names who actually help to sell tickets. But there's *no* reason to pay men more than women for similar work.

Maybe you think that audiences simply want to see more men than women onscreen. It's true that The Rock is a hugely likeable star and box-office draw, capable of getting people out to see *Rampage* or *Skyscraper*, let alone good films like *Jumanji*. What's not true is the idea that no woman can match him. If you look at return on investment, comparing box-office gross against a star's salary, and rule out superhero stars (who benefit as much from character recognition as their own appeal), Forbes found in 2018 that the two best bets in Hollywood were Amy Adams, who brought in $69.90 for every $1 she was paid, and Julia Roberts.[6] Women are underpaid *relative to* their box-office appeal.

If money is power and power is money, and if women get less money than men, then women will always have less power in Hollywood. So it matters that women get paid fairly for their work. The real question is what constitutes 'fair', because so many factors go into determining pay in movies and so many of them are based on nebulous, subjective criteria that are easily influenced by sexism, racism and homophobia. As they did when confronted with their failure to hire female directors, Hollywood studios tend to throw their hands up and proclaim that it's all decentralised and subjective, negotiated on too artisanal a level to possibly compare like with like. Yet this thorny thicket of excuses has been used like the hedge around Sleeping Beauty's castle to hide real discrimination. We can absolutely have a conversation about fairness and the relative size of people's roles, but only if we're looking at *all* the forces that tend to allot more money to men than women. That means unpacking the whole system that assigns more value to men than women, to white people than people of colour, and often to straight and cis people over out-LGBTQ+ people.

Let's deal with the stars first, since they're still usually the most highly paid figures on a film. When a big-name actor is 'in talks' for a film, that person will have a pay 'quote', based on their last pay cheque, which forms the basis of negotiation. It may have wiggle room. Perhaps they worked for less than usual because it was a tiny indie film, and now they're being offered the lead in the – let's say – $200 million Michael Bay adaptation of *Peppa Pig*. Or maybe last time, the star took a piece of the 'back end', the profit that the movie made, so that their initial (or 'upfront') salary was not reflective of their whole remuneration. These caveats aside, what you got last time shapes what you will get this time.

That means if you are underpaid from the off, you're likely to stay underpaid even if your agent argues for steady bumps with each new career milestone. We know that actresses are often underpaid early on because their roles are small, thinly written and much sought-after, since fewer than 35 per cent of all speaking roles go to women.[7] Oh, and an actress's earning power peaks at the age of thirty-four, while male stars don't reach their peak earning level until fifty-one.[8] That's seventeen extra years of building up your quote.

The scarcity of roles means that actresses might be willing to take a pay cut to land one of the few meaty parts out there. Taraji P. Henson said of her role in *The Curious Case of Benjamin Button*, for which she was paid low six figures and no accommodation costs, 'There are way more talented Black actresses than there are intelligent, meaningful roles for them. This is exactly how a studio can get away with paying the person whose name is third on the call sheet of a big-budget film less than 2 per cent what it's paying the person whose name is listed first. I knew the stakes . . . If I pushed for more money, I'd be replaced and no one would so much as blink.'[9]

So there has, in recent history, been a race to the bottom with actresses willing to take a bad deal for a decent role. That only changes with more roles for women, when the percentages climb from 30-ish per cent to something closer to 50 per cent of speaking parts. That statistic holds true even for crowd scenes, by the way: even extras are mostly men.

There's also, one suspects, an element of perceived fairness involved. If someone knows they have a small, supporting role, they likely won't demand parity with the lead – who may have far more work to do. The problem is that small, supporting roles are often all that's available for women. So if you don't demand parity for playing the love interest and that's all that is open to you, you're always going to be underpaid. It's like tennis: for years the argument was that you couldn't pay women the same as men because they only played three-set matches while the men (in some tournaments at least) played five. But if you're not going to *allow* the women to play five sets (and it would send the schedule all to hell if you did) then that argument won't stand. You can't set up a system that denies women decent roles and then argue that the lack of good-sized roles is a reason not to pay them. Maybe female stars need to do what female tennis players ultimately did, and demand parity anyway.

Even success doesn't always come with financial rewards for women – which can deprive us of fun movies. The leading ladies of *First Wives Club* took a pay cut to get the film made, because they were women 'of a certain age' and the concept was unproven. But when the film did well and the studio started work on a sequel, 'they wanted to offer us exactly the same deal,' said star Goldie Hawn.[10] 'We went back to ground zero. Had three men come in there, they would have upped their salaries without even thinking about it. But the fear of women's movies is embedded in the culture.'

The difference is exacerbated when men can lead big franchise movies and women are left with supporting roles as yet another girl-friend, or making a career in indie movies. Agents will argue that a big role in a successful film deserves an uplift, so if you're Chris Hemsworth you go from an estimated five figures on 2009's *Star Trek* to about $150,000 on the first *Thor*, to about $15 million by *Thor: Ragnarok*. Few actresses have the same opportunities. And even when they do, it doesn't always pay off in the same way.

Take, for example, Jennifer Lawrence, a rare woman that the franchise gods smiled upon. She broke through around the same time as Hemsworth, with an eye-catching and Oscar-nominated role in *Winter's Bone*. It landed her in 2011's *X-Men: First Class* as the mutant shapeshifter Mystique, and then she was cast as Katniss Everdeen in 2012's adaptation of bestselling young-adult book *The Hunger Games*. The latter *did* offer big money: from a reported $500,000 salary on the first film, she went up to $10 million for the sequels. Kristen Stewart did similarly on *Twilight*, getting a reported $25 million and 7.5 per cent gross for those sequels, while Emma Watson was on $15 million for the last two *Harry Potter* films. But there are fewer such franchise roles for women than men, and they're often still paid less than the male equivalents.

While her two franchises rolled on, Lawrence turned to challenging roles for the likes of director David O. Russell, winning an Oscar for *Silver Linings Playbook* in 2012. This is smart strategy: to continue the comparison, Hemsworth spent his *Thor* downtime working with Michael Mann on *Blackhat* and Ron Howard on *Rush*, albeit to less awards acclaim. This sort of work proves that you're a Serious Actor concerned about more than money, enhancing your credibility and showing range. In short, it enables you to make more money. Lawrence now had further awards glory *and* two big franchises, and was a prime target for *every* sort of media outlet, equally at home on the cover of *Vogue*, *Time* or *Rolling Stone*.

Yet when Lawrence reteamed with Russell for *American Hustle* the following year, she didn't get quite the compensation you might expect. Late in 2014, there was a hack into high-level Sony emails, hundreds of which were published online. This revealed one December 2013 email showing that Lawrence and her co-star Amy Adams were both on 7 per cent 'points' (profit participation) for that film, while 9 per cent each went to director Russell, co-stars Christian Bale and Bradley Cooper, and supporting actor Jeremy Renner.[11] Lawrence had actually been bumped *up* from 5 per cent to put her on equal footing with Adams, but the studio clearly decided it would be a bridge too far to put the two female leads on the same level as their male contemporaries – though Renner has a smaller role than either woman, and the women had more Oscar nominations between them than all the men.

This hack laid bare the calculations that go into salary debates in stark black and white. All three male leads, of course, had huge franchises behind them, from *Avengers* to *The Hangover* to *The Dark Knight*. But Lawrence was one of the biggest draws in the world and Adams already had four Oscar nominations (she would get another for *Hustle* and later a sixth for *Vice*), as well as commercial success with films like *Enchanted*. On size of role, and size of appeal, they were easily equal to the men in the film's success.

Amy Pascal, head of Columbia at that time, admitted that the emails were authentic – 'There is truth here'[12] – and stayed only long enough to manage the immediate fallout before resigning two months later. You might think that Pascal should have fought harder for pay parity for women – and maybe she would agree in retrospect – but arguably as studio head it was her job to pay as little as she could get away with. Parity will only come if the reputational damage of underpaying women outweighs the savings *and* if the chance of discovering the inequality is high. Right now, the risk of damage is there but there's precious little transparency.

Writing about the affair, Lawrence tended to blame herself. 'When the Sony hack happened and I found out how much less I was being paid than the lucky people with dicks, I didn't get mad at Sony. I got mad at myself. I failed as a negotiator because I gave up early. I didn't want to keep fighting over millions of dollars that, frankly, due to two franchises, I don't need.'[13]

She worried about being seen as 'spoiled' or 'difficult' if she asked for more, in a way that – she guessed – her male co-stars did not. But then men don't get called spoiled or difficult very often, not even Christian 'it's fucking distracting' Bale, a man caught on tape ranting at his *Terminator: Salvation* director of photography during production. Women, however, *do* get castigated for asking for too much. Elizabeth Taylor became the first woman to take a one-million-dollar salary for *Cleopatra* in 1963 and said in response to general gasps that, 'If someone's dumb enough to offer me a million dollars to make a picture, I'm certainly not dumb enough to turn it down.'[14]

Yet her milestone came eighteen years after the first man to do the same: that was Claude Rains, funnily enough on 1945's *Caesar and Cleopatra*. There must be something about ancient Egypt.

Sharon Stone's asking price rose from $500,000 to $4 million after the success of *Basic Instinct*, and a snippy *People* magazine article called her 'cocky' (if not even Sharon Stone is allowed to be confident, who is?).[15] Demi Moore was nicknamed 'Gimme Moore' after her asking price climbed to $12 million for *Striptease*. But as she points out in her autobiography, her then-husband Bruce Willis had just earned $20 million for *Die Hard with a Vengeance* and 'nobody gave him a grabby, greedy nickname'.[16] And note the disparity in their stellar wages. As Moore says, 'In Hollywood at that time – and, unfortunately, still – for some reason a man is worth almost double what a woman is.'

It's not as simple as Lawrence needing to negotiate harder. If you don't know what the men are getting – and you almost certainly don't – then you can't tell whether you are being 'spoiled' or 'difficult' or just asking for your fair share. The Sony email hack caused shockwaves precisely because it proved what people had only suspected: that women and men with comparable (or arguably greater) levels of box-office appeal were being paid at vastly disparate rates.

There's one more Lawrence film worth mentioning: 2016's *Passengers*. There she received a higher salary than her male co-star, Chris Pratt: $20 million to his $12 million, plus 30 per cent of the gross. Contemporary reports explained that Lawrence was the more established star and an Oscar winner, and pointed out that Pratt's asking price had just increased by $2 million following the success of 2015's *Jurassic World*.[17] But it's tempting to see an element of compensation for Lawrence in the Sony-produced film, and her much-trumpeted higher salary as an assurance that other female stars could now trust the studio on fair pay.

Often, parity has happened only when well-intentioned male stars actively took pay cuts to ensure it. Susan Sarandon had equal pay with Paul Newman on 1998's *Twilight* (no relation to the vampire one) only because Newman took a pay cut to fund it.[18] The late, great Chadwick Boseman did the same for co-star Sienna Miller on *21 Bridges*.[19] Emma Stone revealed, in an interview with *Out* magazine, that, 'In my career so far, I've needed my male co-stars to take a pay cut so that I may have parity with them . . . If my male co-star, who has a higher quote than me but believes we are equal, takes a pay cut so that I can match him, that changes my quote in the future and changes my life.'[20] But active sacrifice on the part of individual men shouldn't be what determines fairness.

While some stars, male and female, announced in the immediate aftermath of the Sony hack that they would henceforth be asking for assurances of equal pay across gender lines, the noise died away to a whisper and it's not clear if much real change has followed. Agencies could do much to address the disparity if they chose to do so, since they often represent several people on the same film thanks to 'packaging' deals (see below) and could compare and contrast fees. Comparison can be an instant game changer: genius TV showrunner Michaela Coel's career changed because she asked to look at other creators' contracts, and found that she had sometimes been offered far less than people 'who are perhaps middle-class, male, Anglo-Saxon'.[21] Removing secrecy instantly enhances the chance of change.

But agencies don't always fight hard for all their clients. When Ridley Scott's *All The Money in the World* required last-minute reshoots to replace Kevin Spacey with Christopher Plummer, stars Michelle Williams and Mark Wahlberg were needed back on set. Williams figured it was her duty to help the film and her director, and worked for scale: less than $1,000 in total for the extra shooting days. 'It wouldn't have occurred to me to ask for money for the re-shoots. I just wanted to do the right thing on [Anthony Rapp's] behalf,' she said.[22]

Wahlberg, however, reportedly held the reshoots 'to ransom' (by not approving Plummer, as his contract allowed him to do) while he negotiated a $1.5 million payout for the extra work.[23] The kicker is that both stars were represented by the same agency, WME, which did nothing to alert Williams to the disparity, let alone to close the gap. Even if Williams wanted to 'do the right thing', it was, you might think, up to her agents to alert her to the disparity with her star – but she found out at the same time as the whole world. 'You feel totally de-valued,' she told *Vanity Fair*. 'But that also chimes in with pretty much every other experience you've had in your workplace, so you just learn to swallow it.'[24]

When the story broke, Wahlberg, to his credit, donated the money to Time's Up – but it should never have come to that.[25] The problem is that it's not necessarily in an agency's interest to rock the boat too hard for equality, and potentially jeopardise a huge deal for their bigger-name talent.

The Writers Guild of America (WGA) alleged as much when they threatened strike action in 2019 and 2020. That campaign saw hundreds of writers leave big agencies in protest at the packaging of their scripts. This is an old practice, dating back to the 1950s, that sees agents put together an attractive combination of screenplay, director and star names. In theory, it gives studios something almost ready to shoot, but it can also pay a massive windfall to talent agencies. The writers alleged that their interests were being sacrificed for this greater pay-day, and that they were pressured to take whatever fee was offered rather than having their agent truly negotiate for their individual best interests. If there is any truth to the writers' allegations – something that the agencies concerned largely deny – then it could also be the case that less established, less well-paid stars (for example, women) are also losing out when agencies rush to package them with a bigger name.

For writers, the gender pay gap actually got *worse* between 1999 and 2005, according to a 2009 study.[26] Women's earnings declined by 6 per cent and men's went up by 16 per cent. A 2016 WGA report found that the guild's female members earned $0.68 for every dollar that men did, a decrease of 13 per cent between 2012 and 2014.[27] Black and ethnic minority writers were underemployed, outnumbered five to one by their white peers, and there is a racial pay gap too: that same 2016 report found that 'minority film writers earned 61 cents for every dollar earned by white male film writers'.

The Writers' Guild of Great Britain found a similar result in their report into Gender Inequality and Screenwriters, which looked at films released up to 2016 and found that only 16 per cent of working screenwriters were women – despite the fact that their female-written films outperformed the male average to a 'startling' degree.[29] General Secretary Ellie Peers said in her introduction that, 'Film is not, as popularly believed, driven by the motive to make profit. If it were, women writers would be doing better.'[30] According to the WGGB research, the female-written films were better received by audiences, better reviewed and bigger at the box office than comparable efforts. Yet female writers were almost entirely absent from bigger genres, and made fewer films than their male counterparts.

The fact that women and minority writers are hired in smaller numbers than white men also has a knock-on effect for everyone else's employment prospects. Scripts by women have 8.7 per cent more female characters, for example. Hire a female director and the number of women onscreen goes up even further, by 10.6 per cent – and as already discussed, they hire more female crew members, too.

If most scripts are by white men that exacerbates a lack of roles for women, which in turn means fewer job opportunities for female stand-ins and stuntwomen – who then struggle to build the necessary experience to become senior stunt performers and stunt coordinators. That in turn leads to the grotesque and still current practice of men 'wigging up' to cover women's stunts, and white women being 'painted down' to stunt double for women of colour (someone must have figured that 'painting down' sounds less offensive than 'blacking up', but it shouldn't).[28]

These disparities affect everyone in Hollywood and they're pervasive. Trade paper the *Hollywood Reporter* surveyed average salaries in 2014 for a vast number of different jobs in film, and found that the standard salary, on a big film, for a costume department supervisor was $91 thousand.[31] Not bad, but this traditionally female-dominated role is therefore paid less than a best boy ($92 thousand) or camera operator ($96 thousand). A hairstylist, also a heavily female profession, earned $77 thousand, well below make-up artist, which is male-dominated, at $101 thousand.

If you're wondering why more women don't abandon costume for more lucrative fields, well, here's the kicker. Research beyond the film industry shows that it's not that women choose lower-paying fields; it's that fields *become* lower paying when women go into them.[32] Professions like teaching and social work dropped in status and salary *because they became female-dominated*. Maids earn less than janitors; HR directors less than IT directors. Salaries in IT went *up* when men took over the field. Women's work is not valued *because women do it*, not because it is not important or not done well or because women choose to go into the wrong jobs. If costume departments became male-dominated overnight and camera was taken over by women, those salaries would likely reverse.

Sometimes, outright sexism pushes women into those lower-paid jobs. Much as the field of animation has a cheery, happy-clappy air, it's long been an area where women complained of open discrimination. Selby Kelly, who worked on *Snow White and the Seven Dwarves* for Walt Disney, was told back then that women couldn't animate because they had 'no sense of timing', according to animation professor Nancy Beiman, who knew Kelly well.[33] Kelly had applied to be an animator, but was confined to inking (transferring animators' pencil-drawn work into ink on the finished cels). 'She said in those days, if a woman even walked into the animation building, she was fired. Unless she was a model.'

Not everywhere was so hostile – Chuck Jones hired for talent, including the first Black animator in Hollywood. Beiman got her start at Jack Zander's Animation Parlor. There Beiman was judged on her talent, but not always paid for it. 'After about six months, I was still officially a trainee, but I was redoing animation for older animators who were getting much more money. When I found this out, I went to see Jack and said, "I would like to please have a raise." Jack said, "Well, you're making good money for a girl." I looked him in the eye and said, "Jack, I'm not making good money for an animator. And if you hired me as a girl, I'm charging you double!"'[34]

Beiman forged a successful career, working on the likes of *Hercules* and *Treasure Planet*. But many studios retain the air of a boys' club even now. An animator who has worked at both Disney and Pixar in recent times, and who wishes to remain anonymous, points out both studios' historical paucity of female production designers and solo female directors, the most senior and prestigious roles in the team. Domee Shi became Pixar's first solo female director, on short film *Bao*, only in 2018.

It's no longer the case (if it ever was) that women are a small minority of those trying to get into animation. As with directors, the colleges teaching animation often see a 50–50 gender split, and in some cases have a female (plus non-binary) majority. Yet women still report being sidelined into the lower-paying, and less creatively prestigious, jobs like clean-up artist and PAs or coordinators 'whose job is to be like the mother hen to all the creative geniuses', says that animator.[35] Roles that are female-dominated, like costume designer or shading art director, are the first to be cut or combined with other jobs when there's a downturn. There's even age discrimination against women in the industry despite the fact that – as Disney's Nine Old Men showed – you can animate into your eighties. Animation doesn't rely on physical strength or physical beauty, and companies like DreamWorks, who *do* have friendlier conditions for women, are not noticeably suffering for it. So what's needed to effect actual change is a fundamental shift in the culture.

Things can be different. They even *were* different, sometimes in Hollywood history. Mary Pickford earned about as much as her male compatriots, and set up production deals and ultimately her own studio, United Artists, to ensure that that remained the case. Women also used to have more opportunity for better leading roles. Quigley Publishing's Top Moneymaking Stars, an annual list published between 1912 and 2013, ranked the stars that exhibitors considered the biggest box-office draws, a rough measure of star power across the century.[36] Until the 1940s the top ten was fairly evenly split, with small variations year on year (plus dog star Rin-Tin-Tin, who made a whopping $2,000 per week in his heyday. For what it's worth, he was male). But by 1957 the list turned entirely male for the first time. Women rebounded in the 1960s, thanks to Doris Day, Elizabeth Taylor and Julie Andrews, but the 1970s were a wasteland aside from Barbra Streisand, while the '80s and '90s were heavily male-dominated.

There's an element of subjectivity in these lists: they were compiled from standardised questions sent to exhibitors, who might buy into prevailing social narratives about which films did 'well' beyond expectations. Will Smith didn't top the list until 2008, long after his mid-90s run of hits like *Independence Day* and *Men in Black*, and Denzel Washington didn't appear on it at all until 2001. Voters might see success where they expect to see success: among white men. No women of colour or out-LGBTQ+ stars have appeared on the list this century (the latter have not appeared at all), and only two women, both white, made the number one spot between 2000 and 2013 (Sandra Bullock and Jennifer Lawrence, one year each). It's a snapshot of a film industry that stopped making female-led films a priority in the late 1940s and never went back.

In the studio era, pay was discussed relatively openly, which sometimes allowed women to fight for a better deal. Even so, the pay disparities can be striking. On 1927's *Flesh and the Devil*, male lead John Gilbert made $5,000 per week, while Greta Garbo – already a sensation on only her third US film – earned just $600. Garbo demanded parity, and MGM boss Louis B. Mayer threatened to have her deported to Sweden. The divine Garbo didn't give a hoot, and took a suspension rather than work at the lower rate. At the behest of his marketing department, desperate for her magic touch, Mayer brought her back. On $5,000 a week. Garbo had the great advantage that she was indifferent to Hollywood, and her bosses knew it.

When Myrna Loy asked for a raise, based on the success of her *Thin Man* series and the fact that she was paid half as much as co-star William Powell (he was on $3,000 for the first picture), she was threatened with replacement by Rosalind Russell. She persisted, and won. Incidentally, Loy was also an advocate for better racial representation, objecting publicly to MGM's policy of casting Black people almost exclusively as servants and arguing for, say, briefcase-carrying Black extras in courtroom scenes. (Lest you think that this is giving her praise for doing the absolute least, she continued her advocacy for racial equality throughout her life, later becoming co-chair of the Advisory Council of the National Committee Against Discrimination in Housing and an active UNESCO campaigner).

Ginger Rogers also had to fight for a raise on *Top Hat* with Fred Astaire. The musical favourite was their fourth film together, but her salary still lagged behind his. She had gone from $1,100 per week during their second film, *The Gay Divorcee* (barely more than she had made years before on Broadway), to $1,550. She declined to work on *Swing Time* until she was bumped up to $2,635 per week, and for fifty-two weeks per year rather than the usual forty.[37] After *Top Hat* proved a huge success, she received a $10,000 bonus and another raise to $3,000 per week. Pretty sweet – yet on the same outing Astaire got 10 per cent of the film's profits, or about $238,000.[38]

Such huge deals eventually caused a backlash. In 1938, a guy called Harry Brandt, president of the Independent Theater Owners Association, took out a full-page ad in the *Hollywood Reporter* to complain about stars who were 'box office poison': that is, overpaid relative to their appeal. Brandt's piece named twelve stars, some of the biggest in town. They were: Greta Garbo, Marlene Dietrich, Mae West, Joan Crawford, Kay Francis, Norma Shearer, Luise Rainer, Dolores del Río, Katharine Hepburn, John Barrymore, Edward Arnold and Fred Astaire.

Two-thirds of the list are women, though they were by no means a majority of the best-paid stars even then. You have to wonder if Brandt had based his views entirely on the figures or, to some extent, on an antipathy to successful women. Gossip queen Louella Parsons described the piece as '[throwing] a bombshell into peaceful Hollywood' in her end-of-year review; she called the stars named 'top-notchers' and pointed out that several had already disproved Brandt's 'bitter' piece with hits in its immediate aftermath (Davis's *Jezebel* would have been in cinemas as he wrote, and was a smash; Arnold's *You Can't Take It with You* soon followed).[39] Those hits incidentally proved Parsons' own reaction to the piece correct, where she sniffed that, 'There is nothing the matter with any of these stars that a good picture won't cure.'[40] But not all got that chance; most of del Río's later hits were in Mexico, while Hepburn, dropped from her contract after the affair, had to craft a huge Broadway hit with *The Philadelphia Story* to get back on to the A-list. West and Dietrich were both dropped by Paramount, and the latter was then hired by Universal but at a significantly lower salary. The list may have come from Brandt, but the studios embraced it as a chance to cut their stars down to size.

*　　*　　*

At least those stars could earn big money. Black actors were typically paid *much* less than their white counterparts, with a few notable exceptions. Hattie McDaniel earned perhaps $450 per week on *Gone with the Wind*, but negotiated herself up to a solid $2,000 per week by the time of her hugely successful *Beulah Show* radio performances by the late 1940s.[41] Dorothy Dandridge, on *Carmen Jones*, earned $10,000 a week for the shoot, according to her manager Earl Mills, a good salary by any standards.[42] Her non-exclusive Twentieth Century Fox contract in 1955 then gave her three pictures, one per year, at a salary escalating from $75,000 to $125,000, and star billing above the title. It was a landmark for a Black performer – though with the colour barrier still in place, her actual opportunities were limited, and the interracial romance of *Islands in the Sun* had to be watered down to get past the Production Code.

That colour barrier, and lack of opportunity, still exists. Amma Asante says she is sure that she has been paid less than comparable white men, and that when pushing back on this encountered people who seemed to think that she should be grateful to be able to make a film at all – so she can't *also* expect an equal wage for equal work. All the other structural inequalities working against women amplify one another, particularly the scarcity effect and the lack of reward for success. 'That's how work and pay goes,' Asante says.[43] 'You get paid for your experience, you get paid for your accolades to a certain extent and for the attention and quality of cast you are able to attract towards your film. If you can't do that as well as a man, who has had many times more opportunity than you, that's really not our fault. That's just the way it is.'

Again, the problem of opportunity is magnified for trans women, disabled women and women of colour, as Viola Davis pointed out in 2018. 'I got the Oscar, I got the Emmy, I got the two Tonys, I've done Broadway, I've done off-Broadway, I've done TV, I've done film, I've done all of it,' she said.[44] 'I have a career that's probably comparable to Meryl Streep, Julianne Moore, Sigourney Weaver . . . They had the same path as me, and yet I am nowhere near them, not as far as money, not as far as job opportunities, nowhere close to it.' Davis's estimated net worth of $12 million is less than a quarter of Moore's estimated $50 million; Streep is worth an estimated $150 million.

At least Davis, Streep and Moore have careers that have lasted into their fifties, allowing them to keep building up their accolades and steadily improve their quotes. That wasn't always possible in Hollywood history, because women's careers are not just lower-paid but, usually, shorter. In a town that prizes the beauty of youth rather than the beauty of age, roles for women historically dried up as they passed into the second half of their thirties – because they were objectified by the male gaze, valued as objects rather than people. It's not that women stop being talented as they get more experienced, it's that they're simply not given the roles to prove it.

Once again, that's in stark contrast to men. There's a general rule that actors don't win the Best Actor Oscar before they're forty. Adrien Brody is the youngest-ever winner, at twenty-nine, and even DiCaprio had to wait until he was forty-one, after four nominations. But for women, twenties and thirties are the sweet spot: thirty-two women won Best Actress in their twenties, more than twice the number who won it in their forties. After that there's a serious dearth of opportunity until after their sixtieth birthday. Throughout the whole twentieth century, only one actress won an Oscar in her fifties, Shirley Booth in Come Back, Little Sheba (Julianne Moore and Renee Zellweger have recently joined her). The average age for a female Oscar winner is thirty-six, eight years younger than the average male winner, and that's *after* eighty-year-old Jessica Tandy pulled up the average and Katharine Hepburn won three times in her sixties.

The Oscars, in this respect, illustrate the kind of roles women get to play: love (or sex) interests, young mothers and then skip a few steps to get to quirky grandmothers. Not authority figures or protagonists in adulthood; nothing too threatening. If anything, the Awards undercount the number of roles only open to women in their twenties and thirties, since many of them are too flimsy to attract a nomination.

Lana Turner once said, 'It used to be that when an actress reached thirty she was considered almost washed up . . . The most dreadful thing was when a star had to play a mother. That was the beginning of her professional end.'[45] According to director Rob Cohen a sticking point for Rachel Weisz, in returning for 2008's *The Mummy 3*, was that she did not want to play the mother of a grown man (she was thirty-seven at the time so the maths of an adult son didn't even make sense).[46] Weisz's explanation was a scheduling conflict. There is still at least the fear of a career penalty when you're seen to be ageing.

On the other hand there is a venerable tradition of male stars acting opposite significantly younger women as they age. Fred Astaire (born 1904) starred opposite Ginger Rogers (1911) in the 1930s, Rita Hayworth (1918) in the '40s and Audrey Hepburn (1929) in the '50s. Cary Grant (also 1904) started off playing against the slightly older likes of Mae West (1893), Marlene Dietrich (1901) and Irene Dunne (1898), and Katharine Hepburn (1907) in the '30s. Then he too slid the other way, working with Ingrid Bergman (1915) and Ann Sheridan (also 1915) in the late '40s, and Grace Kelly (1929) and Sophia Loren (1934) in the '50s.

When women date younger men onscreen, like Gloria Swanson and William Holden in *Sunset Boulevard*, it's usually a plot point that ends in tragedy. Men dating younger women is just an average Tuesday. Nor is the phenomenon purely historical: Tom Cruise's leading ladies started off occasionally older (*Top Gun*, *Risky Business*) but more recently have hovered around the two-decades-younger mark: Sarah Wright in *American Made* (twenty-two years younger), Annabelle Wallis in *The Mummy* (also twenty-two years) and Rebecca

Ferguson in the *Mission: Impossible* franchise (twenty-two years again). At thirty-seven, Maggie Gyllenhaal was told she was 'too old' to play the wife of a fifty-five-year-old leading man.[47] The casting of Monica Bellucci, fifty, opposite Daniel Craig, forty-seven, in *Spectre* was much heralded as a groundbreaking older Bond woman – but she had perhaps five minutes of screentime before he spent the film with Léa Seydoux (thirty). Also, is it really a stretch if she's Monica freakin' Bellucci? Nobody's picky enough to check her date of birth.

But this sort of casting just reflects reality, right? A world where powerful older men fetishise young women. And maybe it reflects the unstoppable studliness of Tom Cruise/Cary Grant/whoever. A certain amount of male ego-boosting certainly seems to be involved. But there's a chicken-and-egg question of causation there: is Hollywood normalising and glamourising this sort of age differ-ence? Either way it's a patriarchal and anti-feminist stance that ties a woman's value to her youth, while allowing a man to gain the power that apparently renders him irresistible to women born when he was in college.

What are older women to do? The role of love interest to men their own age is largely closed to them, and as *The First Wives Club* cast discovered, Hollywood persists in treating ladies of a certain age as a risk *even when they have a hit behind them.* Historically the only remain-ing path was to play grotesque – and even that took some selling. When director Robert Aldrich set out to make *What Ever Happened To Baby Jane?*, the horror classic starring Joan Crawford and Bette Davis, he found financing difficult. 'They didn't want to put their money on two old bags,' said Davis, who was then fifty-four – the same age as Nicole Kidman or Halle Berry in 2021.[48] Before the film came out (it was a smash), Davis took out an ad in *Variety* on her own behalf, claiming not only thirty years of experience but that she was 'mobile still and more affable than rumor would have it'. She was poking fun at her fiery reputation, but underneath there's a sincere plea. 'I've gone from being "most wanted" to "help wanted",' she joked in a TV interview.[49]

Meryl Streep's entire twenty-first-century career has disproved the idea that no one wants to watch older women, but she's still written off as an outlier so Hollywood can cling to the old myths. Each time a female-led film succeeds, especially one with an older lead, it's treated as a freakish sleeper hit that no one could have seen coming, or credit is assigned elsewhere somehow. *The Devil Wears Prada; Mamma Mia; Eat, Pray, Love;* back to *Thelma & Louise* and *A League of their Own.* Female-led movies come out, become smash hits – and yet each is discounted as a model for future success.

The situation *is* beginning to change, but oh so slowly. Streep's continued career helps. So does the work of actresses like Sandra Bullock, Julianne Moore, Nicole Kidman, Geena Davis, Julia Roberts and Reese Witherspoon. Many of these women have started to take active producing roles to ensure that there is material to play and decent money for it – and that's often netted a fortune for the studios that support them as well as the stars themselves. Studies by the USC Annenberg Inclusion Initiative, Geena Davis Institute on Gender in Media, Center for the Study of Women in Television and Film at San Diego State University and others have *proved* that much of the received wisdom about women's diminished box-office appeal is myth and not fact, and that is beginning to change the picture, while the post-#MeToo willingness of women to speak out means they're not putting up with the same old excuses.

But to be sure that all women are getting equal pay and equal opportunities for equal work, *everyone* needs to step up. Studios need to do the right thing and not the cheap one; they need to share salary information, most of all. They need to screw their courage to the sticking place and tell stories *not* about white men, making room for diverse voices. Privileged people – whether male or white or more established – need to be transparent about their compensation so that their colleagues have a chance to negotiate for a fair wage. Look at Jessica Chastain who, on discovering that co-star Octavia Spencer habitually earned less than she did, tied their salaries together and insisted on equal pay.[50] Don't just say you're an ally; do the work.

Everyone needs to be conscious of their bias, to ensure that women and other current minorities can negotiate freely and have equal opportunities. Agents need to work as hard for marginalised groups as they do for the male A-listers. Ideally, the Byzantine systems of compensation would be simplified – or at least clarified.

Then we need to change the film ecosystem a little further, to ensure that everyone's story gets the same chance at success. We need to look at the industry's gatekeepers beyond the studio gates, the forces that award the accolades and acclaim that pay systems rely on. We need to look at festivals, critics and awards.

12

Gatekeeping
Or, who critiques the critics?

IMAGINE YOU'RE a director who has just made your first independent feature. After, most likely, a decade or more making short films and corporate efforts, you convinced someone to trust you with the tens of thousands of dollars needed for even a micro-budgeted film and decided whether you're more of a baseball-cap director or a scarf-wearing director (they're all one or the other). You have survived bad weather, temperamental actors, sleep deprivation and probably a minor panic attack. Congratulations, you have achieved something extraordinary.

To convince people to let you do it again, maybe with a bit more money, it would help to make a splash. That means you have to get past the industry's gatekeepers and convince festivals, critics and awards bodies that your film matters. All three can prove serious obstacles for women. Because festival programmers, film critics and awards voting bodies have all been white male-dominated for most of their history, and the films that they anoint skew accordingly.

Only one film by a female director has ever won the Palme d'Or at Cannes (Jane Campion's *The Piano*). Only one woman has ever won Best Director at the Oscars (Kathryn Bigelow, with 2009's *The Hurt Locker*). Only *five* women have even been nominated in that category, all of them white. Out of ninety-two Best Picture winners, only seventeen have been female-led. Studies show[1] that male film critics outnumber women by almost two to one, and judge films with female leads more harshly than those with male protagonists (also more harshly than female critics judge male-led films).

So not only do female directors and female stars struggle to get their films made, they then struggle to have them taken as seriously as those about, or led by, men. There's a sort of gatekeeping in the industry that keeps writing off women.

But there's cause for hope. Gatekeepers, by nature, are less opaque in their choices than the financiers who decide which films get made: gatekeepers' choices are out in the open, and that means that the wider public has become aware of the disparities that exist, and has begun to exert pressure for change.

'The thing that has been so problematic is the language that people use,' says Melissa Silverstein, founder and editor of Women and Hollywood and Artistic Director of the Athena Film Festival. 'They always use "best", "most qualified", and all those things. They [say they] don't look at women, they don't look at race, and things like that. Firstly, I think that's not true. Secondly, I believe people have to be pro-actively inclusive. And that is something that the industry has been very worried about because that will create an industry that's not dominated by white men.'[2]

For many young filmmakers, festivals are their first key step towards an audience. Getting your film into a film festival can win useful plaudits that may help you get a distributor who will put it in cinemas; the distributors may even be in attendance, looking to purchase films. The reality for most early-career filmmakers is that they will not be going to the big festivals like Cannes, Venice or Toronto. Sundance has a better record of promoting first-time (American) filmmakers, at least, but all of these mega-festivals have limited spaces, and hold some slots for established names who can bring in the punters. But those huge festivals still set the tone for the film industry, so they're worth considering.

The yen for established names means – for now – lots of men. Festivals have a tendency to share the rest of the industry's veneration for auteurism, and it means they look for a certain kind of filmmaker even among newcomers. Think about it: much of the storied reputation of Cannes, Sundance or Venice lies in the fact that these were the first places where you could see films by major cineastes. But in all their history those cineastes have been lured along by an environment made to appeal to men.

Cannes bills itself as the home of the auteur. It was designed to welcome filmmakers from all over the world in the 1930s as a pointed rejoinder to the then-fascist-controlled Venice Film Festival. To the Festival's credit it's been a European gateway for many Asian filmmakers and some South American auteurs, and an enormous step up on to the world stage for many talented voices. But it decidedly has favourites who are invited back again and again. If Tarantino's new film is ready by May, he can be pretty sure of an invite. Ditto the Dardenne brothers, Pedro Almodóvar, Ken Loach, Xavier Dolan. Very few of the regular Cannes darlings are female. Festival director Thierry Frémaux bemoaned the lack, saying that he always welcomed new films from Kathryn Bigelow and Jane Campion – which is all well and good but perhaps insufficient.

In recent years Cannes has invited regular controversy in its attitude to women. There has been a consistent paucity of places for female-made films in the main competition, and of course the great shoe controversy of 2015 – which saw some women stopped from attending galas because they weren't wearing heels – didn't help. Yes, in the year of our lord two thousand and fifteen, Cannes security guards 'sur le tapis rouge' stopped women in flat shoes because they considered them insufficiently glamorous for the dress code.[3] Those women included Danish producer Valeria Richter, who opted for flats because part of her foot and big toe had been amputated a few years before. Most tragically of all, Richter battled through this sexist bureaucracy to watch Gus Van Sant's *The Sea of Trees*, which was dreadful.[4]

As regards the programme, Thierry Frémaux reacted to all criticism of the festival's diversity with, essentially, an elegant Gallic shrug. 'I continue to find it difficult to consider films based on gender,' he told *Variety* in 2019, when the festival featured a then-record twelve films from thirteen female directors, out of forty-seven. 'I'm a supporter of having women filmmakers express a certain artistic, creative and feminine sensibility. Some things are purely feminine. [Gender parity]'s a question that has to be addressed to the rest of the industry. Cannes is only at the end of the cycle and reflects the fact that for a long time – and it is absurd – our society has been dominated by men . . . How could Cannes be the miracle of a potential parity if the film world as a whole has yet to accomplish it?'[5]

Let's assume he doesn't *only* support women expressing a 'feminine sensibility' for our own peace of mind, but the statement does smack of some hand-waving of responsibility. It's true that the industry as a whole enables fewer women to make films than men, so at the present time there could be a disparity in Western films (less so in some other countries; Senegal has always punched above its weight in terms of female filmmakers, for example, and Middle Eastern countries sometimes have a better gender balance). But then again Cannes prides itself on discovering new talent, and if you were *really* looking for new voices to shake things up, you'd be looking beyond white men.

Tricia Tuttle, Director of BFI Festivals including the London Film Festival, also noted the pipeline problems in terms of female-made films. They're easily 50 per cent of shorts and often documentary submissions, but fall away the further up the budget ladder you go. Still, the LFF has still managed to increase the percentage of female-made films in the programme from 30 per cent in 2017 to 38 per cent in 2019.

Frémaux's interview followed, but did not reflect, a rather more coherent statement in 2018, when eighty-two female filmmakers, including Eva Husson and Ava DuVernay, walked the Cannes red carpet to draw attention to the Festival's treatment of women. That year's festival jury president, actress Cate Blanchett, was among the protest's leaders and said, 'We are eighty-two women, representing the number of female directors who have climbed these stairs since the first edition of the Cannes film festival in 1946. In the same period, 1,688 male directors have climbed these very same stairs.'[6] Agnès Varda, the Cannes veteran, added, 'Women are not a minority in the world, and yet our industry says the opposite. We want this to change.'[7] In response, Cannes pointed out that they had (finally) ensured a gender balance on their selection committees (which choose the films in competition), a move that followed a challenge by two 2017 jurors, actress Jessica Chastain and director/actress Agnès Jaoui.

Cannes' older neighbour, Venice, is if anything more glamorous – there's something special about arriving by boat – and a win is only fractionally less prestigious these days. The good news is that Venice has done a little better by female directors in terms of prizes: the Golden Lion has gone to women four times out of fifty-four, with awards for Agnès Varda, Margarethe von Trotta, Sofia Coppola and Mira Nair. But in terms of competition it's rarely better: in 2019 Venice had just two films made by women out of twenty-one. The year before it had just one.

'If the Venice festival is an example of toxic masculinity because they have just one film by a woman in competition, then I don't understand why a festival that instead has two should not be considered toxic,' said Paolo Baratta, president of La Biennale, which runs the Festival. 'In that case, all we would have to do is have three women in competition next year and the problem would be solved. This would be ridiculous!'[8]

It would – because the problem would not be solved until the Festival is as likely to be female-dominated as male-dominated. Both Cannes and Venice signed up to a 5050 by 2020 pledge in 2016 – but that in no way commits them to a 50–50 per cent quota on films. As Cannes saw it, the pledge committed them to greater transparency on the composition of their selection panels and programmers, statistics on submissions, and to 'work towards parity' on their executive boards.[9] Venice was similarly reticent, committing to transparency but no suggestion of quotas.[10]

Perhaps it's not festivals that should have quotas, but funders. Tuttle says, 'When you're investing in films, like the BFI [British Film Institute], it's really important to have quotas. But when you're programming a festival, it has to be quality first.'[11] The issue for all these festivals is ensuring that 'quality' doesn't equal 'looks like other, familiar male- and male-made films'.

'Sometimes women might see things differently,' says Joana Vicente, co-head of the Toronto International Film Festival (TIFF). 'Or, you know, what has been defined as a "quality" film might also be debatable. It's interesting, sometimes people say that, "We just judge on the quality of film and some of the films directed by women were just not at that level." Says who?! The man in charge? What is this idea of quality? Who's defining what that is? I think [a balanced team] makes for better conversations.'[12]

This question is particularly stressful for young filmmakers. Are their films rejected because they're not good enough, or because they're just not familiar? Claire Oakley's impressive debut feature, *Make Up*, was widely submitted to build its profile. 'In some ways it's quite a feminine film in that it's a female lead and it's quite introspective. I don't know, if it was about a young boy or had more masculine themes, whether it would have got into more festivals. It's been accepted now to three festivals; we're just at the beginning of our run. But all three, it was programmed by a woman, which was interesting.'[13]

'Quality' and 'diversity' just can't be in opposition. Arguably TIFF has succeeded in finding both. Venice's loss was their gain in 2019, since they got to launch highly successful female-made films like *Hustlers* and *A Beautiful Day in the Neighbourhood*. Vicente, who became co-head from 2019, found a gender-balanced programming team already in place. She blames the pipeline of production for the remaining disparity but explains that, 'Every year the number of women submitting is going up. Even now, 30 per cent [of features] seems such a low number, but ten years ago was a lot smaller so there's progress. [When] we give a platform to these films, the platform that we give male directors, people were incredibly responsive, so I think it pays to lift them up. The talent is there. We were close to the 50 per cent mark [in 2019] on the more high-profile sections.'[14]

TIFF also has serious cachet as an Oscar launch pad. The People's Choice Award has become a strong Oscar bellwether, with eight winners between 2008 and 2018 going on to win the Oscar for Best Picture. Any mission to promote inclusivity of talent at TIFF has to balance what its large, paying audience (450,000 people a year) is going to want to see. Yet that can be an advantage for new female filmmakers too: *if* your film plays well at TIFF, that's a sign not only of artistic strength but potential mass appeal. Include enough films by women here and you might even change the sort of film that is taken seriously and treated as important.

But of all the major festivals, perhaps the best placed to change the picture is Sundance, which was designed as a showcase for American independent filmmakers and a nursery for new talent. Sundance exploded in popularity after launching or helping to launch the careers of a generation of American men including Tarantino, Soderbergh, Thomas Anderson, Aronofsky and Jarmusch. A place at this sort of festival is a mark of not just talent but cool.

For Catherine Hardwicke, with her first film *Thirteen*, Sundance was a big deal.[15] 'When your film gets into the competition, your life instantly changes. You've got to do everything you can to parlay that into a lasting career.' At that point you're on track: you have a slot at a major festival and a good chance of being picked up by a distributor.

Hardwicke was working 24/7 to finish in time – 'the print was pretty much still wet' – and reached the festival 'overwhelmed, exhausted' and thrown into a publicity whirl. She won the Directing prize (drama), and landed a distributor in Fox Searchlight. All went just as it should, in that sense – though the film's tiny release meant that it never made much money.

Marielle Heller was selected as a Writing and Directing fellow at the Sundance Institute in 2012 to workshop her first film, *Diary of A Teenage Girl*, which then debuted at the Sundance Festival in 2015. 'Sundance was my creative family and I felt so supported by them,' she says. 'I think it does help women and non-binary filmmakers to feel like they have a platform and a place where they will be given a fair shot.'[16]

Heller made lasting creative friendships at the Sundance Institute – Chloé Zhao, Ryan Coogler and David Lowery were all there around the same time – but for her it's the potential of festivals like this to widen the scope of storytelling that really matters.

'The indie, lower-budget world can feel a little bit like second-class citizen, or like we're not being given the same budgets, perhaps, as our male, white, hetero counterparts,' says Heller. 'But in many ways, we're leading the way [and] Hollywood studios with such interest in money are a little slower on the uptake when it comes to recognising that diverse stories matter. People want these stories; they want to see themselves reflected in film.'

That's the importance of festivals, their potential to create new marquee names of a more varied type to draw in the next generation of moviegoers. And it is in 'defence of the new' that critics come into their own. Or at least, where they should. But criticism is also dominated by a certain sort of person.

'When a man gives his opinion he's a man, but when a woman gives her opinion she's a bitch,' Bette Davis once said.[17] It's bad news for female critics, who give nothing else. In the English-speaking world, about two-thirds of film critics are male, and these men write a majority of reviews across every genre, according to research by Dr Martha Lauzen at the Center for the Study of Women in Television and Film at San Diego State University.[18]

Like film directors, then, this cohort is not a representative cross-section of the audience, but a small slice of it. It's the same slice that is also represented in onscreen heroes, in Hollywood boardrooms and in directors' chairs, and it's tempting to see at least correlation there. These are the people that Hollywood lavishes its attention upon, and tells stories about. Is that why they grew up loving film, and went into a relatively low-paying profession, so they can talk about movies all the time? Critics are, almost without exception, passionate about their field, even the vicious ones. But did more men fall for film than women because so many films speak directly to them? Certainly middle-aged male critics and middle-aged male filmmakers end up in a mutually reinforcing circle that determines what films get made, what films get attention and what films are considered 'important'.

That may make it sound like film criticism is a weird secret society with strange robes and eldritch symbols, and of course it's nothing of the sort (that I know of – possibly I'm just not invited). But if cinema has been speaking to you your entire life in your own language; if men who look just like you have often been the centre of the narrative, you might feel more fervent about the power of cinema than someone who has only ever seen themselves reflected as a terrorist, a sex object or a figure of pity. That sense of being personally invested in cinema might lead you into a career where you watch and write about films rather than a more sensible job in law* or banking.

You may think that this doesn't matter, that critics are no longer relevant in a world with IMDb scores set by audiences. But critics, or at least the critical consensus, *do* matter in Hollywood and *do* affect how films and filmmakers are treated. Since the very earliest days, studios need money but also crave acclaim. After all, sometimes acclaim brings in dollar bonuses. The ticketing company Fandango bought Rotten Tomatoes in 2016, and thereafter started to put RT's 'rotten' or 'fresh' tomato logos next to film titles, adding to the importance that studio executives attached to a 'fresh' verdict. Even before that, in 2015, executives credited part of the success of films like *Mission: Impossible – Rogue Nation* and *Straight Outta Compton* to high RT scores, and the underperformance of films like *The Man from U.N.C.L.E.* to lower ones. There's an obvious complicating factor to such conclusions – good films tend to score higher than bad films, and audiences generally respond better to good films, so the score may be correlation rather than causation – but the numbers are a nice, simple qualifier for overworked executives, so they are adopted by some as an easy measure of quality.

White male critics are the group most invested in the success of the cinema we have now, and despite a general effort at open-mindedness and feminism, it shows. The 'canon' of important, influential, must-watch films is anointed by these men; they collectively set the parameters of discussion. Then, being the majority, they become the model of what a critic looks like, and minority critics can find the environment less welcoming than their white male peers.

---

* I was a lawyer once. Sometimes I think how much richer I'd be if I'd stuck with that. Mostly, though, I'd rather spend my days arguing about whether *Tenet* really makes sense or not.

'There's the element of, if she can see it, she can be it,' says critic Anna Smith, host of the Girls On Film podcast and former Chair of the London Film Critics' Circle. 'So a lot of young women are growing up with the misperception that film criticism is a male game. And, of course, men are growing up with that unconscious bias about what a film critic looks like, and those men become editors and those men then hire people – just as we have those issues about directors and other jobs in the industry.'[19]

Women in media may be paid less for equal work (or even paid less when in more senior positions), and there have been claims in media of women being forced into redundancy at a higher rate than men – especially older women in TV work.[20] Assuming you can get a job as a critic, and earn a living (not always easy, especially for writers of colour), then you may still find yourself sidelined into less prestigious areas, stuck writing the 130-word round-up review of the minor kids' movie rather than the 800-word think piece on Christopher Nolan's latest. Akua Gyamfi of The British Blacklist points out that critics writing for Black publications, or similarly focused titles, are sometimes only invited to the films related to that identity and not the big, general titles. 'It's fighting to say actually, some Black organisations aren't just about the Black audience and they want to review everything,' says Gyamfi. 'Same as women don't just want to see *Little Women*; don't put a barrier on who you think of.'[21]

At least women have always managed to exist in criticism – albeit mostly white, middle-class women (Hi!). Dorothy Parker dabbled in film criticism when she wasn't writing about theatre or literature, before she joined the Dark Side and went to Hollywood to write movies. In the early days of Hollywood there were writers like Geraldyn Dismond, Djuna Barnes and Iris Barry, and female critics have often been influential. B. Ruby Rich coined the term 'New Queer Cinema' in 1992 to describe filmmakers like Todd Haynes and Gregg Araki;[22] bell hooks in 1996 accused Tarantino's films of representing only 'white cool' (ouch: nothing could hurt him more);[23] Claude-Marie Trémois challenged the French New Wave's treatment of women.[24]

There were even a few decades, mid-century, where women dominated major jobs in film criticism because reviews had been exiled to the women's or lifestyle pages. In the UK, the mid-twentieth century was coloured by the rival tastes of Dilys Powell at *The Sunday Times* and C. A. Lejeune at the *Observer*. In the US of the late 1960s there was Pauline Kael holding forth at the *New Yorker* and in the women's magazine *McCall's*, championing her favourites and shaping film debate. Kael was controversial, often outspoken and sometimes plain wrong, but she proved influential in speaking out for new, underdog filmmakers. Her example inspired many of the young men who would come to dominate film criticism in her wake. Lili Anolik, writing in *Vanity Fair*, went further: she said that Kael 'was an artist, always and invariably, the equal to any director or actor she covered, the superior to most'.[25]

Yet when film started to be taken more seriously as an art form, film reviews shifted into a more prestigious niche, and serious young men found their spot. The 'movie brats' who didn't make films would explain to the world why they mattered and would come to dominate film criticism.

'I grew up reading Pauline Kael and then Stephanie Zacharek, women that I just gravitated towards,' says Jo Robinson, a podcaster, critic and pop culture writer at *Vanity Fair*. 'They're so bright and fantastic. I didn't realise until I got into the profession how few there were, how I had to actively seek them out. Actually, it was more non-white critics than female critics who really helped me understand [that] when criticism is so masculine and so white, it has such power to shape our perception of what are the valuable stories to tell.'[26]

If female critics have never been entirely alone, as female directors like Ida Lupino or Dorothy Arzner were, often we've been alone at our publications. Being in such a minority is odd. You're often challenged on your knowledge, and have to prove your familiarity with the canon of films accepted as great cultural or commercial touchstones – almost all of them male-led and male-directed. If your road to criticism started with *Clueless, But I'm A Cheerleader* or *Drumline* rather than *Star Wars*, that should not hold you back – yet film criticism culture sometimes treats only one of these routes as legitimate.

This can affect how you write. Making a representational critique of a film, as a woman or LGBTQ+ person or person of colour, is still sometimes treated as niche, 'identity politics' – but viewing everything through a white, straight, male lens is somehow seen as normal. Film critic and psychology student Wendy Lloyd made a study of the disparity in how her male and female peers write about film as part of her Masters dissertation. She found female critics significantly more likely to balance feminist criticism of a film with more positive references to a film's cinematography or good performances. 'It's like, in order to navigate what's presumed to be necessary analysis for a film critic,' says Lloyd, 'I'm going to have to park the social [criticism] for a minute and separately consider the aesthetics.' In contrast, she found male critics 'much more emboldened and confident discussing this stuff . . . which highlighted the greater privilege for the male voice. [There's] this default position of authority.'[27] That was the case even when they were dead wrong, e.g. in assigning all the blame for *Red Sparrow*'s shortcomings to star Jennifer Lawrence rather than the wider filmmaking team.

While 'the canon' embraces foreign films, it's far slower to embrace English-speaking films that are female-led, or teen-focused, or about people of colour. The films that a critic is supposed to know, and probably admire, are mostly about white, straight men – and that's only now beginning to open up. A female critic's enthusiasm for this male-led canon is not necessarily disingenuous or fake – you will prise Billy Wilder's films from my cold dead hands and all those '80s action films with them – but then we're the ones who have made it into the profession. How many people who would have made great critics were put off by all the gangster movies they had to endure to earn their stripes? And how much is the profession failing audiences by failing to look beyond the majority's own frame of reference?

In 2019, Anne Cohen at Refinery29,[28] a magazine site aimed at young women, began to address that question with a series called 'Writing Critics' Wrongs'. She aimed to reassess female-focused and teen movies (*She's All That*, *Pretty Woman*, etc.) that critics panned even as their target audiences embraced them. 'Going back and reading the reviews, the disrespect that most critics have for that demographic, especially of young girls, is so striking,' says Cohen. 'It's crazy because women are taught to empathise with men's stories, but men aren't taught the opposite. It's as if they can't compute something that is not specifically tailored to them.'[29]

It's that failure of empathy that keeps coming up. If women have little choice but to learn to empathise with male leads in films, men seem to struggle with it; witness critic Richard Brody's lament in his review of *Hustlers* that we didn't hear more from some of the male victims of the girl gang.[30] That's even aside from critical grotesquerie about female stars, sometimes from giants of the profession: David Thomson's assertion that Nicole Kidman's eyes are so wide she could 'do blow jobs with them' in *To Die For* (er, what?!),[31] or Andrew Sarris complaining that *The Notorious Bettie Page* did not turn him on and was 'smugly anti-erotic'[32] (the point of that female-directed biopic was to reclaim the pin-up as a person). Then there's Anthony Lane drooling over Elastigirl in *Incredibles 2*[33] or Todd McCarthy sexualising the teenage *Dora the Explorer*[34] or Harry Knowles reviewing *Blade 2*[35] via an extended cunnilingus metaphor. Sometimes male critics assume they're guys talking to other guys about guy stuff, and women are not even considered as an audience.

The whiteness and maleness of criticism can cause them to miss great films. bell hooks wrote of Julie Dash's *Daughters of the Dust*, a gorgeous, dreamlike film about Black women, 'This focus caused critics (especially white males) to critique the film negatively or to express many reservations. Clearly, racism and sexism so overdetermine spectatorship – not only what we look at but who we identify with – that viewers who are not black females find it hard to empathize with the central characters in the movie. They are adrift without a white presence in the film.'[36]

This fault of empathy is why female critics, when dispatched to see the rom-com, teen movie or family film, take the job. One female critic I spoke to loves sci-fi movies more than anything – but is usually assigned romances and family movies (she has no children, incidentally). You take it because you know that some men will be so turned off by the basic form of the genre that they could be more negative than the film deserves.

That's not wild speculation, incidentally; male critics really are harsher on films with female leads than the reverse. Dr Lauzen's research has consistently found that male critics are less positive about films with a female protagonist than female critics, whereas women are roughly as positive as men when reviewing films with a male protagonist.[37] Women were more likely to review female-made films, but then that doesn't help the careers of female critics if there are fewer female-led films.

This is not to say that only women should review female-led films, or only Black people should review Black-led films, or anything else. When Brie Larson said, 'I do not need a forty-year-old white dude to tell me what didn't work for him about *A Wrinkle in Time*. It wasn't made for him,'[38] she was expressing a good point in an overstated way. It's not that white men have nothing to say about Ava DuVernay's film, or that they can't have a valid opinion on it. The point is that they should not be the *only* people discussing it, or the dominant group, as they currently are. It might still have had lacklustre reviews, but with a little more diversity there might be a more nuanced discussion of what works and what does not. And as *LA Times* critic Justin Chang asked, 'Who gets to say for whom a film is made, in the end – the filmmakers? The marketing executives? What about those viewers who love a movie, whether or not they fit the target demographic? How seriously do we take the forty-year-old white dude for whom *A Wrinkle in Time* worked beautifully, versus, say, a thirty-year-old Black woman who found it disappointing?'[39] Maybe we need both, and in about equal numbers.

There is one more reason that white men dominate criticism, however; a more pernicious one. Criticism is all about opinions: no review is anything more, however much analysis or informed comparison it includes. And women are not socially awarded for having strongly held opinions; it's not seen as *feminine*. Some men react to a clearly expressed female opinion as if their entire being has just been insulted, and all defences must be brought to bear immediately. Yet by definition critics flaunt their opinion-having, and they attempt to bolster their opinions with knowledge – and again, what's less feminine than flaunting your knowledge?

So a woman who goes into criticism *will* be called shrill, bossy, bitchy, stuck up, humourless (you also 'must be joking' about your views), unqualified, fat (it keeps coming up, even if you are thin) and ugly. We are 'biased', 'not objective', 'rude', every queer slur word going, or an 'uneducated SJW savage', in one delightfully nonsensical claim.* We get death threats. We're told we should be fired, or that people will try to have us fired, or that we must have slept our way into the job. Letters are written to our editors complaining about us.

---

* I asked female critics on Twitter what insults had been thrown at them; all of these were quoted in the responses.

Critics of colour get the worst abuse; even mildly critical reviews from them can trigger racist comments. Queer critics also receive particularly vicious attacks. You'll be told that you care too much or know too little. You'll be overthinking it or failing to understand its subtleties. You'll be told that the film is simply not aimed at you because of your skin colour or gender identity or sexuality, and that you're spoiling everyone else's fun. Some men will call you a slut for not liking *Joker* – again, rather mystifyingly. Surely it would be sluttier to like *Joker*? Someone call Harley Quinn and ask.

A poll of fellow critics revealed a world of gendered hostility to female reviews, particularly over certain films that riled up a certain kind of man. One critic was called 'clueless', 'talentless' and 'amateurish' after writing a positive review of *Star Wars: The Last Jedi*; another was told that 'cancer should have killed her' and that she was singlehandedly responsible for the 'pussification' of her country (impressive work, really. All on her own?). I've personally been told that I shouldn't review films like *Ghost Rider* 2 because I can't possibly understand them (I don't think it's wildly arrogant to claim my intellect is up to *that* challenge).

Men write blog posts thousands of words long explaining why we are incapable of appreciating *Game of Thrones* and therefore why our reviews are wrong. The *New York Post* published an entire article claiming that 'Women are not capable of understanding *Goodfellas*', which must have come as a shock to its legions of female fans.[40] Some fandoms are more like cults than mere passing fancies, and they react accordingly to any criticism from those they perceive as outsiders – even if we are also fans. And they are *much* more offended if criticism is coming from women.

'[Listeners]'ll say, I can't believe Joanna was so hard on X,' says Jo Robinson. 'And I feel sort of gaslit by it because I swear to you, my male co-hosts were even harder on this exact same opinion. But I am the awful, unreasonable one.'[41]

Listeners will police women's tone more than men's, or (on audio formats) their vocal fry, or their appearance on TV formats. Of course, this comes from a small proportion of consumers, and while it can take a toll on critics' mental health this is still a wonderful job that we are privileged to do. But it's worth noting that this exists, because our white, straight male colleagues don't get it on the same scale. They get argument and abuse, of course, but the particular assumption that they are not qualified, or mean, or somehow physically unfit, which colours so much abuse of female critics, is largely absent.

The good news is that things *are* improving. The #MeToo movement opened the eyes of some editors to the need for more female writers, and Black Lives Matter has made the urgency of looking beyond the white middle classes clear. It's getting easier for women and under-represented groups to break through, says Anna Smith. 'I think the advent of social media has been really good, because there are a lot of women who've been able to get heard and some [are] major critics now on national newspapers. I'm finally getting asked about female directors, I'm getting asked about female film critics, I'm getting asked about female-focused films, and why aren't there more.'[42]

More widely, social media helped women realise that we're not alone, that we're not completely crazy to think that we need to cover *Twilight* as well as *Transformers*, and that we can argue back with all the senior white men because – whatever they think – their opinions are not law. 'It can be intimidating as a young woman,' says Anne Cohen, 'because you're constantly second guessing yourself and your opinions, but ultimately the thing to keep in mind is that really they're the wrong ones.'[43]

A more diverse critical base might cheerlead a more diverse range of films, and help a wider selection of films to build awards momentum and gain the career possibilities that come with that acclaim.

Then there's just one more barrier to negotiate: the fact that awards bodies also seem to think that male-focused films matter more.

'Good morning to everyone that's writing me about the #goldenglobes I feel you but know this. I was on the inside for the first time this year. These are not our people and they do not represent us. Do not look for justice in the awards system. We are building a new world.'

So wrote Alma Har'el on 19 December 2019, after the 2020 Golden Globes nominations were announced and her brilliant first feature, *Honey Boy*, missed out on a nod.[44] She wasn't speaking out of bitterness, but in acknowledgement of a truth that is often overlooked for fear of appearing to be a sore loser: the odds are stacked against films made by, with or for women. The people that awards shows acknowledge tend to be male, their subject matter tends to be male and their leads tend to be male. The rather self-conscious grasp that cinema makes at importance every awards season is guided by voters who are mostly – sing it with me now – old, white men.

Directors UK, the professional association for UK screen directors, has been talking to BAFTA about the question. 'There are issues around what people consider to be worthy of merit,' says spokeswoman Natasha Moore. 'How do you divide what is meritorious and what is not? Is there a subconscious pre-selection to automatically include the things you like?'[45]

No female directors were nominated in 2020's Globes; at the time of writing the last one was Ava DuVernay for *Selma* in 2015. Only five have *ever* been nominated (though two were nominated twice), and Barbra Streisand is the only female winner, for *Yentl* in 1984.

The 2020 Oscars brought more disappointment. The Academy trumpeted the fact that 'almost one third' of the year's nominees were women, which is, depressingly, more than usual. But there were no women in the Best Director race in a year that included Greta Gerwig's *Little Women*, Marielle Heller's *A Beautiful Day in the*

Neighbourhood, Lorene Scafaria's *Hustlers*, Celine Sciamma's *Portrait of a Lady on Fire*, Lulu Wang's *The Farewell* and Har'el's *Honey Boy*. There were, however, eleven nominations for Todd Phillips' *Joker*, somehow including Best Director. It's hard to disagree with Har'el's assessment that there is 'no justice'.

Now of course, it's always easy to pick apart criticism of a single year. Some of those female-directed films come from small distributors who perhaps didn't put campaign weight behind them. There were stunning achievements by male directors that were also overlooked: Noah Baumbach for *Marriage Story*, and Pedro Almodóvar for *Pain and Glory*. With the possible exception of *Joker*, there are no obvious howlers among the nominees.

Still, it's a list of nominees that feels symptomatic of deference to long-standing authority. Martin Scorsese is a nine-time Best Director nominee and former winner for *The Departed*; Sam Mendes is a former winner for *American Beauty*; Quentin Tarantino is on his third nod. Only Bong Joon-ho feels like a deserving surprise – and he is already a Palme d'Or winner and one of the most storied directors in South Korea, a country that has always punched well above its weight in cinematic terms. We're not exactly widening the definition of who gets to be a 'great' director here.

So maybe voters don't want to. The Best Director nominations are chosen by the directing branch only, and that is, historically, overwhelmingly male. To be eligible to join you have to have directed two features in the past decade, a rate of work beyond the reach of many female directors until recently. It looks suspiciously as if members of the branch are continuing to reward the films to which they've always been instinctively drawn. If that's the case, the situation will take decades to change, and throughout those years we'll continue to grant auteur status only to these same men.

Another factor is the kind of film that gets recognition. War movies, crime dramas, gangster stories, biopics of great men, portraits of damaged men, men's struggles. Not just male stories, but stories about male anger and male violence. Vulture's Rachel Handler wrote about the 2020 nominated films asking, 'Why is this [white] man mad, and is it my fault?'[46] The same could be said for most years in Oscar history.

Films about female ambition (*Little Women*), men working towards some sort of grace or peace (*A Beautiful Day in the Neighbourhood, Honey Boy*), or female anger (*Hustlers*) are not considered as important. That also explains the oversight of *Marriage Story* and *Pain and Glory* above, and makes the 2017 win for *Moonlight* even more extraordinary (though that too is a story about violence). We've been told that films about men doing things, possibly violently, are more important than stories about women, in any capacity, ever since the silent era, after all. There's a far greater overlap between Best Actor and Best Picture than between Best Actress and Best Picture as a result.

In the last twenty years, only two Best Picture winners have had female protagonists, *Chicago* and *The Shape of Water* (some might argue for *Million Dollar Baby*, but that's still his film). The good news is that the Best Actress nominees are a more representative and varied bunch than they were: it was once the case that you were most likely to win if you played a sex worker, a nun or someone with a disability. If we have moved on from the days of judging women by the frequency with which they use their genitalia, that can only be a good thing, and hopefully the vogue for able-bodied actresses faking a disability has also passed (thirty-odd actors have won Oscars for playing someone with a disability, but only two winners actually had one).

Only thirty-five Black women have ever been nominated for an Acting Oscar out of over 900 nominees. Of those, Rotten Tomatoes editor Jacqueline Coley calculated that over half played slaves, maids or women living in abject poverty.[47] Many of the rest were principally defined as the wife or mother of a male character. That is not a representative view of Black women, let alone an inspiring one. It's telling that in 2020 the Oscars overlooked Lupita Nyong'o's two-pronged role as a middle-class success story/monster in *Us*, and Awkwafina's role as a middle-class Chinese-American stand-up in *The Farewell*, and Jennifer Lopez's supremely proud, fiery Ramona in *Hustlers*, in favour of Cynthia Erivo's performance as slave-turned-liberator Harriet Tubman in *Harriet*. That film has great work from Erivo, but it's hardly broadening the sort of roles that the Academy considers Oscar-worthy for women of colour.

Only seven Asian women or women of Asian descent have been nominated in the Acting categories, six of them as Supporting Actress. There have been only three women of Hispanic descent nominated in the Acting categories, though one, Hillary Swank, won Best Actress twice (her maternal grandmother is of Mexican descent, though she is perhaps not the most obviously Latina nominee). There have been only three indigenous nominees, including *Whale Rider's* Keisha Castle-Hughes and *Roma's* Yalitza Aparicio.

It all suggests that awards honour – consciously or not – a certain type of person rather than a certain quality of work. Partly it's because awards provide a sketch of who's getting the big roles, and there the picture is basically white, with a few faint lines of colour almost hidden on the canvas (like the painting in *Art*[48]). Worse, many nominees of colour miss out on the sort of career uplift that their white contemporaries get. Mahershala Ali, winner of two Best Supporting Actor nods, is at the time of writing still waiting for the big leading roles that should result. After winning her Best Supporting gong for 2013's *12 Years a Slave*, the stunning Nyong'o wasn't cast to appear onscreen in her own skin until 2016's *Queen of Katwe*: everything in between was performance capture or voice work for films like *The Jungle Book* and *Star Wars: Episode VII – The Force Awakens*.

The conversation about likely winners starts early, with critics who are more inclined to be sniffy about female-focused stories and awards pundits more likely to portray women of colour, for example, as long shots. That narrative afflicted Lupita Nyong'o in 2020. Despite having won Best Actress from six major critics' groups, more than anyone else, the story was still that she was a long shot for an Oscar nomination. *Vanity Fair* writer Mark Harris, in one of his 2020 Oscar columns, pointed out that voters don't like to waste their vote – so the punditry's poor assessment of her chances becomes a self-fulfilling prophecy.[49]

This might all seem academic. It's just a statue, right? It doesn't *mean* anything, not here in the real world where there are people with actual problems. If you're even close to a nomination you're probably earning a good living doing what you love in film. Who cares if you also get a little gold man for your mantelpiece? Of course, awards are not the ultimate arbiter of quality, or the best measure of accomplishment, and box-office success will be enough to keep you in work if you never even win Best Kiss at the MTV Awards. As *Parasite* director Bong Joon-ho said about the Oscars in 2019, 'The Oscars are not an international film festival. They're very local.'[50] For all the Academy acts like the centre of the film universe, they really do focus on only a narrow slice of English-speaking cinema. Then again, Hollywood remains the world's biggest film industry by box office despite challenges from India and, increasingly, China, and it retains a degree of cultural power unlike any other. If you want to make films in the English-speaking world, it's cold comfort to tell yourself that that isn't all there is.

But look at the Best Director winners and you'll see ninety-one men and one woman who are generally given the freedom and support to be auteurs (problematic as the term is), who are permitted to develop their own stories and presumed to be competent. A Best Director or Actor nomination is still, rightly or wrongly, a marker within the profession, and if it is not a blank cheque for future projects it is at the very least an increased chance of a meeting, and a greater likelihood that someone takes your idea seriously. Someone gave Tom Hooper the money to make *Cats* after he won Best Director. Presumably on purpose. These statuettes are a prop to wave in the face of anyone who tries to argue with you; think of the gag where Steven Spielberg does exactly that at the start of *Austin Powers in Goldmember.*

'As much as I don't give a damn about BAFTA on the surface of it,' says writer, actress and director Alice Lowe, 'it has the power to change my career and change my life. I won't get recognised as a director until I get whatever nomination. It's that Catch-22 situation where it's harder for you to get your next film funded and you have a bigger gap between projects. I get the sense that there are male directors out there that people treat like, "Oh his films don't make any money but he's an artist so we just keep funding him." I'm like, "Well mine did make some money but you're not funding mine!" How do I get to be this auteur who does whatever they like?'[51]

At every stage of the process, the markers of 'significant' film-maker status are held back from female filmmakers, by critics, festivals and finally awards. And still we're assured that it's all done on merit. The voters claim that any attempt to change the status quo smacks of forced diversity and quotas that do a disservice not only to the art form but also to the minority filmmakers thus allowed into the ranks of nominees. Never mind that every interview with an anonymous Oscar voter proves the opposite, showing that voters don't watch all the nominated films and do vote for their friends.

It also shows how resistant the voters can be to anything that smacks of challenge to the existing system. Comments in *The Hollywood Reporter*'s anonymous Oscar voter interviews include declarations like, 'Part of the reason why I liked *The Shape of Water* . . . is it's only "topical" in that it deals with outsiders, not racism or sexism or anything else.'[52] Another (female) voter said that *Get Out*, 'played the race card, and that really turned me off'.[53] Way to miss the point, madam.

Yet it's still all done on merit, right? If that's the case, let's take up a suggestion Mark Harris made on Twitter and take turns with the voting. If the white, straight men are really just consistently better and there's no bias among the white, straight men voting for them, they'll still come top in the years where only women vote, right? Or the years where only people of colour vote? Or the years where only LGBTQ+ people vote?

Now you might think – if you're one of these men – that this proposal smacks of identity politics. How could it possibly be fair to restrain the voting body to just women, or just people of colour? Of course that wouldn't be fair. Which is why the current situation, where *all* of these bodies are dominated by old white men, is so unacceptable. It's identity politics even if the identity is white and straight and male. That's not a human default, just an identity group who have usurped power for themselves.

Steps *are* finally being taken to change this. One milestone was the #OscarsSoWhite debacle, where a social media outcry rose on the hashtag created by April Reign, a Black lawyer and pop-culture tweeter who was struck by 2015's all-white acting nominees. She told the *New York Times* in 2020 that, 'It could've been a bunch of different things – there were no women in the directors category, there were no visibly disabled people nominated – so #OscarsSoWhite has never just been about race. It's about the under-representation of all marginalised groups.'[54]

In response, the Academy of Motion Picture Arts and Sciences (AMPAS) that runs the Oscars started to widen its membership, inviting in a larger and more diverse pool in every year since 2016 in an attempt to bring down the average age, average maleness and average whiteness of its membership. BAFTA has followed, and in 2018 brought in diversity standards that required every film up for Best

British Film or Outstanding Debut by a British Writer, Director or Producer to meet two out of four BFI-set diversity criteria. They're not onerous standards and can apply to onscreen as well as crew membership, but they require at least *some* thought.[55] In June 2020 BAFTA announced that it was expanding that requirement to all categories.[56] Also in June 2020 AMPAS announced similar standards that should foster more diverse hiring, and encourage unconscious bias training.[57]

Both awards bodies trail the British Independent Film Awards, which introduced unconscious bias training for its already younger and more diverse membership in 2018. Amy Gustin, co-director of BIFA with Deena Wallace, made the training compulsory for voters, 'because it's not a hard skill, trying to get people to find time to do it would be a lot harder if we hadn't made it compulsory'. Wallace added, 'We ask a lot of the voters, they have an enormous number of films to watch, so it is one of those things that would be easy to fall by the wayside.'[58]

The response was almost entirely positive, especially when voters realised that the training *did* show up biases they all carried. It wasn't just sexism and racism: unconscious bias training may also show that you are more negative on films watched right before lunch, so you need to take more breaks between screenings when cramming in dozens of films in the week before the nomination deadline.

The initiative isn't just about making awards fairer, though that's a huge part of it, of course. Voters for Oscars, BAFTAs, BIFAs and the like all work in the film industry, commissioning ideas or producing as well as voting once a year. There's a potential halo effect to this sort of policy. As Gustin says, 'Not only would we be able to make a positive impact on the results of voting, and therefore platform diverse voices, which obviously has a beneficial impact on emerging filmmakers, but we would also be able to perhaps shift, a little bit, the kind of media that's being made. The long-term impact might be that commissioners and script developers develop a broader range of stories, which in turn would hopefully make this training totally unnecessary because we're all brought up surrounded by stories that you know, are multicoloured and multicultural. So we're hoping that we can change the world.' Gustin laughs. 'One step at a time.'[59]

Every step forward matters. The recent Oscar wins for films like *Parasite* and *Moonlight* suggest that things are changing, that these wider and more diverse voting pools are making a difference and that the industry is looking beyond the traditional, stale old subjects. Now is the time for people who want – like Gustin and Wallace – to change the world, and Hollywood, for ever.

13

Who's the Boss?
How we can change the picture

I T's A strange moment to finish a book on women in Hollywood, because so much is on the brink of change. The percentage of female directors is finally shifting upwards, even on the biggest films. Female cinematographers and even composers – two areas where women are massively under-represented – are gradually getting a chance. The media's making active efforts to include diverse voices, which will change the stories we tell about Hollywood, about what constitutes success and failure. Myriad campaigns like Time's Up and #MeToo and #OscarsSoWhite mean that no one can claim they're not aware of inequality anymore, or that they didn't think it was a big deal. Profound structural change has not happened, yet, but a steady erosion of the old norms is ongoing.

This is also a dangerous time, because it's tempting to think that the hard work is done and that change will now continue uninterrupted – and history shows that's not the case. It's going to take continual pressure to make this progress permanent, because it could still all stumble and fall away as the push for women directors did in the 1970s, or the discussion about equal pay did after Patricia Arquette's Oscar speech in 2015, or the talk of inclusion riders did after Frances McDormand's Oscar speech in 2018. There's an economic contraction following the coronavirus epidemic of 2020, and that could see the old excuses come out and women's concerns sidelined. Still, there's cause for hope.

While the rolling revelations of #MeToo were horrifying, and triggering for many survivors, they accomplished one essential thing: they helped the women of Hollywood to realise that they could accomplish more together than alone. For decades, the system had encouraged women – had encouraged *everyone* – to see success as a zero-sum game. For one person to succeed, another had to fail. What #MeToo has shown beyond doubt is that women united can accomplish what singular women could not.

Social media changed the picture, united all the 'minority' voices around the world who were once marginalised by the white, straight, cis male establishment and enabled them to work together to make some noise for representation. As director Amma Asante puts it, '[Representation] is absolutely moving in the right direction and I do put a lot of that down to social media and the galvanising of opinion. Twelve years ago I could feel very lonely and alone, and now I can have a conversation with a filmmaker in Atlanta and a thousand people could read that conversation on Twitter. When I made my [first] film it was a pretty lonely experience. Now I feel far less lonely.'[1]

Beyond social media, there are moves to formalise these ties between women in the creative arts – though they don't want to get *too* formal. Both Film Fatales, in the US, and Cinesisters, in the UK, offer a framework where female directors can meet, talk and support one another – often in deliberately casual environments like each other's homes or local pubs. It's like Frances Marion's cat parties, one hundred years later.

Film Fatales, the older of the two organisations, was founded by Leah Meyerhoff to give feature directors, specifically, a supportive community.

'I'm guardedly optimistic,' says Meyerhoff. 'People are talking about [equality] a lot more right now, but it's not actually going to change until there's a mandate for it to change. It feels like for a very long time, there were myths that became ingrained about what did and did not sell, about people of colour as well as women. And all of these things then become self-fulfilling prophecies because they base their decisions on them. It takes someone coming along challenging that.'[2]

Cinesisters began as a sister organisation to Film Fatales, but has spun off independently. 'It feels very much like the community is building this thing rather than anyone deciding,' says co-founder Claire Oakley. 'We didn't want a governing body. Our whole ethos is to meet up in the pub and share experiences and hopefully through that help each other make more and better films.'[3]

The more high-profile Time's Up organisation also grew from mass action, women realising how bad the situation was in industries far beyond Hollywood. Its UK Chair, Dame Heather Rabbatts, says that, 'Times Up UK is really trying to ensure that we shift the culture in film and television and theatre. And to shift that culture, we fundamentally believe that we need to have equity. We need to have a much better balance between men and women, people of colour, LGBT, people with disabilities.'[4] They focus on establishing procedures to protect people involved in film and TV, and on fighting for pay and equity. They've worked with Ita O'Brien to normalise the use of intimacy coordinators, campaigned for Black Lives Matter and tackled workplace sexual harassment.

What if producers want to diversify their crews but still don't know where to start? Enter Victoria Emslie and her network Primetime, a database of women in film that aims to make it easier to hire qualified people. As an actress, and fired up by the Time's Up movement, Emslie figured that the best way to improve representation onscreen was to improve representation behind the camera, so she built a site where women could essentially advertise their skills and experience. 'There are so many excuses that fly around the industry about not being able to find women, and if I can take one of those off the table then that's a step in the right direction.'[5]

Alma Har'el's Free The Work, like Primetime, also puts women and other under-represented groups on the radar of those looking to hire them. 'I started to get invited into the rooms of all these studios and production companies,' says Har'el. 'I chose to come in and just really push this initiative into TV and film and see if they're aware of it. A lot of the stagnation was that people were making the decision to change, but didn't have the time to research new talent. We gave them a tool.'[6]

If you're developing your own independent film, Breaking the Lens offers practical ways to pitch your film to investors. That started when director Emily Carlton and her producing partner Daphne Schmon were given the chance to throw a big party during the Cannes Film Festival, and decided to open the doors to other young female filmmakers. They now curate a yearly selection of female-made projects and present them to financiers. 'There's not just one seat at the table,' says Carlton. 'You need to be able to share the luck. I've really felt that in the last couple of years with this explosion of female organisations, we can do that same thing [men do] of helping each other out. These new organisations are not in competition.'[7]

For work with marginalised communities, organisations like The British Blacklist and BEATS are raising profiles, highlighting successes and campaigning against racism. Akua Gyamfi set up The British Blacklist in 2012 to celebrate the achievements of the Black community in the UK, and then turned it into a database of Black talent. 'The grand thing is yes, it's put the spotlight on certain careers, it's helped the industry connect with this so-called hard-to-reach audience. People have crewed up, cast up and found writers and directors from the early database. People are collaborating and communicating and finding their tribe.[8]'

BEATS, an organisation for British East and South East Asians in the Screen and Stage Industry, was born after the Royal Shakespeare Company staged a production of *The Orphan of Zhao*, often described as the Chinese *Hamlet*, with majority white actors and only a few East Asians in minor roles. 'British Asian actors were like, we can't play traditionally white roles, and we can't play our own roles,' says co-founder Chi Thai. 'It kicked off a massive ruckus.'[9] From there, the group has become a force in advocacy for better onscreen representation for Asian people in the UK. 'Generally in America when they talk about representation for all things it's very binary,' says Chi. 'It's like male or female, black or white, able-bodied or disabled, gay or straight. Then the true diversity of everything gets missed out.'

These efforts are not just setting up mailing lists and monthly meetings and changing the world, they're a huge step forward. These are practical people focused on practical solutions, mentoring one another just as white men have mentored each other for decades, and advocating for lasting change on one another's behalf. And it *is* lasting: not a moment but a movement.

Another key area that has to be transformed is in executive suites and producing: the people who control the money, who oversee hiring, who greenlight and develop stories. There have been female studio heads in history, and they made films very successfully for female audiences. But they couldn't change the still male-dominated picture – not least because some female executives came slowly into their feminism. Sherry Lansing, the first woman to become studio head of production since the silent era, while still an executive at MGM, was promoted to vice president at the same time as a male colleague, but was paid less. 'So I went in and asked for a raise,' she recalled. 'The head of business affairs said, "Well, I understand why you feel you deserve it, but you're single and he's married and has kids, so he deserves a raise and you don't." The terrible thing is, I accepted it. I was so conditioned to think that I was worth less money that I actually went, "Oh, OK." [10]

Lansing dealt with sexism in those early days by 'denying it': she felt she could either 'stand on a picket line and burn my bra' or navigate the system to a point where she could be heard. She chose the latter, but that came with its own pressures: at a party given in celebration of her appointment to head Fox Productions in 1980, a woman stood up, jabbed her finger at Lansing and said, 'You represent all of us. And if you fail, you fail for all of us. You have to succeed more than anybody's ever succeeded.' Another guest, actress Marlo Thomas, responded, 'Jesus! Give her a break. If a guy lasts a year in that job, it's considered a miracle.' [11]

Dawn Steel, the first female President of Columbia Pictures, once said about her career that, 'I did feel threatened by other women in those early years. If there was only room for one woman in a room, I wanted to be her.' [12] Steel initially made her way by being as sweary, shouty and abusive as the men, but she evolved. Her friend Nora Ephron, who got her first directing gig from Steel, said in Steel's obituary that, 'Dawn certainly wasn't the first woman to become powerful in Hollywood, but she was the first woman to understand that part of her responsibility was to make sure that eventually there were lots of other powerful women. She hired women as executives, women as producers and directors, women as marketing people. The situation we have today, with a huge number of women in powerful positions, is largely because of Dawn Steel.' [13]

For these women in a man's world, it didn't pay to kick off about locker-room talk or make a fuss about sexual harassment or what would nowadays be called micro-aggressions (some were undoubtedly macro-aggressions). Steel, Lansing, agent Sue Mengers and their generation of agents and executives (the lines between the two groups blurred as former agents went into production) got ahead by playing by the rules of a man's game, by 'leaning in' as Sheryl Sandberg would later put it. But they also spotted opportunities that the men might have missed. Both Steel and Lansing championed films aimed at women during their tenures, and had big hits as a result: things like *Fatal Attraction*, *The Accused*, *When Harry Met Sally* and *Titanic*. Mengers represented both stars of *Love Story*, the weepy romantic mega-hit that was a career landmark for Ali MacGraw and Ryan O'Neal, and put together the stars and director of *What's Up, Doc?*, packaging another female-friendly hit. But these women remained, for a long time, a tiny minority. And they faced sexism, sometimes in their own workplace but certainly out in the wider film world. Amy Grossman, an agent at CAA in the late 1970s, said that, 'In those days, if you received an unwanted advance from a man, pretty much the only appropriate response was to let it roll off your back.'[14]

With motherhood, the picture got even tougher. Steel was fired from her job as president of production at Paramount Pictures (try saying that three times fast) while she was in labour in March 1987.[15] She became president of Columbia less than six months later, and then founded her own company, where she brought us *Cool Runnings* and *Sister Act 2* (both milestones for audiences of a certain age). Her daughter, Rebecca Steel Roven, is now a producer and worked with her father Charles Roven on movies like *Wonder Woman*, so maybe Steel had the last laugh.

Yet this scattering of female executives couldn't transform the picture; it requires a tipping point in numbers (both numbers of executives and numbers at the box office) to fundamentally reset the scales. 'Quite honestly, ten years ago, when women were in big positions, they were not supporting other women,' said director Julie Taymor of the situation. 'They were terrified of losing their job and they had to support the boys' films ... It wasn't necessarily better that women were at the top because they were frightened of making a mistake and that they would then be called out for having supported chick flicks or women's things. It was fear.'[16] The culture needs to change because even heads of studio don't have complete autonomy when they try to do something as radical as paying women equally to men, or announcing a slate with an equal number of female to male leads. They need the money men and their boards to support them too – and those remain male-dominated without exception.

Still, it's important that there are more women producing now, and more female directors who also produce. Jessica Hausner, the Austrian director of *Little Joe*, has produced as well as directed almost since the start, and says that, 'I was always sort of intimidated and did feel, in the beginning of my career, out of place. But . . . I founded my own production company. That was a big important step for me. I didn't realise back then. I only thought it's artistic control that I had to find. But now I also think it was good that I was never dependent on any other producer. I was always in power.'[17]

Female producers are more likely to think of hiring female crew members, and generally balanced crews – as Cate Shortland found on all her Australian films and was surprised to find was *not* the case when making a Marvel movie in the UK.[18] Joana Vicente of TIFF says, 'It's just having that person advocating. I bring in people that I think are great for the job; we probably give [directors] a choice of equal numbers of men and women. It was just a natural orientation to me.'[19]

An increasing number of stars have also turned to producing – and not just the vanity efforts of twenty-five or thirty years ago. Reese Witherspoon, Margot Robbie, Viola Davis, Charlize Theron and Kerry Washington have all started up production companies that look for movies with great roles for women, and not *just* for their star owners. The model is less Ryan Phillippe's underperforming Lucid Films, which made its first film in 2020, nearly two decades after its founding, and more Brad Pitt's astonishingly successful Plan B, supporting overlooked filmmakers and telling non-male and often non-white stories. (Pitt, incidentally, is that non-problematic fave who supports the movement, saying in 2019 that, '. . . we, Hollywood specifically, but the workplace, men and women's dynamics is being recalibrated in a very good way that is long overdue'.[20])

Witherspoon's Pacific Standard started after she toured the six major studios in about 2012 to ask how many female-led films they had in development. On learning that only one studio had even a single film in development for a female lead over thirty, she decided to act. She and partner Bruna Papandrea began by seeking out books to adapt and projects to develop, leading to films like *Wild* and *Gone Girl* and the TV mega-hits *Big Little Lies* and *Little Fires Everywhere*.

Witherspoon largely stuck to tried-and-tested directors initially – so, men – but she blasted the idea that no one wants to see female-led films, and her more recent TV efforts have had female directors. Kerry Washington, starting out as a producer, called Witherspoon for advice. Washington remembered, 'I said to her, "You're killing it now, but tell me all the mistakes you made so I don't have to reinvent the wheel."'[21] Once again, women are helping each other. Of course, women have acted as producers, whether in name or in fact, since the studio era (see Joan Crawford on *Johnny Guitar*, for example), but the difference now is a desire to look beyond one's own career: so Margot Robbie produces *Promising Young Woman* with Carey Mulligan starring, or Charlize Theron works on *Mindhunter* on TV but the female lead is played by Anna Torv.

Recent history also shows that a small number of producers *can* make a big difference. Megan Townsend of GLAAD points out that 14 per cent of *all* LGBTQ+ representation on broadcast, cable and streaming TV came from shows by just four creators: Greg Berlanti, Lena Waithe, Shonda Rhimes and Ryan Murphy, two Black women and two gay men. 'There's great progress being made in TV,' says Townsend, 'but it's still this small group of creators and producers who are prioritising inclusion that are really driving it.'[22] The good news is that so few can do so much to change the overall picture.

The bad news is that it has taken so long for these few to get their chance.

So what do we do to make this change permanent, short of making a few billion and buying some studios? The first and most important thing we can do is to vote with our wallets. See films by women, starring women, and particularly films by marginalised women. If there are few or no such films in your preferred genres, start agitating on social media to see them. Write letters or tweets or Instagram captions to the people who make stuff you like, and ask them to consider hiring diversely for their next outing.

You'll get the most bang for your movie-going buck if you can see these films in the cinema, though of course that isn't possible for everyone. But wherever you watch media you can speak up, and ask the person in charge to show more diverse films – *and then turn up to them*, even if that means tuning in on your sofa. Encourage your friends to do the same. It will make a difference. I maintain that the only reason that *Booksmart* didn't end up with a shelf full of awards and forty-two sequels is that people didn't see it. Don't let the next smart, funny, *true* exploration of girlhood slip by as lightly.

It's also great if you can become an advocate for female-led work. Don't be intimidated by the men in your life, who may have been accustomed to setting the agenda for film-watching. Challenge husbands, boyfriends, brothers, sons, fathers and male friends to try films by women. Question their beliefs if they claim that such works are not 'for' them. Does every film 'for' them need a male lead? Does he have to be white? Do they have to limit their empathy so tightly? You will probably get some pushback. Shrug it off and keep trying (if you can; don't do anything that makes you feel unsafe). Be difficult. Difficult women get stuff done. Even if people push back, the pressure still grows for them to reassess, reconsider and justify their exclusionary habits (even to themselves).

And, especially for those of us who are white, cis, straight, middle-class, able-bodied, hearing, sighted, educated or comfortably off, we should think about our relationship to others onscreen and our own privilege. It's not enough to carve out a space for white women and then claim that equality has been achieved. The result of that is a system every bit as unfair as the one we have now. We have to try to remember how it feels to be marginalised and consigned to girl-friend roles, sex-object roles, mother roles, whatever, and ensure that we don't limit anyone else's opportunities in our turn. If you have ever been frustrated that your story wasn't being told onscreen, you *have* to fight to get everyone's story told. More diverse stories mean better art for everyone.

It's been proven over and over again, in films as varied as *Coming to America* and *Get Out* and *The Farewell* and *Crazy Rich Asians* and *Wonder Woman* and *Little Women* that simply flipping the script and introducing a different culture creates a different film experience, one with the potential to shock and surprise us all over again. Introducing fresh voices makes even hackneyed old stories sound new again because those voices come with different attitudes, different life experiences, different backgrounds and a different take on the old genres. That's why the tensest moment of *Get Out* comes at the end when the police car turns up. It's why the most thrilling moment of *Wonder Woman* comes when someone goes over the top of a First World War trench.

If your social group – whether that's a company board, a brain trust or a group of producers – is homogenous and similar in outlook, you're missing out on the insight of everyone outside that group. Your prejudices and biases become self-reinforcing, bouncing off people with no reason to challenge them, and you're all likely to make the same mistakes and not to spot them. If you have a more diverse group, you benefit from the mathematical concept called the 'wisdom of the crowd': across all those viewpoints and opinions you're more likely to find the right answer. If there were African-American executives in Hollywood, it would not have taken decades to realise the hunger that existed for films like *Black Panther* or *Friday* or even the *Madea* series. If there were more female executives, maybe it wouldn't have taken nearly forty years after *Superman* to make a *Wonder Woman* movie.

Any sensible industry should be clamouring for new blood, new takes, new stories from old cultures. If *Emma* can be transferred to a Beverly Hills high school for *Clueless* (by a female director, note), then why not to any other subculture? If we've seen every possible take on Shakespeare, why not adapt one of the four great classical novels of China? *Love, Simon* could have been just another teen rom-com – except that the teen was gay and so it felt different. *Hustlers* could have been just another crime drama – except that the criminals were women and so it felt original. Why not a big swoonsome romance starring someone with a disability? Why not an action movie starring an older woman after all the geri-action-ers that followed *Taken*? Or a trans woman saving the world from alien invasion?

Even if you don't believe that diversity is a moral good, that people deserve to see themselves onscreen or to have a chance to tell their own stories without being reined in by people who don't understand their identity or culture, even if you think that people talk too much diversity these days, it simply makes for better stories. Forget about all those internet trolls bleating about 'wokeness' or 'social justice warfare' or 'virtue signalling'. Act out of pure self-interest. If you truly believe in the power of cinema, then you should want to hear a plurality of voices in your local multiplex because there is more chance that something extraordinary will occur. If you truly care about film, you should want to be transported into the lives of people quite unlike yourself – and that doesn't just mean white-coded wizards and aliens. Roger Ebert called cinema a machine for creating empathy. It's up to us to actually use it to build empathy for everyone, and not just, or mostly, straight white men.

Hollywood needs to diversify because it's right, and because otherwise they risk embarrassing future generations the way that *Song of the South* embarrasses Disney now. The Hollywood histories to come will not be kind to the studios that fought to add a white protagonist to Black stories, or fought against female leads and female directors. They won't be kind to science-fiction films that imagine a sexist future; it will look as ridiculous to them as elements of *Metropolis* do to us. The days when your place in history was assured by financial success or professional accolades are over. The generations growing up now care about more than that; they care about the kind of person you are, and that is a good thing. It's not being a snowflake; it's not being overly sensitive. It's a moral evolution for humanity.

For a very long time, most women in Hollywood accepted the myth that this skewed playing field was simply the way things were and that they'd have to play by those rules. Now they're changing the rules. It's not quick and it's not easy. Those who have fought most visibly have still paid the greatest price, so that those too scared to speak out can prosper. But slowly the structures are changing. If the prejudiced system is still standing, it shows cracks that were never there before. It may not look like much, but there *is* hope.

The men who ruled Hollywood for decades and those who invested vast sums in their work assumed that women had nothing extra to offer the film business, that film was not missing out on anything important. But that's the great mistake: we do, and it is.

References

Introduction

1 In an interview with the author.
2 In an interview with the author.

Chapter 1

1 https://babel.hathitrust.org/cgi/pt?id=coo.31924013929876&view=
  1up&seq=12
2 Quoted in *Red Velvet Seat: Women's Writing on the First Fifty Years of Cinema*,
  edited by Antonia Lant with Ingrid Periz, Verso.
3 In his book *American Traits*, 1901, quoted in *Red Velvet Seat*.
4 https://wfpp.columbia.edu/essay/exhibiting-women-gender-showman-
  ship-and-the-professionalization-of-film-exhibition-in-the-united-
  states-1900-ndash-1930/
5 There's considerable controversy about this, as you might imagine when
  a female director claims to have made the very first narrative film. There
  are two surviving films that reflect elements of Guy's description of her
  Cabbage Fairy film, but the archives that hold them dated them to 1897–
  1900 and 1902 respectively. Guy herself was consistent in her memory of
  the date and disputed the Swedish archive's catalogue of the earlier film,
  but in those same memoirs described a film plot the later, 1902, film
  actually titled *Sage-femme de première classe* (First-Class Midwife). Her
  1895 film may have been lost, misdated or simply misremembered, but
  be aware that claiming credit for the first narrative feature on her behalf
  may result in endless argument.
6 From a French interview done in the 1960s and quoted in 1995 documentary *The Lost Garden*: https://www.youtube.com/watch?v=zliomysaUeU

7 Also in the interview in *The Lost Garden*.
8 *Moving Picture World*, July 1914.

Chapter 2

1 Quoted in *Red Velvet Seat*.
2 Quoted in *Lois Weber in Early Hollywood*, Shelley Stamp, University of California Press.
3 Quoted in *Universal Women*.
4 Quoted in *The Silent Feminists: America's First Women Directors*, Anthony Slide, Scarecrow Press.
5 Quoted in *Lois Weber in Early Hollywood*.
6 Quoted in Charles Affron's *Lillian Gish: Her Legend, Her Life*, University of California Press.
7 Quoted in *Silent Women: Pioneers of Cinema*, Melody Bridges and Cheryl Robson (eds), Supernova Books, and on the Columbia Woman Film Pioneers Project.
8 *The Motion Picture World* magazine, 17 July 1917.
9 https://www.nytimes.com/2014/02/17/books/passing-with-panache-and-feeling-little-guilt.html
10 https://archive.org/stream/motionpicturenew153unse#page/2317/mode/2up
11 https://wfpp.columbia.edu/pioneer/ccp-lule-warrenton
12 This section draws from *Silent Women: Pioneers of Cinema*, and the article on Shipman therein, and also Joseph B. Walker's autobiography, *The Light on her Face*, ASC Holding Corp.
13 Quoted in the BFI's *Mabel Normand: A Documentary*.
14 Historian Anthony Slide edited Guy's *The Memoirs of Alice Guy*, with her daughters Simone Guy and Roberta Guy, published by the Scarecrow Film Series; Shipman's memoir was published posthumously as *The Silent Screen and My Talking Heart*, Boise State University Bookstore.
15 In an interview with the author, 2020.
16 https://www.theguardian.com/film/2015/may/23/i-spent-most-of-my-life-as-a-nobody-the-last-of-the-silent-movie-stars
17 In an interview with Pamela Hutchinson, 2020.
18 Quoted in *Universal Women*.
19 https://vinepair.com/articles/the-secret-history-of-women-distillers/ – for centuries, distilling was women's work.
20 Most cloth-making was done by women in family units prior to the Industrial Revolution; after that, many women were employed in weaving and cloth-making, but at a lower wage than men.
21 In an interview with the author, 2020.

Chapter 3

1 Steven Soderbergh has made more films since 'retiring' than most film-makers manage before it, though the most productive living director (who's also good) is probably Japan's Takashi Miike, who averages nearly three per year.
2 In *The Whole Equation*, David Thomson, Abacus.
3 https://www.buzzfeednews.com/article/annehelenpetersen/loretta-young
4 *Mae West: It Ain't No Sin*, Simon Louvish, Louvish Hollywood Biographies.
5 Quoted in *Marilyn Monroe: The Biography*, Donald Spoto, Cooper Square Press.
6 *Conversations with Classic Film Stars*, James Bawden and Ronald G. Miller, the University Press of Kentucky.
7 *Clara Bow: Runnin' Wild*, David Stenn, Rowman & Littlefield.
8 'It Happened One Night . . . at MGM', *Vanity Fair*, April 2003.
9 *The Girl: Marilyn Monroe, The Seven Year Itch and The Birth of an Unlikely Feminist*, Michelle Morgan, Running Press.
10 Quoted here: https://www.vanityfair.com/hollywood/2016/07/classic-hollywood-abortion
11 *Swanson on Swanson*, Gloria Swanson, Random House.
12 www.glamourgirlsofthesilverscreen.com/show/50/Jeanne+Crain/index.html
13 Quoted in *Hitchcock*, Francois Truffaut, Faber & Faber; Lo's name confirmed in the *New York Times* obituary here: https://www.nytimes.com/2012/10/26/movies/anita-bjork-once-the-new-garbo-dies-at-89.html
14 https://www.buzzfeednews.com/article/annehelenpetersen/loretta-young
15 In *Bette Davis Speaks*, Boze Hadleigh, Barricade Books.
16 In *The Whole Equation*, David Thomson, Abacus.
17 Technically the winning name was 'Joan Arden', but an actress of that name threatened to sue, so the second-place entry became her new moniker.
18 *The Lonely Life*, Bette Davis, Macdonald.
19 In her foreword to *The Films of Olivia de Havilland* by Tony Thomas, Citadel Press.
20 https://www.latimes.com/opinion/op-ed/la-oe-stipanowich-de-havil-land--20160701-snap-story.html
21 *The Films of Olivia de Havilland*.
22 *MM – Personal: From the Private Archive of Marilyn Monroe*, Lois Banner, Abrams.

23 Quoted in *Marilyn Monroe: The Biography*, Donald Spoto, Cooper Square Press.

24 *The Girl: The Seven Year Itch and the Birth of an Unlikely Feminist*.

25 *The Secret Life of Marilyn Monroe*, J. Randy Taraborrelli, Sidgwick & Jackson.

26 *The Girl: The Seven Year Itch and the Birth of an Unlikely Feminist*.

27 *The Girl: The Seven Year Itch and the Birth of an Unlikely Feminist*

Chapter 4

1 Wanda Tuchock managed two films in the 1930s, while American-born Esther Eng made several Chinese-language films in Hong Kong and the US, but Arzner was the only female member of the Directors Guild of America during her career.

2 agnesfilms.com/interviews/interview-with-dorothy-arzner

3 *Ida Lupino, Director: Her Art and Resilience in Times Of Transition*, Therese Grisham and Julie Grossman, Rutgers University Press.

4 The Filmmakers' 'Declaration of Independence', published in *Variety* on 20 February 1950.

5 *Ida Lupino: A Biography*, William Donati, University Press of Kentucky.

6 From an essay she wrote for *Action*, quoted in *Ida Lupino, Director*.

7 *Off With Their Heads: A Serio-Comic Tale of Hollywood*, Frances Marion, Macmillan.

8 Loos' travails with Emerson are extensively documented, notably in Gary Carey's *Anita Loos: A Biography*, Bloomsbury.

9 *Anita Loos: A Biography*.

10 'The Negro Actor and the American Movies', reproduced in *Red Velvet Seat*.

11 https://www.npr.org/templates/story/story.php?storyId=5245089

12 Quoted in *Mae West: It Ain't No Sin*.

13 A smaller all-Black film called *Hearts in Dixie* beat it to release.

14 Quoted here: https://www.nytimes.com/interactive/2019/obituaries/nina-mae-mckinney-overlooked.html, from Vidor's memoir, *A Tree Is a Tree*, Longmans, Green.

15 Quoted in *Lulu In Hollywood*, by Louise Brooks, University of Minnesota Press.

16 'The Color Fad', Ruby Berkley Goodwin, quote in *Red Velvet Seat*.

17 Quoted in *Red Velvet Seat*, itself quoting a *Pittsburgh Courier* article of 15 April 1939, which was in turn cited in Alfred Singer Buchanan's 'A Study of the Attitudes of the Writers of the Negro Press Towards the Depiction of the Negro in Plays And Film, 1930–1965', dissertation.

18 From *A Pictorial Biography of Paul Robeson: The Whole World in His Hands*, Susan Robeson, Citadel Press.

19 Quoted in *Paul Robeson: A Biography*, Martin Duberman, Knopf.

20 Quoted in https://www.nytimes.com/2010/05/10/arts/music/10horne.html?pagewanted=all

21 https://twitter.com/HumphreyBogart/status/994273093508972544?s=20; and also https://www.theguardian.com/music/2010/may/10/lena-horne-profile-tributes

22 Quoted in *That's Entertainment III*.

23 Quoted in *Hazel Scott: The Pioneering Journey of a Jazz Pianist from Café Society to Hollywood to HUAC*, Karen Chilton, University of Michigan Press.

24 www.openculture.com/2020/03/what-happened-hazel-scott.html

25 https://www.newyorker.com/culture/culture-desk/the-wizard-of-oz-the-last-munchkin-and-the-little-people-left-behind

26 *Toms, Coons, Mulattoes, Mammies, and Bucks: An Interpretive History of Blacks in American Films*, Donald Bogle, Bloomsbury Publishing.

27 *Sydney Morning Herald*, 1 May 1939. https://www.newspapers.com/clip/14242198/1st-may-39-sydney-morning-herald

28 *The Anniston Star*, 15 December 1959, https://www.newspapers.com/clip/33857157/anna-may-wong-alaskan-thousand-deaths

29 Quoted in *Conversations with Classic Film Stars*.

30 From an interview with EW in 2011. https://ew.com/article/2011/05/08/johnny-depp-tonto-lone-ranger/. He has also mentioned Chickasaw heritage here: www.canada.com/entertainment/Johnny+Depp+Tonto+leader+Lone+Ranger+follower/8576134/story.html .

31 www.bbc.co.uk/culture/story/20151006-when-white-actors-play-other-races

32 *From Reverence to Rape*, Molly Haskell, University of Chicago Press.

Chapter 5

1 *Movie Censorship and American Culture*, Francis G. Couvares (ed.), Smithsonian Institution Press. This from 'Mothering the Movies' by Alison M. Parker.

2 Quoted in 'Black Films, White Censors' by Charlene Regester, in *Movie Censorship and American Culture*.

3 Discussed in *Movie-made America: A Cultural History of American Movies* by Robert Sklar, Vintage Books.

4 *Monitoring the Movies* by Jennifer Fronc, University of Texas Press.

5 'The Morals of the Movies', Karl Kitchen, *Photoplay* magazine, July 1920

https://babel.hathitrust.org/cgi/pt?id=umn.31951002808791g&view=1up&seq=46

6 https://books.google.co.uk/books?id=c8ih7OuhdugC&pg=PA201&lpg=PA201&dq=karl+kitchen+photoplay&source=bl&ots=pNbtLDvsKx&sig=ACfU3U1corIu16CGVMQBozmDfc83vMBQoA&hl=en&sa=X&ved=2ahUKEwj4t_Dn6t3nAhWUUBUIHc23CwkQ6AEwAnoECAkQAQ#v=onepage&q=karl%20kitchen%20photoplay&f=false

7 *The Sins of Hollywood*, Ed Roberts, Hollywood Publishing Co, quoted in *Movie-made America.*

8 Quoted in *The New Yorker*, here: https://www.newyorker.com/culture/richard-brody/a-brilliant-unknown-memoir-about-classic-hollywood

9 Donald Young, a sociologist writing in *The Annals of the American Academy of Political and Social Science*; quoted in *Movie-made America.*

10 'Mothering the Movies'.

11 Quoted in 'Mothering the Movies'.

12 Quoted in 'Mothering the Movies'.

13 *Film Censorship: Regulating America's Screen*, Sheri Chinen Biesen, Wallflower Press.

14 *Monitoring the Movies.*

15 Quoted in *Pre-Code Hollywood: Sex, Immortality and Insurrection in American Cinema 1930–1934*, Thomas Doherty, Columbia University Press.

16 Quoted in 'Black Films, White Censors' in *Movie Censorship and American Culture.*

17 Ibid.

18 Quoted in *Conversations with Classic Film Stars.*

19 Quoted in 'Goodness Had Nothing To Do with It' in *Movie Censorship and American Culture.*

20 *Red Velvet Seat.*

21 Ibid.

22 Quoted in 'Goodness Had Nothing To Do with It'.

23 Quoted in *Mae West: It Ain't No Sin.*

24 Quoted in 'Goodness Had Nothing To Do with It'.

25 Quoted in *She Always Knew How: Mae West, A Personal Biography* by Charlotte Chandler, Simon & Schuster.

26 Quoting *High Society: Grace Kelly and Hollywood*, Donald Spoto, Random House, in *Hitchcock's Heroines* by Caroline Young, Insight Editions.

27 *Dressed: A Century of Hollywood Costume Design*, quoted here: https://www.thevintagenews.com/2018/06/09/bra-designer/

28 From *Vanity Fair* article 'The Lipstick Jungle', Laura Jacobs, March 2004.

29 https://www.lipstickalley.com/threads/famous-who-modeled-for-vogue-slept-with-famous-men-and-married-an-aristocrat.405450/

30 Chronicled in her autobiography, *My Story*, Caroline Cossey, Faber & Faber.

31 This is all quoted via *Gay People, Sex and the Media*, Michelle A. Wolf and Alfred P. Kielwasser (eds), Harrington Park Press.

32 https://www.filmratings.com/History

33 Interview with Peirce in Kirby Dick's 2006 documentary *This Film Is Not Yet Rated*.

34 https://www.espn.com/wnba/story/_/id/29069339/an-oral-history-love-basketball-20-years-later

35 https://web.archive.org/web/20130513073601/blog.moviefone.com/2010/12/08/blue-valentine-rating-nc-17/

36 https://www.flavorwire.com/430289/why-did-wolf-of-wall-street-get-a-pass-from-the-mpaa-when-feminist-films-dont-a-conversation-with-jill-soloway

37 https://qz.com/1335380/eighth-grade-shows-the-difference-between-how-the-us-and-europe-think-about-teens-and-sex/

38 https://ew.com/movies/2018/12/21/disney-aladdin-cultural-authenticity/

39 https://deadline.com/2018/01/disney-aladdin-criticized-media-browning-up-1202237376/

40 I hope I am being quite careful with language here. Some sources suggest that Gill was not a trans man but a masculine-presenting lesbian, and I don't wish to misgender Gill either way. Even were Gill not trans, the point stands that a straight, femme cis actress is probably not the best choice for the role.

41 Quoted at https://www.theguardian.com/film/2018/jul/13/scarlett-johansson-exits-trans-role-rub-and-tug

42 https://variety.com/2020/film/news/halle-berry-trans-role-apology-transgender-film-1234699605/

Chapter 6

1 Quoted in *The Silent Feminists*, Anthony Slide, Scarecrow Press.

2 *Quoted in Lois Weber: Interviews*, Martin F. Norden (ed), University Press of Mississippi; further quoted in *The New Yorker*: https://www.newyorker.com/culture/the-front-row/a-real-director-should-be-absolute-lois-webers-prescient-thoughts-on-filmmaking-a-century-ago

3 In *Une certaine tendence de la cinema française*, François Truffaut.

4 https://archive.org/details/Sarris_Andrew_The_Auteur_Theory/page/n5/mode/2up

5 filmmakeriq.com/wp-content/uploads/2014/06/Circles-and-Squares-the-Joys-and-Sarris.pdf

6 https://www.empireonline.com/movies/features/irishman-week-martin -scorsese-interview – please do not ask for my position on this take. This is not a discussion in which I wish to pick sides.

7 https://www.vulture.com/2017/09/liman-speaks-about-tom-cruise-and- american-made-crash.html

8 On the Empire Podcast.

9 Quoted in *Hitchcock's Heroines*.

10 From *The Glamour Factor: Inside Hollywood's Big Studio System*, Ronald L. Davis, Southern Methodist University Press, quoted in *Hollywood's Second Sex*, Aubrey Malone, McFarland & Co.

11 Quoted in *Spellbound by Beauty: Alfred Hitchcock and his Leading Ladies*, Donald Spoto, Random House.

12 Quoted in *The Dark Side of Genius: The Life of Alfred Hitchcock*, Donald Spoto, Plexus.

13 https://variety.com/2016/film/news/tippi-hedren-alfred-hitchcock- sexual-assault-1201904500/

14 https://cinephiliabeyond.org/marnie-hitchcocks-controversial-explor- ation-of-sexual-violence-and-the-complexity-of-the-human-psyche/

15 Both quoted in *Spellbound by Beauty*.

16 Quoted in *Conversations with Classic Film Stars*.

17 https://www.newyorker.com/magazine/2008/01/14/balance-of-terror

18 *Hollywood's Second Sex*.

19 *Hollywood's Second Sex*

20 Quoted in *Being Rita Hayworth: Labor, Identity and Hollywood Stardom*, Adrienne L. McLean, Rutgers University Press.

21 https://www.gq-magazine.co.uk/article/orson-welles-quotes-citizen- kane-100-birthday-anniversary

22 https://www.theguardian.com/film/2013/jun/29/orson-welles-criticism- hollywood-stars-tapes

23 https://www.theguardian.com/theguardian/2012/oct/05/jean-seberg- saint-joan-preminger-archive-1956

24 Quoted in *Hollywood's Second Sex*.

25 Quoted in *Otto Preminger: The Man Who Would Be King*, Foster Hirsch, Knopf.

26 Ibid.

27 'Second Chance for Jean', *The Age*, 8 October 1957.

28 https://www.nytimes.com/1974/06/16/archives/a-showbiz-saint-grows- up-or-whatever-happened-to-jean-seberg-jean.html

29 Quoted here: https://www.thevintagenews.com/2018/11/12/sternberg- and-marlene-dietrich/

30 Quoted here: https://www.newyorker.com/culture/richard-brody/the- front-row-marlene-dietrich-in-dishonored

31 Mentioned here: https://www.newyorker.com/magazine/2015/10/19/bombshells-a-critic-at-large-pierpont

32 'To Have and Have Not', *Vanity Fair*, March 2011.

33 Quoted in 'To Have and Have Not', *Vanity Fair*.

34 Quoted in *Leading Lady: Sherry Lansing and the Making of a Hollywood Groundbreaker*, Stephen Galloway, Crown.

35 Quoted in *Easy Riders, Raging Bulls: How the Sex 'n' Drugs 'n' Rock 'n' Roll Generation Changed Hollywood*, Peter Biskind, Bloomsbury.

36 Ibid.

37 reprints.longform.org/death-of-a-playmate

38 https://www.vulture.com/article/thandie-newton-in-conversation.html

39 From *InStyle* magazine, 2011, quoted here: https://www.dailymail.co.uk/tvshowbiz/article-1394105/Thandie-Newtons-affair-16-film-director-John-Duigan-23-years-older-her.html#ixzz1OJZDGTuJ

40 https://www.thetimes.co.uk/article/winona-ryder-on-turning-50-missing-keanu-reeves-and-being-saved-by-normal-people-o7rppmj3t

41 https://www.thetimes.co.uk/article/winona-ryder-on-turning-50-missing-keanu-reeves-and-being-saved-by-normal-people-o7rppmj3t.

42 https://www.smh.com.au/entertainment/movies/downhill-ride-for-maria-after-her-tango-with-brando-20060622-gdnt2a.html

43 https://www.ansa.it/web/notizie/rubriche/spettacolo/2013/09/17/Bertolucci-confessione-shock_9312378.html

44 https://web.archive.org/web/20110105081412/daily.greencine.com/archives/007965.html

45 https://www.youtube.com/watch?v=RMl4xCGcdfA

46 All quoted here: https://www.telegraph.co.uk/films/0/original-fifty-shades-painful-story-behind-nine-half-weeks/

47 https://www.theguardian.com/film/2003/aug/03/features.review

48 https://www.thedailybeast.com/the-stars-of-blue-is-the-warmest-color-on-the-riveting-lesbian-love-story

49 https://www.vulture.com/2013/10/timeline-blue-is-the-warmest-color-controversy.html

50 https://www.newyorker.com/culture/culture-desk/did-a-director-push-too-far

51 https://www.interviewmagazine.com/film/rooney-mara-and-david-fincher

52 https://www.moviemaker.com/eli-roth-10-golden-rules-of-moviemaking/

53 https://www.slashfilm.com/megan-fox-was-an-extra-in-bad-boys-2/

54 Originally from *Wonderland* magazine, quoted here: https://www.theguardian.com/film/2011/jun/20/steven-spielberg-megan-fox-transformers

55 https://deadline.com/2009/09/transformers-crew-talk-back-to-megan-fox-15879/

56 https://www.insider.com/megan-fox-explains-made-up-transformers-director-michael-bay-2018-11

57 https://www.vanityfair.com/news/2008/01/heigl200801

58 https://www.vulture.com/2009/07/even_seth_rogen_now_hating_on.html

59 https://www.hollywoodreporter.com/news/seth-rogen-katherine-heigl-knocked-up-feud-918640

60 https://www.newyorker.com/magazine/2019/10/28/adam-driver-the-original-man

61 https://variety.com/2019/film/news/celebrity-salaries-leonardo-dicaprio-margot-robbie-dwayne-johnson-will-smith-1203200508/

62 https://variety.com/2019/film/columns/netflix-you-have-a-problem-the-irishman-is-too-good-martin-scorsese-1203353105/

63 https://www.hollywoodreporter.com/news/behind-martin-scorseses-killers-flower-moon-apple-deal-1296394

Chapter 7

1 Quoted in *Popcorn Venus: Women, Movies & the American Dream*, Marjorie Rosen, Coward, McCann & Geoghegan.

2 https://www.theguardian.com/film/2013/jun/13/steven-spielberg-george-lucas-film-industry

3 https://www.nytimes.com/1970/05/27/archives/movies-leaving-holly-wood-behind-studio-system-passe-film-forges.html

4 https://www.independent.co.uk/arts-entertainment/films/features/dennis-hopper-peter-fonda-on-his-easy-rider-co-star-9605915.html

5 Quoted in *Godfather: The Intimate Francis Ford Coppola*, Gene D. Phillips, University Press of Kentucky.

6 *Popcorn Venus*.

7 *Easy Riders, Raging Bulls*.

8 From *Shirley MacLaine*, Roy Pickard, Spellmount Books, quoted in *Hollywood's Second Sex*.

9 https://www.theparisreview.org/blog/2017/06/16/summers-and-swim-mers/

10 https://www.nytimes.com/1970/05/27/archives/movies-leaving-holly-wood-behind-studio-system-passe-film-forges.html

11 Quoted in *Liberating Hollywood: Women Directors and the Feminist Reform of 1970s Cinema*, Maya Montanez Smukler, Rutgers University Press.

12 All Angelou quotes from here: https://www.theparisreview.org/inter-views/2279/the-art-of-fiction-no-119-maya-angelou

13 https://www.nytimes.com/2020/07/10/movies/the-old-guard-gina-prince-bythewood.html

14 Quoted in *Liberating Hollywood*.

15 Ibid.

16 *Empire* magazine, October 2019, reproduced here. https://www.empire-online.com/movies/features/irishman-week-martin-scorsese-interview/

17 In an interview with the author, 2020.

18 In *The New Masses*, 14 July 1942.

19 *Popcorn Venus*.

20 In an interview with the author, 2020.

21 In *Reel to Real: Race, Sex and Class at the Movies*, bell hooks, Routledge.

22 This word is used in reviews on the BBC, the Dissolve, the Atlantic, and many more. Roger Ebert considered the film simultaneously 'homo-erotic and homophobic'.

23 https://www.vocativ.com/culture/celebrity/hollywood-movies-strong-female-roles-make-money/

24 https://www.theguardian.com/world/2013/nov/06/swedish-cinemas-bechdel-test-films-gender-bias

25 In an interview with the author, 2020.

26 https://twitter.com/photopuck/status/607259980631273473

27 https://www.nytimes.com/1991/04/07/magazine/hers-the-smurfette-principle.html

28 In an interview with the author, 2020.

29 https://www.newstatesman.com/2013/10/after-bechdel-test-i-propose-shukla-test-race-film

30 https://www.theguardian.com/film/2016/jan/18/hollywoods-race-prob-lem-film-industry-actors-of-colour

31 https://www.nytimes.com/2016/01/30/movies/sundance-fights-tide-with-films-like-the-birth-of-a-nation.html?_r=0

32 www.npr.org/blogs/monkeysee/2008/09/the_bechdel_rule_1.html

33 https://www.glaad.org/sri/2020

34 https://uniteyouthdublin.files.wordpress.com/2015/03/is-there-a-transgender-text-in-this-class-1-1_pages.pdf

35 https://slate.com/culture/2018/10/cinemability-disability-representation-hollywood-jenni-gold-director-interview.html

36 https://www.forbes.com/sites/andrewpulrang/2020/02/13/disability-movies-arent-what-they-used-to-be-thats-good

37 https://www.theclittest.com/about

Chapter 8

1 Quoted in *Conversations with Classic Movie Stars.*
2 Producer who asked to remain anonymous, in an interview with the author, 2020.
3 Statistics courtesy of Box Office Mojo.
4 https://catalog.afi.com/Catalog/MovieDetails/30199 –This film was made by a company called American Mutograph, which would eventually become the Biograph Company, a giant of the silent era.
5 *Blockbusters: Why Big Hits and Big Risks are the Future of the Entertainment Business,* Anita Elberse, Faber & Faber.
6 See previous chapter.
7 In an interview with the author, 2019.
8 https://www.investopedia.com/financial-edge/0611/why-movies-cost-so-much-to-make.aspx
9 https://www.boxofficemojo.com/title/tt6266538/?ref_=bo_se_r_1
10 https://www.boxofficemojo.com/title/tt0473705/?ref_=bo_se_r_1
11 https://www.boxofficemojo.com/title/tt1341188/?ref_=bo_se_r_1
12 Marston's life is chronicled in *The Secret History of Wonder Woman,* Jill Lepore, Scribe Publications. which is fascinating even if you are not a comics fan. For an even quicker primer, try Angela Robinson's 2017 film, *Professor Marston and the Wonder Women.*
13 Ibid.
14 https://lby3.com/wir/
15 www.lby3.com/wir/r-4_2899.html.
16 https://www.theguardian.com/books/2015/sep/18/female-comic-book-readers-women-avengers-a-force
17 https://www.pajiba.com/film_reviews/the-writers-of-deadpool-2-didnt-know-what-fridging-was.php
18 https://womenandhollywood.com/marvel-ceo-doesnt-believe-in-female-superheroes-fcdbc3d80c50/
19 https://www.vanityfair.com/hollywood/2015/09/marvel-studios-ike-perlmutter-kevin-feige
20 https://www.vanityfair.com/hollywood/2015/09/marvel-studios-ike-perlmutter-kevin-feige
21 https://collider.com/iron-man-3-rebecca-hall-character-details-original-version/
22 https://deadline.com/2020/07/daredevil-peter-shinkoda-jeph-loeb-asian-racist-comments-1202995534/
23 https://www.wired.com/2009/01/women-steer-bat/
24 https://www.thedailybeast.com/doctor-strange-director-owns-up-to-whitewashing-controversy

25 https://www.theverge.com/2013/7/21/4542974/gravity-director-alfonso-cuaron-defends-casting-sandra-bullock-female-lead-sci-fi

26 In an interview with the author, 2019.

27 https://www.boxofficemojo.com/movies/?id=ghostbusters2016.htm

28 https://www.theguardian.com/film/2019/feb/27/rotten-tomatoes-captain-marvel-brie-larson-review-trolls

29 https://www.theatlantic.com/entertainment/archive/2019/03/rotten-tomatoes-captain-marvel-review-ratings-system-online-trolls/584032/

30 https://www.wired.com/story/trolls-are-boring/

31 In an interview with the author, 2020.

32 https://www.dailyscript.com/scripts/alien_early.html

Chapter 9

1 *New York Times* magazine, 21 July 1957, quoted in *Hollywood's Second Sex*.

2 https://timesmachine.nytimes.com/timesmachine/1943/06/27/85107893.pdf?pdf_redirect=true&ip=0

3 https://womenintvfilm.sdsu.edu/files/Women per cent20@ per cent-20Box per cent20Office.pdf

4 Quoted in *Lois Weber in Early Hollywood*.

5 Ibid.

6 *Liberating Hollywood.*

7 https://www.dga.org/-/media/Files/Diversity/DGAvsWarnerBrosandColumbiaRymer1985.ashx?la=en&hash=B9615A00BE5D239779250AF6FE07F6C239CB63FC

8 From participants in both meetings, interviewed by the author.

9 https://socialsciences.ucla.edu/wp-content/uploads/2020/02/UCLA-Hollywood-Diversity-Report-2020-Film-2-6-2020.pdf

10 https://www.theguardian.com/film/2013/jan/23/women-independent-film-sundance-survey

11 https://www.filmla.com/wp-content/uploads/2018/04/2015_film_study_v5_WEB.pdf

12 https://variety.com/2015/film/news/colin-trevorrows-comments-on-lack-of-female-blockbuster-directors-draw-criticism-1201576364/

13 In an interview with the author, 2020.

14 *My First Movie*, Stephen Lowenstein (ed.), Faber & Faber.

15 These quotes from an interview I did with Asante for the now defunct online magazine *The Pool*, on the release of *A United Kingdom*.

16 In an interview with the author, 2020.

17 Quoted in *Is That a Gun in Your Pocket? Women's Experience of Power in Hollywood*, Rachel Abramowitz, Random House.

18 In an *Empire* podcast interview with the author, December 2019.
19 *Liberating Hollywood.*
20 In an interview with the author, 2020.
21 In an interview with the author, 2020.
22 https://www.hollywoodreporter.com/news/study-finds-80-percent-female-directors-made-one-movie-10-years-970896
23 In an interview with the author, 2020.
24 In an interview with the author, 2020.
25 https://www.vogue.com/article/greta-gerwig-cover-january-2020
26 In an interview with the author, 2020.
27 From an interview with the author, 2020
28 https://www.nytimes.com/2007/03/20/movies/20roth.html
29 https://variety.com/2007/film/columns/julie-taymor-flies-across-the-universe-1117971531/
30 https://www.vulture.com/2018/07/evan-rachel-wood-across-the-universe-scared-people.html
31 https://www.hollywoodreporter.com/thr-esq/grey-s-anatomy-crew-member-700950
32 In an interview with the author, 2020.
33 https://www.vanityfair.com/hollywood/2020/03/wonder-woman-1984-director-patty-jenkins-on-knowing-when-to-fight
34 https://www.vanityfair.com/hollywood/2018/09/director-mimi-leder-on-the-basis-of-sex
35 https://film.avclub.com/wayne-s-world-director-penelope-spheeris-on-leaving-hol-1833211775/amp?__twitter_impression=true
36 https://www.nytimes.com/2019/07/03/movies/black-directors-1990s.html#click=https://t.co/4PMv7BjtbH
37 In an interview with the author for now-defunct website The Pool, 2018.
38 https://www.hollywoodreporter.com/features/barbra-streisand-hollywoods-double-standard-845819
39 In an interview with the author, 2020.
40 https://www.hollywoodreporter.com/features/bryan-singers-traumatic-x-men-set-movie-created-a-monster-1305081?utm_source=twitter&utm_medium=social
41 https://www.hollywoodreporter.com/features/thrs-producer-year-charles-roven-future-dc-films-what-happened-between-george-clooney-david
42 https://www.nytimes.com/1998/12/27/magazine/restless.html?pagewanted=all
43 https://www.salon.com/2016/03/14/david_o_russell_made_amy_adams_life_a_living_hell_5_sadistic_male_directors_who_treat_their_actors_like_garbage/

44 https://deadline.com/2017/08/patty-jenkins-highest-payday-female-director-historic-deal-wonder-woman-2-1202151303/
45 In an interview with the author, 2020.
46 Quote from hip hop producer Russell Simmons in *Vanity Fair*, March 2007.
47 https://deadline.com/2015/05/directors-guild-aclu-investigation-female-directors-martha-coolidge-1201430374/
48 In an interview with the author, 2020.
49 https://twitter.com/NetflixFilm/status/1007645994123751425
50 In an interview with the author, 2020.
51 https://womenintvfilm.sdsu.edu/wp-content/uploads/2020/01/2019_Celluloid_Ceiling_Report.pdf
52 https://www.harpersbazaar.com/uk/celebrities/news/a31269567/gugu-mbatha-raw-international-womens-day/
53 In an interview with the author, 2020
54 In an email interview with the author, 2020.
55 https://variety.com/2017/film/news/diversity-box-office-winners-hollywood-1202603438/

Chapter 10

1 In an interview with the author, 2020.
2 https://www.lamag.com/culturefiles/hollywood-highland-casting-couch/
3 In season 6, episode 14, 'Kidnapped By Danger'.
4 https://www.independent.co.uk/news/courtney-love-harvey-weinstein-2005-clip-a8001551.html
5 https://www.nytimes.com/2017/10/19/movies/tarantino-weinstein.html
6 *Modern Screen*, February 1941, quoted in *The Girl*.
7 Quoted in *The Girl*.
8 *Marilyn Monroe: My Story*, Marilyn Monroe, Taylor Trade Publishing.
9 Quoted in *Conversations with Classic Film Stars*.
10 Quoted in *Hollywood's Second Sex*, originally from *The Casting Couch*, by Selwyn Ford, Grafton.
11 Quoted in *Conversations with Classic Film Stars*.
12 *Dorothy Dandridge: An Intimate Biography* by Earl Mills, Holloway House Publishing.
13 *Easy Riders, Raging Bulls*.
14 https://www.theguardian.com/film/2009/sep/29/roman-polanski-whoopi-goldberg
15 *Easy Riders, Raging Bulls*.

16 Quoted here https://www.newyorker.com/magazine/2009/12/14/the-celebrity-defense#:~:text=At%20this%20age%2C%20Polanski%20wrote,of%20contrition%20about%20his%20actions.

17 https://nypost.com/2010/05/15/new-polanski-sex-shock/

18 https://www.theguardian.com/film/2019/nov/11/pressure-mounts-on-roman-polanski-over-new-sexual-assault-allegation https://www.vox.com/culture/2017/8/17/16156902/roman-polanski-child-rape-charges-explained-samantha-geimer-robin-m

19 https://web.archive.org/web/20091002184012 blogs.telegraph.co.uk/news/michaeldeacon/100011795/roman-polanski-everyone-else-fancies-little-girls-too

20 On Facebook, quoted here: https://www.rollingstone.com/movies/movie-news/arnold-schwarzenegger-praises-eliza-dushku-after-true-lies-molestation-accusation-200323/

21 https://www.theguardian.com/film/2018/jan/15/eliza-dushku-accuses-true-lies-crew-member-of-sexually-assaulting-her-aged-12

22 https://deadline.com/2018/01/joel-kramer-sexual-assault-accusations-stunt-women-eliza-dushku-1202243343/

23 https://www.nytimes.com/2000/03/30/books/finding-new-cracks-in-an-exposed-life.html

24 https://nationalpost.com/entertainment/celebrity/ill-break-you-judy-garland-faced-her-own-harvey-weinstein-in-mgm-head-louis-b-mayer

25 https://deadline.com/2012/06/youth-talent-manager-martin-weiss-pleads-no-contest-sentenced-in-molestation-case-280828/

26 https://www.hollywoodreporter.com/news/jjabrams-super8-sex-offender-child-casting263287

27 https://www.hollywoodreporter.com/news/corey-feldman-elijah-wood-hollywood-897403

28 https://www.newyorker.com/culture/culture-desk/in-showbiz-kids-alex-winter-weighs-the-costs-of-child-stardom

29 https://www.buzzfeednews.com/article/adambvary/anthony-rapp-kevin-spacey-made-sexual-advance-when-i-was-14#.eoDnqn8nB

30 https://www.theguardian.com/film/2017/oct/11/actor-terry-crews-sexually-assaulted-by-hollywood-executive

31 https://www.gq.com/story/what-ever-happened-to-brendan-fraser/amp?__twitter_impression=true

32 https://www.salon.com/2017/10/12/james-van-der-beek-tells-his-story-of-sexual-abuse-a-powerful-reminder-that-men-can-be-victims-too/

33 https://www.theguardian.com/film/2017/dec/15/peter-jackson-harvey-weinstein-ashley-judd-mira-sorvino

34 https://www.theatlantic.com/entertainment/archive/2020/01/rose-mcgowan-on-the-exhausting-road-to-the-weinstein-trial/604522/

35 https://www.theguardian.com/film/2019/aug/26/rosanna-arquette-they-said-i-was-a-pain-in-the-ass-its-not-true

36 https://www.newyorker.com/news/news-desk/from-aggressive-over-tures-to-sexual-assault-harvey-weinsteins-accusers-tell-their-stories

37 https://variety.com/2017/film/columns/heather-graham-harvey-wein-stein-sex-for-movie-role-1202586113/

38 https://www.newyorker.com/news/news-desk/weighing-the-costs-of-speaking-out-about-harvey-weinstein

39 https://www.nytimes.com/interactive/2017/12/13/opinion/contributors/salma-hayek-harvey-weinstein.html

40 *Bette Davis Speaks.*

41 https://www.hollywoodreporter.com/news/british-actress-sophie-dix-speaks-harvey-weinstein-harassment-1048337

42 https://www.nytimes.com/2017/10/05/us/harvey-weinstein-harassment-allegations.html

43 https://www.nytimes.com/2017/10/05/us/harvey-weinstein-harassment-allegations.html

44 https://www.rainn.org/statistics/criminal-justice-system

45 https://variety.com/2018/film/news/salma-hayek-says-harvey-weinstein-only-responded-to-her-and-lupita-nyongos-harassment-claims-because-women-of-color-are-easier-to-discredit-1202808828/

46 https://www.independent.co.uk/arts-entertainment/sharon-stone-me-too-sexual-harassment-times-up-cbs-sunday-lee-cowen-laugh-mosaic-a8159781.html

47 https://www.nytimes.com/2017/10/19/opinion/lupita-nyongo-harvey-weinstein.html

48 https://variety.com/2018/film/news/cate-blanchett-cannes-weinstein-metoo-diversity-1202791914/

49 https://www.indiewire.com/2019/09/brad-pitt-threatens-kill-harvey-weinstein-gwyneth-paltrow-1202175152/

50 https://variety.com/2018/biz/news/jennifer-lawrence-harvey-weinstein-wanted-to-kill-sexual-misconduct-1202710412/

51 https://www.nytimes.com/2017/10/09/movies/dench-close-streep-wein-stein.html

52 https://www.nytimes.com/2018/01/03/movies/meryl-streep-tom-hanks-the-post-metoo.html

53 https://variety.com/2020/biz/news/harvey-weinstein-emails-quentin-tarantino-jeff-bezos-mike-bloomberg-1203529459/

54 https://metoomvmt.org/2020/02/24/me-too-releases-statement-in-the-wake-of-weinstein-verdict/

55 https://www.newyorker.com/news/news-desk/weighing-the-costs-of-speaking-out-about-harvey-weinstein

56 Quoted in *She Said* by Jodi Kantor and Megan Twohey, Penguin Press.

57 https://www.theguardian.com/world/2019/dec/14/lawyer-lisa-bloom-harvey-weinstein-jeffrey-epstein-hadley-freeman

58 *She Said.*

59 https://www.hollywoodreporter.com/news/john-lasseters-pattern-alleged-misconduct-detailed-by-disney-pixar-insiders-1059594

60 https://www.theguardian.com/film/2017/nov/21/john-lasseter-taking-leave-from-pixar-citing-missteps-and-unwanted-hugs

61 https://variety.com/2018/film/news/pixar-boys-club-john-lasseter-cassandra-smolcic-1202858982/

62 https://pagesix.com/2019/12/15/harvey-weinstein-i-deserve-pat-on-back-when-it-comes-to-women/?_ga=2.194675502.2047045191.1576512981
    -281883192.1576512981

63 https://twitter.com/TIMESUPNOW/status/1206420956169854976

64 https://www.nytimes.com/2018/10/30/arts/louis-ck-comedy-cellar.html

65 https://www.nytimes.com/2017/11/10/arts/television/louis-ck-statement.html?module=inline

66 https://www.theguardian.com/tv-and-radio/2018/oct/01/matt-weiner-on
    -sexual-harassment-allegation-i-really-dont-remember-saying-that

67 https://www.theguardian.com/film/2019/aug/29/roman-polanski-venice-accusations-absurd-director-an-officer-and-a-spy-premiere

68 https://www.hollywoodreporter.com/news/john-lasseters-pattern-alleged-misconduct-detailed-by-disney-pixar-insiders-1059594

69 https://www.hollywoodreporter.com/heat-vision/john-lasseter-lead-animation-skydance-1174878

70 https://variety.com/2019/film/news/emma-thompson-john-lasseter-letter-1203149788/

71 'The Rude Warrior', *Vanity Fair*, March 2011.

72 In an interview for *Empire* magazine, 2019.

73 https://www.hollywoodreporter.com/features/ruth-wilson-left-affair-hostile-environment-nudity-issues-1263553

74 https://www.nytimes.com/2015/03/01/movies/shooting-film-and-tv-sex-scenes-what-really-goes-on.html?_r=0

75 https://deadline.com/2007/09/creepiest-email-from-a-blogger-to-hollywood-3216/

76 In an interview with the author, 2020

Chapter 11

1 https://www.cnbc.com/2019/08/27/the-10-top-earning-actresses-earn-273-million-less-than-male-peers.html

2 https://www.wsj.com/articles/SB10001424127887324798904578529682230185530

3 https://www.nyfa.edu/nyfa-news/has-female-equality-in-hollywood-progressed-in-2014.php#.Xt5BY25Fw2x

4 https://www.forbes.com/sites/natalierobehmed/2017/08/22/full-list-the-worlds-highest-paid-actors-and-actresses-2017/#2acf1c537515

5 https://www.theguardian.com/world/2019/sep/15/hollywoods-gender-pay-gap-revealed-male-stars-earn-1m-more-per-film-than-women https://www.eeassoc.org/doc/upload/THE_GENDER_EARNINGS_GAP_AMONG_HOLLYWOOD_STARS20190822201439.pdf

6 https://www.forbes.com/sites/natalierobehmed/2018/12/26/hollywoods-best-actors-for-the-buck-avengers-stars-earn-top-rois-matthew-mcconaughey-and-christian-bale-flop/

7 https://womenintvfilm.sdsu.edu/wp-content/uploads/2020/01/2019_Its_a_Mans_Celluloid_World_Report_REV.pdf

8 timothy-judge.com/documents/Agegenderandcompensation.pdf

9 *Around the Way Girl: A Memoir,* Taraji P. Henson, 37 Ink.

10 https://time.com/3716681/goldie-hawn-first-wives-club/ and https://hbr.org/2015/03/lifes-work-goldie-hawn

11 https://www.theguardian.com/film/2014/dec/12/sony-email-hack-jennifer-lawrence-paid-less-american-hustle

12 https://www.independent.co.uk/news/people/sony-hacking-reveals-bosses-wanted-to-pay-jennifer-lawrence-less-than-american-hustle-male-co-stars-9922623.html

13 https://www.lennyletter.com/story/jennifer-lawrence-why-do-i-make-less-than-my-male-costars

14 https://www.theguardian.com/film/2011/mar/23/elizabeth-taylor-obituary

15 https://people.com/archive/cover-story-lights-action-attitude-vol-39-no-13/

16 *Inside Out: A Memoir,* Demi Moore, 4th Estate.

17 https://www.hollywoodreporter.com/heat-vision/jennifer-lawrence-chris-pratts-sci-802876

18 https://www.bbc.co.uk/news/uk-43330356

19 https://www.empireonline.com/movies/news/chadwick-boseman-boosted-sienna-miller-s-21-bridges-salary-from-his-own-pay/

20 https://www.out.com/out-exclusives/2017/7/06/emma-stone-andrea-riseborough-billie-jean-king-tennis-equality-battle-sexes

21 https://www.vulture.com/2019/02/michaela-coel-black-earth-rising-chewing-gum-interview.html

22 https://www.vanityfair.com/hollywood/2018/07/michelle-williams-marriage-wedding-equal-pay

23 https://eu.usatoday.com/story/life/people/2018/01/11/exclusive-mark

-wahlberg-refused-approve-christopher-plummer-unless-he-paid/
1026347001/

24 https://www.vanityfair.com/hollywood/2018/07/michelle-williams-marriage-wedding-equal-pay

25 https://www.vanityfair.com/hollywood/2018/01/mark-wahlberg-donated-his-hefty-all-the-money-in-the-world-reshoot-salary-to-times-up-michelle-williams

26 https://www.sciencedirect.com/science/article/abs/pii/S0038029609000302?via%3Dihub

27 https://www.thewrap.com/wga-west-study-finds-mixed-results-on-pay-for-women-minorities/

28 https://www.refinery29.com/en-us/2020/08/9939912/black-stuntwomen-hollywood-experience

29 'Gender Inequality and Screenwriters: A study of the impact of gender on equality of opportunity for screenwriters and key creatives in the UK film and television industries', Alexis Kreager with Stephen Follows, ALCS.

30 Ibid.

31 https://www.hollywoodreporter.com/news/hollywood-salaries-revealed-movie-stars-737321

32 https://www.nytimes.com/2016/03/20/upshot/as-women-take-over-a-male-dominated-field-the-pay-drops.html

33 In an interview with Beiman by the author, 2020.

34 Ibid.

35 In an interview with the author, 2020.

36 https://en.wikipedia.org/wiki/Top_Ten_Money_Making_Stars_Poll#1950_Poll

37 *Ginger Rogers: A Bio-Bibliography*, Jocelyn Faris, Greenwood Press.

38 Based on the production cost of $620,000 and box office of $3 million, quoted in *Ginger Rogers: A Bio-Bibliography*.

39 'Drop in 1938 Film Box Office Receipts Parallels Marked Economy In Hollywood', Louella Parsons, *Deseret News*, 31 December 1938. https://news.google.com/newspapers?nid=336&dat=19381231&id=paJTAAAAIBAJ&sjid=tocDAAAAIBAJ&pg=6641,7369525

40 https://hollywoodrevue.wordpress.com/2019/01/21/box-office-poison-the-ad-that-started-it-all/

41 *African American Actresses: The Struggle for Visibility, 1900–1960*, Charlene B. Regester, Indiana University Press.

42 https://www.washingtonpost.com/archive/lifestyle/1988/02/09/the-fragile-flame-of-dorothy-dandridge/9c0eb130-354c-4f1b-8e2f-22d25c33bc76/

43 In an interview with the author, 2020.

44 https://www.refinery29.com/en-gb/2020/07/9895370/viola-davis-wage-gap-viral-video

45 From *Holy Matrimony!*, Boze Hadleigh, Andrews McMeel Publisher, quoted in *Hollywood's Second Sex*.

46 https://www.digitalspy.com/movies/a95411/weisz-criticised-for-mummy-decision/

47 https://www.theguardian.com/film/2015/may/21/maggie-gyllenhaal-too-old-hollywood

48 Quoted in *The Girl Who Walked Home Alone: Bette Davis, A Personal Biography*, Charlotte Chandler, Simon & Schuster.

49 Ibid.

50 https://time.com/5118504/jessica-chastain-octavia-spencer-wage-gap

Chapter 12

1 https://womenintvfilm.sdsu.edu/wp-content/uploads/2020/08/2020-Thumbs-Down-Report.pdf

2 In an interview with the author, 2020.

3 https://www.bbc.co.uk/news/entertainment-arts-32792772#:~:text=Cannes%20Film%20Festival%202015&text=Cannes%20Film%20Festival%20has%20come,Cate%20Blanchett%27s%20new%20film%20Carol.

4 https://www.bbc.co.uk/news/entertainment-arts-32809200

5 https://variety.com/2019/film/news/cannes-thierry-fremaux-record-number-female-directors-american-cinema-1203192890/

6 https://www.bbc.co.uk/news/entertainment-arts-44095914

7 https://www.nytimes.com/2018/05/12/movies/cannes-women-protest.html

8 https://variety.com/2018/film/spotlight/venice-film-festival-signs-gender-parity-pledge-1202922995/

9 https://www.vanityfair.com/hollywood/2018/05/cannes-gender-pledge

10 https://www.screendaily.com/news/venice-film-festival-chiefs-signs-gender-parity-pledge-call-it-a-step-forward/5132174.article?referrer=RSS

11 In an interview with the author, 2020.

12 In an interview with the author, 2020.

13 In an interview with the author, 2020.

14 In an interview with the author, 2020.

15 In an interview with the author, 2020.

16 In an interview with the author, 2020.

17 Quoted in *Good Girls Finish Last*, Sarah Parvis, Andrews McMeel Publishing.

18 https://womenintvfilm.sdsu.edu/wp-content/uploads/2020/08/2020-Thumbs-Down-Report.pdf

19 In an interview with the author, 2020.

20 https://www.pressgazette.co.uk/miriam-oreilly-older-female-journalists-forced-take-redundancy-and-gagged-bbc/
21 In an interview with the author, 2020.
22 *Sight & Sound*, September 1992.
23 https://boysoprano.tumblr.com/post/551725054/cool-cynicism-pulp-fiction-by-bell-hooks-1996
24 See, for example, her 1962 Télérama piece on Brigitte Bardot, quoted in *Sight & Sound*'s 'A pantheon of one's own: 25 female film critics worth celebrating'. https://www.bfi.org.uk/news-opinion/sight-sound-magazine/features/pantheon-one-s-own-25-female-film-critics-worth#tremois
25 https://www.vanityfair.com/hollywood/2017/02/warren-beatty-pauline-kael-love-and-money
26 In an interview with the author, 2020.
27 In an interview with the author, 2020.
28 https://www.refinery29.com/en-us/2019/12/8952462/girl-movies-for-women-reviews-male-film-critics-problem
29 In an interview with the author, 2020.
30 https://www.newyorker.com/culture/the-front-row/review-hustlers-is-a-lurid-crime-story-with-no-edge
31 *Nicole Kidman*, David Thomson, Alfred A. Knopf.
32 https://observer.com/2006/04/buñuel-peeps-through-keyholes-a-cubist-vision-of-deneuve/
33 https://www.newyorker.com/culture/culture-desk/incredibles-2-reviewed-a-sequel-in-the-shadow-of-a-masterwork
34 https://www.hollywoodreporter.com/review/dora-lost-city-gold-review-1227526
35 http://legacy.aintitcool.com/node/11793
36 *Reel to Real*.
37 https://womenintvfilm.sdsu.edu/wp-content/uploads/2019/05/2019_Thumbs_Down_Report.pdf for 2019 and https://www.nytimes.com/2018/07/17/movies/male-critics-are-harsher-than-women-on-female-led-films-study-says.html for the earlier one.
38 https://www.youtube.com/watch?v=9e852S8RvlU
39 https://www.latimes.com/entertainment/movies/la-et-mn-film-criticism-diversity-20180620-story.html
40 https://nypost.com/2015/06/10/sorry-ladies-youll-never-understand-why-guys-love-goodfellas/
41 In an interview with the author, 2020.
42 In an interview with the author, 2020.
43 In an interview with the author, 2020.
44 https://twitter.com/Almaharel/status/1204046786442223616?s=20
45 In an interview with the author for *Grazia* magazine, 2020

46 https://www.vulture.com/2020/01/what-is-a-white-man-mad-about
-in-this-oscar-movie.html

47 https://twitter.com/THATJacqueline/status/1216774744231440384

48 This comical play concerns a serious collector who buys a piece of
modern art that is entirely white – apart, he claims, from some faint
lines in one corner.

49 https://www.vanityfair.com/hollywood/2020/01/oscar-nominations
-preview

50 https://www.vulture.com/2019/10/bong-joon-ho-parasite.html

51 In an interview with the author for *Grazia*, 2020.

52 https://www.hollywoodreporter.com/lists/brutally-honest-oscar-ballot-
call-me-by-your-name-is-wrong-post-got-spielberg-ized-1088406/item/
honest-oscar-ballot-best-picture-1088401

53 https://www.hollywoodreporter.com/lists/brutally-honest-oscar-ballot-
get-filmmakers-played-race-card-just-sick-meryl-streep-1090440/item/
best-picture-2018-brutally-honest-oscar-ballot-2-1090446

54 https://www.nytimes.com/2020/02/06/movies/oscarssowhite-history.
html

55 www.bafta.org/media-centre/press-releases/new-diversity-requirement-
film-awards

56 https://deadline.com/2020/06/bafta-aiming-to-implement-diversity-
eligibility-criteria-across-all-awards-from-2022-1202957849/

57 https://deadline.com/2020/06/oscars-academy-inclusion-best-picture-
ten-nominees-1202957610/

58 Both in an interview with the author, 2020.

59 In an interview with the author, 2020.

Chapter 13

1 In an interview with the author, 2020.

2 In an interview with the author, 2020.

3 In an interview with the author, 2020.

4 In an interview with the author, 2020.

5 In an interview with the author, 2019.

6 In an interview with the author, 2020.

7 In an interview with the author, 2019.

8 In an interview with the author, 2020.

9 In an interview with the author, 2020.

10 Quoted in *Leading Lady: Sherry Lansing and the Making of a Hollywood
Groundbreaker*.

11 Ibid.

12 https://www.nytimes.com/1997/12/22/movies/dawn-steel-studio-chief-and-producer-dies-at-51.html

13 Ibid.

14 Quoted in *Powerhouse: The Untold Story of Hollywood's Creative Artists Agency*, James Andrew Miller, Custom House.

15 https://www.nytimes.com/1997/12/22/movies/dawn-steel-studio-chief-and-producer-dies-at-51.html

16 https://www.vulture.com/2018/07/evan-rachel-wood-across-the-universe-scared-people.html

17 In an interview with the author, 2020.

18 In an interview with the author, 2020.

19 In an interview with the author, 2020.

20 https://www.indiewire.com/2019/09/brad-pitt-threatens-kill-harvey-weinstein-gwyneth-paltrow-1202175152/

21 https://www.instyle.com/celebrity/kerry-washington-march-cover

22 In an interview with the author, 2020.

Further Resources

Rachel Abramowitz, *Is That a Gun in your Pocket? Women's Experience of Power in Hollywood* – Random House, 2000

James Bawden and Ron Miller, *Conversations with Classic Film Stars: Interviews from Hollywood's Golden Era* – University Press of Kentucky, 2016

Peter Biskind, *Easy Riders, Raging Bulls: How the Sex 'n' Drugs 'n' Rock 'n' Roll Generation Changed Hollywood* – Bloomsbury, 1998

Melody Bridges and Cheryl Robson (eds), *Silent Women: Pioneers of Cinema* – Supernova books, 2016

Mark Garrett Cooper, *Universal Women: Filmmaking and Institutional Change in Early Hollywood* – University of Illinois Press, 2010

Anita Elberse, *Blockbusters: Why Big Hits and Big Risks are the Future of the Entertainment Business* – Faber & Faber, 2013

Ronan Farrow, *Catch and Kill: Lies, Spies and a Conspiracy to Protect Predators* – Fleet, 2019

Jane M. Gaines, *Pink-Slipped: What Happened to Women in the Silent Film Industries* – University of Illinois Press, 2018

Stephen Galloway, *Leading Lady: Sherry Lansing and the Making of A Hollywood Groundbreaker* – Three Rivers Press, 2017

Molly Haskell, *From Reverence to Rape: The Treatment of Women in the Movies* – University of Chicago Press, 1973

bell hooks, *Reel to Real: Race, Class and Sex at the Movies* – Routledge Classics, 2008

Jodi Kantor and Megan Twohey, *She Said: Breaking the Sexual Harassment Story That Helped Ignite a Movement* – Penguin Press, 2019

Antonia Lant (Ed) with Ingrid Periz, *Red Velvet Seat: Women's Writing on the First Fifty Years of Cinema* – Verso, 2006

James Andrew Miller, *Powerhouse: The Untold Story of Hollywood's Creative Artists Agency* – Custom House, 2016

Laura Mulvey, *Afterimages: On Cinema, Women and Changing Times* – Reaktion Books, 2019

Marjorie Rosen, *Popcorn Venus; Women, Movies & the American Dream* – Coward, McCann & Geoghegan, 1973

Vito Russo, *The Celluloid Closet: Homosexuality in the Movies* – Harper Paperbacks, 1987

Thomas Schatz, *The Genius of the System: Hollywood Filmmaking in the Studio Era* – Faber & Faber, 1988

Robert Sklar, *Movie-made America: A Cultural History of American Movies* – Vintage Books, 1994 (revised and updated)

Maya Montanez Smukler, *Liberating Hollywood: Women Directors and the Feminist Reform of 1970s American Cinema* – Rutgers University Press, 2019

USEFUL ORGANISATIONS

The Annenberg Inclusion Initiative, University of Southern California
https://annenberg.usc.edu/research/aii
BEATS: British East & South East Asians in the Screen & Stage Industry
wearebeats.org.uk/
The Bechdel Test Fest
bechdeltestfest.com/
BFI Diversity Standards
https://www.bfi.org.uk/inclusion-film-industry/bfi-diversity-standards
The British Blacklist
thebritishblacklist.co.uk/
Center for the Study of Women in Television and Film
https://womenintvfilm.sdsu.edu/research/
Cinesisters
https://www.cinesisters.com/
Film Fatales
www.filmfatales.org/
Free The Work
https://freethework.com/
The Geena Davis Institute on Gender in Media
https://seejane.org/
Girls On Film podcast
https://podcasts.apple.com/za/podcast/girls-on-film/id1439182513
GLAAD Studio Responsibility Index
https://www.glaad.org/sri/2020
Illuminatrix
https://www.illuminatrixdops.com/

Primetime Network
https://primetime.network/
Time's Up UK
https://www.timesupuk.org/

WEBSITES

https://athenafilmfestival.com/
https://www.cemeterytour.com/
https://womenandhollywood.com/
https://hollywoodracism.com/
https://www.itaobrien.com/
bechdeltestfest.com

Acknowledgements

First and foremost I'd like to thank Amanda Keats, my editor, for this book. I asked to take her out for coffee and pick her brain; instead she suggested that we work together on this. My further thanks to all the team at Robinson and Little, Brown: notably Alison Tulett and Beth Wright. Thanks, as well, to my agent Zoe Ross for putting up with me.

My special thanks go to all my interviewees, who were kind enough to take time out of their very busy days of acting, activism, teaching, writing, directing, producing, programming and generally much more important work to speak to me. Thanks to Lexi Alexander, Corrina Antrobus, Geraldine Bajard, Mark Batey, Nancy Beiman, Anne Cohen, Madeline Di Nonno, Paul Feig, Professor Jane Gaines, Charles Gant, Greta Gerwig, Akua Gyamfi, Catherine Hardwicke, Alma Har'el, Jessica Hausner, Marielle Heller, Pamela Hutchinson, Patty Jenkins, Mimi Leder, Maria Lewis, Charlotte Little, Wendy Lloyd, Christopher Marcus, So Mayer, Stephen McFeely, Leah Meyerhoff, Polly Morgan, Jasmin Morrison, Professor Laura Mulvey, Claire Oakley, Ita O'Brien, Dame Heather Rabbatts at Time's Up UK, my sister from another mister Joanna Robinson, Cate Shortland, Anna Smith, Megan Townsend and all her colleagues at GLAAD, Melissa Silverstein at Women And Hollywood, Chi Thai, Tricia Tuttle and her team at the London Film Festival, Joana Vicente at TIFF, Deena Wallace and Amy Gustin at BIFA, and all the interviewees who spoke to me but wished to remain anonymous.

I want to thank Victoria Emslie of Primetime Network who was not only an absolute delight to talk to but also the world's greatest networker, putting me in touch with a who's who of talent and vouching for me (terribly unwise, terribly generous) before I'd even got home from our meeting. The staff at the BFI Reuben Library were also wonderful, at least until bloody Covid closed the place halfway through my research period. I'm also grateful to Karie Bible of the Hollywood Forever Cemetery tour, whose knowledge and advice was enormously helpful even when I didn't quote her directly. Should you find yourself in LA, take the tour; you won't regret it.

For moral support, thanks to Hamilton Club; the 12 Adorable Nerds (especially Amon, who introduced me to Amanda and demanded his own credit); Rhiannon Evans and Angharad Parry for counsel and afternoon tea; the Lincolnites; the Dominicaners, especially Justin for trying to get me to start drinking and Helen for not backing him up; the entire *Empire* gang but especially Terri White, Nick de Semlyen, Chris Hewitt, Ian Freer and James Dyer, who are the best gang of weirdoes the world has ever known; and thanks to all the *Empire* readers and *Empire* podcast listeners who have enabled me to somehow make a career of watching movies. Judging by my experience of other online subcultures, you guys are the best ones. Most of all, thanks to my family for being the best family, sorry everyone else. Special thanks to my sister Maria who cooked for me while I wrote a lot, and my tiny nephew and niece Aiden and Aoife, whose video calls sustained me. My apologies to Aiden for not finding room for more discussion of *Wall-E*, a robot who would undoubtedly fight for better gender representation if only he were real.

And thanks to Hollywood for the movies. You might be dreadful sometimes but I love you really.

Index